Off The Beaten Track
CZECH & SLOVAK REPUBLICS

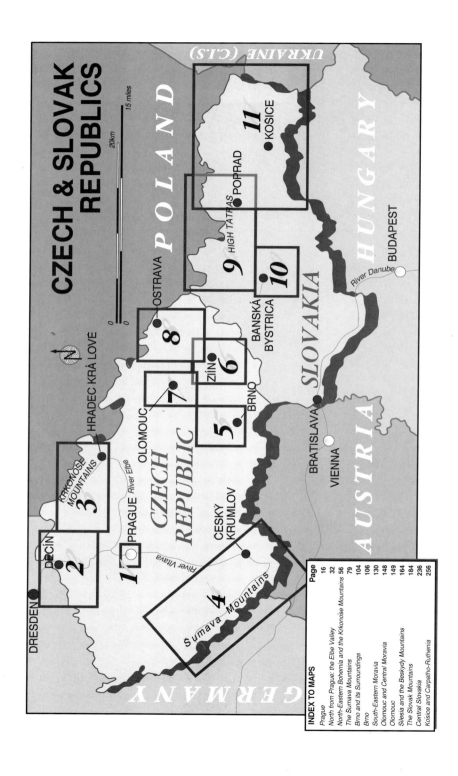

CZECH & SLOVAK REPUBLICS

GERMANY

POLAND

UKRAINE (C.I.S.)

CZECH REPUBLIC

SLOVAKIA

AUSTRIA

HUNGARY

DRESDEN
DĚČÍN
HRADEC KRÁLOVÉ
KRKONOŠE MOUNTAINS
River Elbe
PRAGUE
OLOMOUC
OSTRAVA
River Vltava
ČESKÝ KRUMLOV
Šumava Mountains
ZLÍN
BRNO
BANSKÁ BYSTRICA
BRATISLAVA
VIENNA
River Danube
BUDAPEST
HIGH TATRAS
POPRAD
KOŠICE

1 2 3 4 5 6 7 8 9 10 11

N

0   20km
0   15 miles

Off The Beaten Track
CZECH & SLOVAK REPUBLICS

Andrew Beattie & Timothy Pepper

MOORLAND PUBLISHING

The Globe Pequot Press

Published by:
Moorland Publishing Co Ltd,
Moor Farm Road West, Ashbourne,
Derbyshire, DE6 1HD England

ISBN 0 86190 554 7 (UK)

The Globe Pequot Press,
6 Business Park Road,
PO Box 833, Old Saybrook,
Connecticut 06475-0833

ISBN 1-56440-717-9 (USA)

Black and white illustrations have been
supplied as follows:

Andrew Beattie pp18, 19, 40, 46, 64, 68-69,
81, 83, 86, 92, 151, 188, 199, 201, 206, 208,
212, 218, 221, 227, 229, 231, 244, 258, 264

Timothy Pepper pp22, 27, 34, 37, 59,
109, 111, 113, 116, 119, 133, 135, 137,
154, 156, 157, 159, 167, 173, 238, 248,
249, 266, 268, 270, 273

CM Dixon (Photoresources,
Canterbury, England) 181, 197, 203

Colour illustrations have been supplied
as follows:

Andrew Beattie, Timothy Pepper,
CM Dixon (Photoresources,
Canterbury, England), Copicat Creative
(New Alresford, Hampshire), SM Wragg

Origination by:
ga Graphics, Lincolnshire

Printed by:
Wing King Tong Co Ltd, Hong Kong

MPC Production Team:
Editorial: Tonya Monk
Editorial Assistant: Christine Haines
Design: Ashley Emery
Cartography: Mark Titterton
Authors' proofreader: Helen Nield

British Library Cataloguing in Publication Data:
A catalogue record for this book is available from the British Library.

Library of Congress Cataloging-in-Publication Data
Beattie, Andrew.
   Off the beaten track: Czech and Slovak Republics / Andrew Beattie &
   Timothy Pepper.
       p. cm.
   Includes index.
   ISBN 1-56440-717-9
1. Czech Republic -- Guidebooks. 2. Slovakia -- Guidebooks.
I. Pepper, Timothy. II. Title. III. Title. Czech and Slovak Republics.
DB2010. B4   1994
914.37 '0443 -- dc20
                                                  94-43312
                                                    CIP

Contents

About the Authors

Andrew Beattie read Geography at Mansfield College, Oxford, and now teaches the subject at Eltham College, London, spending most of his time outside the classroom writing and travelling. He is the author and co-author of Moorland Publishing's guide books on the Czech and Slovak Republics, Syria, Hungary and Prague, and has written articles on travel for reference books and journals.

Timothy Pepper was born in Chester and read History at Wadham College, Oxford. He has travelled extensively in Eastern Europe, the Middle East, Southern Africa and Cenral America. With Andrew Beattie he is the author of Moorland Publishing's *Visitor's Guides* to Hungary and to Syria . He has contributed a number of articles to the *International Dictionary of Historic Places*.

An Introduction to the Czech and Slovak Republics

Neville Chamberlain, the British Prime Minister who, in 1938, signed the Munich Agreement which allowed Nazi Germany to appropriate a large part of Czechoslovakia, called the country — which had been in existence for less than 20 years — 'a far-away country, populated by a people of whom we know nothing'. After the end of World War II, Czechoslovakia was in the hands of another foreign dictatorship — this time the USSR, whose control over the country's internal and external affairs lasted until 1989. Locked in behind the watch towers and barbed wire of the Iron Curtain, for over four decades Czechoslovakia was a country visited by few Western travellers; regarded as a hard-line Communist state, particularly after the uprising in Prague against the government in 1968 (the 'Prague Spring'), travel here was once fraught with restrictions and regulations. After the demise of Communism — the so-called 'velvet' (ie bloodless) revolution of November 1989 — the position of the Czechoslovak authorities on tourism was reversed, and travellers from the west, bringing with them hard currency, were actively encouraged to visit the country. Tourism was increasingly seen as a means of helping to bolster the fragile economy of the new market-led economy. In 1993, the country which had been created from an unwanted 'marriage' of Bohemia, Moravia and Slovakia in 1919, formally split into two nations — the Czech and Slovak republics — and gradually the republics grew further and further apart, adopting separate laws, currency and government administrations. Václav Havel, once dissident playwright and bugbear to the Communist regime, and then president of a united and free Czechoslovakia from 1989, returned to Prague Castle to become the first president of the Czech Republic. In Slovakia, very much the poorer and more backward of the two states, political extremism — both to the right and left — began to emerge as the dominant force in politics, as its new rulers tried to work out what to do with its primitive farming and moribund heavy industry; the Czech Republic, however, buoyed up by money from tourism and its (relatively) prosperous engineering and manufacturing industries, set about making itself Western, and the two nations are emerging from the forced unity of Communist days to become very different places.

The division of the old Czechoslovakia into three — Bohemia and Moravia (the Czech Republic), and Slovakia (the Slovak Republic) — forms the basic division of this book into three distinct parts. Each of the provinces has its own characteristics: Bohemia is a mixture of polluted industrial towns and deserted, remote areas of low mountains, with Prague — arguably the most beautiful city in Europe — at its heart; Moravia is the most undiscovered of the three provinces, where the geography is more extreme — the cities are more polluted, but the mountain areas are emptier and less visited than those in Bohemia, and the folklore and traditions have survived much more successfully; Slovakia is a country of high mountains and remote hill villages, baking summers and often fiercely cold winters, poor agriculture and a feeling, in its most remote parts, of decades of neglect and poverty. Each is a fascinating destination for travellers in its own right. A journey which allows one to encounter aspects of all three provinces reveals as great a variety of landscape, architecture and culture as would travelling in any area of a similar size in the whole of Europe.

The aim of this book is to take people 'off the beaten track' as the title suggests. This leads, inherently, to its being written, perhaps more than other guides, according to the subjective judgement of its authors, who are the ultimate arbiters of whether a place merits being described as being on or off the beaten track. In some cases the distinction is obvious; the most visited parts of Prague and West Bohemia are not described here and are covered very fully in other books. In concentrating on less visited areas — such as the Šumava or Krkonoše Mountains in Bohemia, which are described in considerable detail — it is hoped that the book will be able to guide people away from the more obvious tourist destinations towards those which are overlooked by other books. Nevertheless, some popular destinations have been included; for instance, Brno and the High Tatras are favourite places to visit, but their descriptions in this book will hopefully lead visitors away from the main sights in these places — the main streets in Brno or most trodden walks in the Tatras — to the less obviously touristy parts of the city, or the emptier parts of the mountains. The overall picture that the visitor will leave with will hopefully be one of a country of ruggedly beautiful scenery, attractive towns and a friendly people — and all this seen in areas less tainted by the effects of modern tourism compared to the more obvious and visited destinations within the country.

Part One
BOHEMIA

Introduction

The most accessible part of the Czech and Slovak Republics, a region of pleasant and varied countryside with one of the most beautiful cities in the world at its heart, Bohemia is now one of the most attractive destinations for travellers in Central Europe. Most visitors come to Prague — geographically in the centre of Bohemia — and then fan out from there, to the spa towns of Western Bohemia, north to the areas of natural beauty around the Elbe valley, or to the clutch of historic towns and gentle mountain scenery of Southern Bohemia. The region is easily reached from Germany and Austria and many of its principal places of interest (notably Prague) are packed out by tourists in the summer. The places to which everybody seems to head — the West Bohemian spa towns, central parts of Prague, the more obvious day excursions that can be made from the capital, are not described here. The four chapters that follow should lead visitors to the less popular areas of Bohemia: to the more secluded corners of Prague, to the deserted areas of the Šumava or Krkonoše mountains, to the little-visited historic towns along the River Elbe. Getting off the beaten track in Bohemia may sometimes seem difficult but it can be done, if you know where to go away from the honeypots which attract tourists in their swarms, there are some parts of the province that still await discovery.

Bohemia is an ideal place in which to begin any visit to the Czech and Slovak Republics — if only to witness contrast within the country as one travels from west to east. Bohemia is wealthier, more industrialized, more modern than Moravia or Slovakia. It has embraced capitalism and the market economy more quickly than virtually any other area of what used to be Central Europe. Private enterprise is growing and service provision is more efficient than in other parts of the country. The Czech Republic's principal exports — cars, beer, engineering goods — all come from Bohemia, whose industries are quickly being bought up and modernized by Western firms. Everything seems more efficient, less ramshackle, better upkept; but there is a downside to this: tourists are greeted with the same kind of cynicism and indifference that they are in any part of the world which sees a lot of them, and the environment has borne the brunt of

Bohemia's industrialization under the Communists. In parts of Northern Bohemia pollution from outmoded factories causes permanent air pollution which has irreparably damaged the health of inhabitants, whilst forests — again in Northern Bohemia, and particularly in the Krkonoše — have suffered acutely from acid rain. Bohemia is the power-house of the new Czech Republic, but it also poses the new government with the new country's most serious environmental problems.

Most of Bohemia's history is a complex one of wars, rebellion and external control. At various times it has been under the control of the Holy Roman Empire, the Austrian Empire and, in more modern times, as part of Czechoslovakia, a satellite of the Soviet Union — in theory an independent nation, in practice a vassal state which did what it was told by Moscow. The great German chancellor, Otto von Bismarck, said that whoever controls Bohemia, controls Europe, and most of the figures in Central European History seem to have taken this piece of advice to heart. In the fourteenth century, Prague was made the capital of the Holy Roman Empire and experienced a 'Golden Age' when art and culture flourished. Between 1516 and 1918 however, Bohemia was under the control of the Habsburgs, who ruled their vast Austro-Hungarian Empire from Vienna with a cast-iron fist. A number of nationalist movements grew up over the centuries, many of them recalling the traditions of the first Czech Nationalist, Jan Hus (John Huss), a rector of Charles University in Prague who, in the early fifteenth century, had linked desires for Czech independence with calls for religious reform. Bohemia has a strong history of embracing Protestantism: in 1618, the devoutly Catholic Habsburg prince, Ferdinand of Styria, was placed on the throne, in the hope of reconverting wayward Bohemian protestants. However, the small but powerful Protestant aristocracy in Bohemia considered this a bad idea, and a delegation marched into Prague Castle in 1618 and threw two of Ferdinand's deputies out of the window — an event which sparked off the Thirty Years War, one of the bloodiest in the history of Europe, which set the continent alight from 1618 to 1648 and which left many areas of Bohemia devastated.

Nevertheless, despite political turmoil, the Bohemian economy flourished: silver and other ores were mined in various places, and speculators began to settle in the Krkonoše and other mineral-rich areas. Agricultural products such as hops and barley were exported along the Vltava and Elbe to Germany. Trade became important and many towns grew rich because of their position on trading routes. Merchants in many places became very wealthy, and left a legacy in towns and cities in the form of numerous fine churches and other buildings which, in many cases, they paid for. A sizeable aristocracy grew, and turned the hilltop castles which had once guarded important medieval trade routes into fine palaces, and constructed hunting lodges and châteaux in more secluded areas of woodland. In the nineteenth century coal, found principally in the north of Bohemia, was mined, and steel and heavy industry grew; many cities, including Prague, developed extensive industrial facilities and new housing, which still, in many cases, surrounds their old, well-preserved medieval cores.

A lot of the impetus behind this growth came from German speakers. In the Middle Ages, merchants were likely to be of German stock, as were the nineteenth-century industrialists. Many border regions of Bohemia — grouped together as the Sudetenland — were predominantly German speaking. German was the language of commerce and politics until well into the nineteenth century. During the 1930s the Sudetenlanders began to campaign for a state separate from the newly-founded Czechoslovakia. Their protests encouraged Hitler to persuade Britain and France to let him annex Bohemia and Moravia in 1938 (after the infamous Munich agreement). After 1945 virtually all German speakers were expelled from the country on the pretext of 'mass collaboration' with the occupying Nazis, leaving many towns (such as Cheb, right on the border) virtual ghost towns, into which the government was forced to move many Czech speakers to compensate for the Germans that had left. Now there is only a tiny number of German speakers left, but the legacy of there being so many German speakers means that the language is widely spoken and understood throughout the country, and many towns and villages have German names under which they are occasionally still referred to — such as Marienbad, a name still used for the spa town of Mariánské Lázně in Western Bohemia.

Dissent has always been a theme throughout Bohemian history, beginning with Jan Hus and continuing with the rebels who threw the Habsburg dignitaries out of the windows of Prague Castle in 1618. After 1948, when Czechoslovakia became a Communist — or, to be precise, a neo-Stalinist — state, many dissidents started to produce writing which criticized the government. Many writers, composers and intellectuals were prevented from working at their chosen profession and some were forced by the government to take menial jobs, if they were seen as a threat to the regime. Some, like the novelist and screenwriter Milan Kundera, emigrated (in his case to Paris) and took their campaigning abroad to a wider audience, while others, such as Václav Havel, decided to stay and take what was coming to them — often prison, and certainly the prospect of their works being declared illegal, except as strictly controlled *samizdat* (ie privately printed and circulated) publications. Prague became a centre for dissident activity and in 1977 the Human Rights group Charter 77 was founded there; many of its leaders, including Václav Havel, were jailed, but the group's name became a byword for the campaign for freedom of speech and expression all over the world. All this activity came to a head in November 1989, when 10 days of vociferous but non-violent demonstrations in Prague forced the Communist government of Czechoslovakia to resign. Since then, Prague has become a haven for artists, writers, composers and intellectual drifters after a willing audience — as Paris was in the 1960s; it is a city where ideas are generated, discussed and written about as, perhaps, it always has been. The difference now, in the 1990s is that discussion, argument and dissent can now be expressed legally.

The section in this book on Bohemia is divided into four regions. Firstly, there is a chapter on Prague — not on the obvious tourist sights, but on those places of interest which are often overlooked as they are located out in the suburbs of the city. Travelling out to them gives visitors a very different impression of the capital to the virtual museum-piece old town, which is what most visitors see of the city. The other three chapters look at regions on the periphery of Bohemia — around the river Elbe, to the north, where there are a number of remarkable sandstone features and old towns and then at the Krkonoše and Šumava mountains, which occupy the north-eastern and south-western borders of Bohemia respectively, the former higher and more barren, the latter range lower, gentler and dotted with pretty medieval towns which nestle in its docile valleys. In the mountain areas, the emphasis is firmly on walking (the Krkonoše is the best area for walking in the whole of the Czech Republic), and in all the chapters, the unusual and the seldom visited are covered in preference to the more popular places. In summer in particular, many places in Bohemia groan under the weight of tourists coming to see this newly-accessible land, but such is the nature of this country that those who do manage to get off the beaten track will find their efforts amply rewarded.

1 • Prague

The Suburbs

East of the Centre: Žižkov and Vinohrady

These districts, to the east of the main railway station, remained fields until the mid-nineteenth century when the growing industrialization of Prague and the accompanying urban sprawl finally accounted for them. In the 1870s both Žižkov and Vinohrady actually received town charters but their independent lives were relatively brief and in 1920 both were incorporated within the municipal boundaries (though Žižkov residents proudly maintained their own accent until well into the 1950s). Vinohrady is the more palatable of the two, with an array of crumbling but still grand late-nineteenth century mansions and two reasonable parks (the Riegrovy sady and the Havlíčkovy sady) while Žižkov has always been traditionally more working class and earthy, it being a Communist stronghold even before the war (earning itself the nickname 'Red Zizkov') and today being home to a substantial number of Prague's Romany community.

Begin your venture into **Žižkov** from behind the Florenc bus station and ascend to the westernmost point of Žižkov hill (also known as Vitkov) where on 14 July 1420, though quite ridiculously outnumbered, the Hussites under the leadership of the one-eyed general Jan Žižka of Trocnov (from whom the name Žižkov derives) defeated King Sigismund and his Crusader troops. At the summit point of the hill is a superb view over the city and the huge granite Žižkov Monument which is fronted by a 30ft (9m) high equestrian statue of Žižka (complete with mace) erected in 1950, actually the largest equestrian statue in the world. The Monument itself was built 1929-32 according to the design of J. Zázvorka as a celebration of the newly-independent Czechoslovak state but between 1955 and 1989 it was used as the Communist Party mausoleum. Numerous party dignitaries and Presidents Gottwald, Zápotocký and Svoboda were laid to rest here though they were all removed in 1989 for fear of desecration. All the urns were given up to the next of kin except for that of Gottwald whose family wanted nothing to do with it — the precise location of his earthly remains today is not known. Interestingly enough, the building actually contains a whole complex of rooms built in the 1950s for the display of Gottwald's mummified corpse though in the event it proved increasingly difficult to preserve

his body which had to be slowly replaced limb by limb in plastic by the make up department of the Barrandov film studios. By 1962 all that was left of his original body was his head and the project was at last given up.

On the way up to the monument from Florenc one passes, along the steep lane U pámatníku, that part of the city's **Military Museum** (Vojenské Muzeum) dealing with events post 1918. It looks grim and foreboding from the outside but its exhibitions have recently had a sparklingly new post-Communist overhaul and there is talk that shortly the exhibitions may take an even more reactionary viewpoint with sections on 1968 and Charter 77.

Easily the most famous monument in Žižkov is the awesomely space-age **Television Tower** (Televizní vysílač) on Mahlerovy sady — known informally as the Prague Penis (Pražský Čůrák) — at 941ft (287m) tall the highest building in the city. Construction began in 1984 over the grounds of a former Jewish cemetery which had been converted into a park during the 1970s — it had served the community from 1787 to 1891. Only a small section of the cemetery survives today, just to the north-west of the tower, and it is reminiscent of the rather more famous Old Jewish Cemetery in the centre of

Street scenes in Prague (Chapter 1)

Marionettes for sale on the streets of Prague (Chapter 1)

A tram squeezes through the narrow streets of Prague (Chapter 1)

town; but the incongruity of its surroundings and the thought that it once stretched right across the square make it a unique experience in itself, a hauntingly tangible reminder of both history and mortality. The tower itself boats an underground café, a restaurant on the fifth floor and a viewing platform *(vyhlídka)* on the eighth floor (the view is unfortunately not the best to be had in the city and the entrance fee is relatively hefty).

Apart from a trip up to the top of the television tower the reason most people would care to find themselves in this part of town is to visit the huge cemeteries on the border of the Žižkov and Vinohrady districts. Due to the presence of one Franz Kafka by far the most busy of these is the **New Jewish Cemetery** (Nový židovský hřbitov), the entrance to which is by the metro stop Želivského. This was founded in the 1890s when the one at the site of the present day television tower was full. With the huge allotments still to be filled it is thought to be unlikely that Prague will ever find the need for a another site. Kafka's grave is 1,312ft (400m) along the south wall at the end of plot 21; he is buried with his mother and father (he died before both of them). A plaque remembers his three sisters who died in German concentration camps and there are many similar such plaques spread around here. It is well worth a wander through the cemetery as a whole as it is a wonderfully evocative if slightly melancholy place to be — a monument in itself to an age and culture largely lost — and it is not too difficult to escape from the buzz of sightseers around Kafkas grave. Take note that men will be asked to cover their heads upon entering.

Immediately to the north of the New Jewish Cemetery is the highly untouristed **War Cemetery** (Vojenský hřbitov), the entrance to which is along Jana Želivského. Its main attraction is a monument to 436 Soviet soldiers who died on 9 May 1945 during the liberation of Prague. The graves of Czechs who died on the Italian front during the Great War (fighting for the Austro-Hungarian empire) are laid out in a semi-circle nearby. South of the New Jewish Cemetery is the **Vinohrady Cemetery** (Vinohradský Hřbitov) founded in 1885 and boasting at its centre a neo-Gothic chapel consecrated to St Wenceslas and surrounded by arcades built in 1897. The most famous individual to be buried here is probably the architect Jan Kotěra.

The largest of Prague's cemeteries is the **Olšany Cemetery** (Olšanské hřbitovy), nearest metro Flora, which is divided into thirteen districts — at each gate there is a map. It was originally created in 1680 for the victims of the great plague epidemic of that year and the most famous individual to rest here is Jan Palach, the 21 year-old student who famously set fire to himself on 19 January 1969 in Wenceslas Square in protest against the 1968 Soviet invasion. Over three quarters of a million people attended his funeral and five people around the country emulated his behaviour in the proceeding

Space-age Prague: the Television Tower at Žižkov

days. In 1973 in an attempt to prevent the annual congregations at his graveside the Communist authorities dug his body up and reburied him in his home town 37 miles (60km) away, replacing it with that of an unknown woman, Marie Jedličková — the attempt failed for every year on the anniversary of his death mourners just decorated her tomb instead and in 1990 Palach's body was finally returned to Olšany. Today it lies just to the

Franz Kafka's tomb in the New Jewish cemetery in Prague

east of the main entrance on Vinohradská. Perhaps the most evocative time to visit the cemetery is between 31 October (All Saints' Eve) and 2 November (All Souls' Day) when the site becomes alight with candles and silent mourners though at any other time the odd assortment of tombs, obelisks, sarcophagi and crucifixes (including an entire plot from the Russian Orthodox Church) make this a very interesting place to meander through during an afternoon — take the time especially to head for the eastern wall which is lined with literally thousands of urns.

Vinohrady has two main squares, busy náměstí Míru based around the neo-Gothic brick church of St Ludmila (1888-93) and worth a visit for a look at the splendidly Art Nouveau Vinohrady Theatre building (1905-9) designed by A. Čenský, and náměstí Jiřího z Poděbrad which is dominated by the extraordinary **Church of the Most Sacred Heart of Our Lord** (Nejsvětější Srdce Páně) built by Slovenian architect Josip Plečnik (1872-1957) in 1928-32 — it was he who was controversially appointed as the chief architect for the rebuilding of Prague Castle in 1920 (shortly after the foundation of the First Republic). To put it mildly this church features an eclectic mix of architectural styles with contemporary, classical and Gothic elements combined into a highly allusive yet also highly reverential final design. Unfortunately Plečnik's work in Prague managed to offend both traditionalists and Cubists alike and he eventually returned to his native Ljubljana where much of his best work is to be found.

North of the Centre: Holešovice, Bubeneč and Troja

Though most famous for the mainline station, through which one may have entered Prague, Holešovice and Bubeneč are probably most visited for the two huge parks contained here (Letná and Stromovka) and the Výstaviště exhibition grounds from where it is but a short walk over the river to Prague's only genuine château at Troja, next to which is situated the city zoo.

The green expanse of **Letná Plain** was the traditional assembly point for besieging armies and is mentioned in historical records as far back as the eleventh century; King Přemysl Otakar II's coronation took place here in 1261. During the mid-nineteenth century the plain was laid out as a public park but its most recent function was as the site for the May Day parades which went past the 40,000 capacity Sparta stadium. The present day appearance of the park dates back to 1950. On 26 November 1989 three quarters of a million people gathered here to protest against the Communist regime and saw Václav Havel shake hands with Alexander Dubček and in April 1990 one million Catholics gathered to hear Pope John Paul II speak. It was his first visit to an Eastern European country other than his native Poland. Ironically Letná's most famous monument no longer exists, a huge 98ft (30m) high granite statue of Stalin, once visible from all over the city, which was blown up on the orders of Krushchev in a series of nocturnal explosions spread over a fortnight in October 1962. It was the largest Stalin monument in the world and portrayed the great man leading a procession of a Soviet worker, a soldier, a botanist and a woman into the future. Six hundred workers took 500 days to erect the sculpture which was officially revealed on 1 May 1955 to a rapturous public reception. Otakar Švec who designed it obviously had serious misgivings about his work for he shot himself before its unveiling, and anyway within a year the 14,000-ton monstrosity was enveloped in scaffolding following Stalin's denunciation by his successor at the Kremlin Nikita Krushchev. All that remains of it today is a large concrete plinth with a good view over the city and a large metronome marking the progress of time, suitably enough.

In the hillside below the plinth is a nuclear bunker (the only one in Prague) which was built for the Party elite. It has been most recently put to use as a nightclub venue though for a long time it was used to store potatoes. In 1992 the city council put an end to the chemical-induced raving for safety reasons and its most likely future use is as a place to grow mushrooms. If one is seeking a little refreshment in a refined setting head for the nearby Art Nouveau-style **Hanava Pavilion** (Hanavský Pavilón) which was originally built in 1891 for the Prague Jubilee Exhibition. It was moved to its present site in 1898 and there is a late-night disco held here on certain nights.

There is one museum in Holešovice, the **Museum of Technology** (Národní Technické Muzeum) at Kostelní 42, a short walk east of Letná and not nearly so dour as its exterior might suggest, with plenty of knobs and buttons to press and a very reasonably priced café where one may sit and rest one's ears from the merciless onslaught of loud and enthusiastic schoolchildren. The museums very large main hall contains a fascinating array of cars, trains, planes (suspended), bicycles and motorbikes dating from the late-nineteenth century as well as a 1900 railway carriage which was used to transport the royal Habsburgs around. Upstairs there is a very enjoyable acoustics exhibition, an exhibition devoted to the early days of photography, a selection of old gramophones and clocks and a small astronomical collection including instruments used by Tycho Brahe and Johannes Kepler. At 11am, 1pm and 3pm there are guided tours below ground into a mock-up coal mine (well recommended).

A short distance away on route to the Výstaviště exhibition grounds at the corner of Veletržní and Dukelských hrdinů is an interesting seven-storey glass building originally built for the 1928 Trade Fair by O. Tyl and J. Fuchs. One of the Functionalist trailblazers, it managed to make even Le Corbusier feel behind the times when he viewed it for the first time in 1930. There have been plans to house a museum dedicated to modern Czech art in the building since 1975 but so far these have remained unfulfilled.

A couple of minutes walk north of here up Dukelských hrdinů is the entrance gate to the **Výstaviště**, the citys funfair (at the far end from the entrance) and main exhibition space, originally created for the 1891 Prague Exhibition. The Communist Party held its conferences here from 1948 until the late 1970s. The canopy over the main entrance dates from the rebuilding for the 1991 Prague Exhibition (a circular theatre and large blue pyramid were also added). The place is unfortunately usually very quiet except on summer weekends when a family atmosphere pervades though there are a

The château at Troja, in the northern suburbs of Prague

few permanent attractions in the vicinity such as the **Planetarium**, the small funfair for children and the **Maroldova Panoráma**, a giant circular diorama of the Battle of Lipany 1434 which effectively brought the Hussite Wars to a close — essentially a mixture of painting, battle-scarred foreground and poor quality sound effects. Also on offer just to the right inside the main gates to the Výstaviště is a **Sculpture Museum** featuring many of the original statues from the Charles Bridge.

Adjoining the Výstaviště is the **Stromovka Park**, actually Prague's largest, originally founded in the fourteenth century by King John of Luxemburg as part of the royal hunting grounds and converted into a public park only in 1804. The lake was artificially created in 1593 by Rudolf II (a canal connects it to the Vltava), an outstanding technical achievement for the times. Features in the park include a Summer Pavilion, whose present day appearance dates from 1804 to 1806, and an Imperial Mill, originally a fourteenth-century structure rebuilt in Empire style in the nineteenth century. Rudolf II's château has long since gone but from the park one can walk on to the Troja Château and zoo by following the signposted path that leads northwards onto Emperors Island (Cisařský Ostrov) and then across the Vltava.

Troja suburb is a world away from the bustle of central Prague with a provincial, almost Italianate air to it, consisting as it does of rolling hillsides, vineyards and small chapels. The very red early baroque château was built for Count Wenceslaus Adalbert of Sternberk by Jean-Baptiste Mathey at the end of the seventeenth century and has recently been substantially renovated — the very smart French-style gardens are open all year round and were the first of their kind in Bohemia.There are regular guided tours round the interior only; there is a large collection of nineteenth-century Czech art inside but the Grand Hall is the highlight with its amazing frescoes by Dutchman Abraham Godin depicting the victories of the Emperor Leopold I over the Turks at the end of the seventeenth century — the triumph of Christianity over the evils of Islam (painted 1691-7).

The entrance to the **city zoo** is directly opposite that of the château. It was founded in 1931 by professor J. Janda and boasts 2,000 different specimens but unfortunately it has a very bad reputation though thankfully a programme of modernization is under way. In the summer a ski-lift *(lanová dráha)* operates from the duck pond to the top of the hill upon which the Przewalski miniature horses (which no longer exist outside captivity) are situated. Bus #112 presently runs from outside the entrance to the zoo back to Holešovice station (metro) or alternatively boats call about every half hour along the Vltava.

The Western Suburbs

The suburb of **Dejvice** came into existence during the 1920s principally to house the First Republic's new army of civil servants and military officials. Its main square is the busy public transport inter-change Vitězně náměstí at the end of metro line A. Except for a small eighteenth-century rococo château at Šárecká 2915 there is not really an awful lot in this part of town but one may care to head north to the Baba villa colony (named after the hill upon which it is situated). The thirty-three Functionalist houses located within the streets Nad Pat'ankou, Průhledová, Matějská and Jarní all came into existence after a radical town-planning project organized by Cubist Pavel Janák in 1928 in an effort to create a model community (which was based upon a similar scheme in Stuttgart). Leading Czech architects including Gočár, Žák, Starý, Grus, Černý and Janák himself all designed houses intended to provide for the needs of the ordinary family and building work was carried out between 1932 and 1940. Blessed with a wonderful view looking south over the city the colony has worn slightly better than might have been feared though as not one of the houses is open to the public it is not exactly easy to judge the success or failure of the project for oneself. A short walk away on the hillside overlooking the Šárka valley is the late baroque church of St Matthew (1771) designed by I.J. Palliardi. From the graveyard there is a great view over the valley.

The suburb of **Střešovice** is dominated by the Ořechovka villa quarter, built between1920 and 1923 and originally demarcated by the streets Pod vyhlídkou in the west, U laboratoře in the east, Pod Ořechovkou and

Dělostřelecká in the north and Na Ořechovce in the south. During the years 1923 to 1930 the quarter was considerably enlarged with the construction of large isolated villas, the most famous of which is the box-like Müller Haus (1930) at Na hradním vodojemen 14 which was designed by the Brno Functionalist architect Adolf Loos. Again there is no entry and without a look inside it is not much of an actual sight (it was not after all designed to 'look' good) but there is talk of turning the building into a memorial to Loos, one of the most important of the modern architects.

The only place of any real interest in the suburb of **Břevnov** is the baroque monastery and Church of St Margaret (Klášter a kostel sv. Markéty) along Markétská. This Benedictine monastery was founded in AD933 by the Czech prince Boleslav II and the Prague Bishop (and Saint) Adalbert. It was the first male cloister in Bohemia. Only the crypt of the original Romanesque church survives today, the present day structure dates from the first half of the eighteenth century and was designed by Christoph Dientzenhofer. The monastery is surrounded by a garden with a well and a baroque pavilion dating between 1722 and 1725. The main road that runs past the monastery has been named after Jan Patočka (1907-77) who was one of Charter 77's original spokesmen. Patočka died of heart failure on 11 March 1977 following an 11-hour interrogation by the secret police.

A short walk westwards of the monastery along Zeyerova alej is the park of **Hvězda**, one of Prague's most peaceful with a combination of wide green avenues and wild woodland. Originally called the New Royal Enclosure and founded by Ferdinand I in 1530, it was converted into a public park in 1797. At its centre is an interesting star-shaped Renaissance building personally designed in 1555 by the Archduke Ferdinand of Tyrol as a summer palace for his wife (*hvězda* means star). Fully restored during the 1950s it today houses a museum with exhibitions concerning the reactionary writer Alois Jirásek (1851-1930), the historical artist Mikuláš Aleš (1852-1913) and the 1620 Battle of Bílá Hora (or White Mountain) which took place nearby, though it is the building itself which is the main attraction. Look out for details of the occasional chamber music concerts that are staged here.

A short walk south-east of the park is the limestone summit of **Bílá Hora** itself, the scene, on 8 November 1620, of the first battle of the Thirty Years War in which in under an hour the Czechs lost their aristocracy, sovereignty and religious independence to the Catholic troops of the Habsburg Emperor Maximilian — a situation that would continue for the next 300 hundred years. At the top of the hill there is a good view stretching across to Ruzyně airport and a small stone monument (*mohyla*), while along Karlovarská one may find the Catholic Church of Our Lady Victorious (Panna Marie Vítězná) which originally started out life as a small chapel erected soon after the battle — the present day structure dates between 1704 and 1730 and is the work of K. Luna. The so-called Large Ale-house (Velká Hospoda) at Karlovarská 41 (over the other side of the tram stop) originally started out life as a Servite monastery, construction work began in 1628 but was never completed though aspects of the original architecture are clearly visible in the exterior.

If you really want to get away from the hub of the city without actually leaving it then probably the best place to head for is the **Šárka Valley** limestone gorge, a shortish walk north of the Hvězda park. By far the most dramatic section is the Divoká Šárka where there is a café and open-air swimming pool for good measure; the Kartografie Praha 120,000 city map shows the walking paths in the area. Heading along the valley back up in the direction of Dejvice one can only walk along the path as far as it meets the road Horoměřicka after which one can either catch a bus back to the centre or walk along the quiet road V Šáreckém údolí to where the Šárka stream flows into the Vltava.

The Šárka Valley actually derives its name from a Czech legend sometime in the seventh or eighth century after the death of Libuše, the founder of Prague and the country's first and last female ruler, the women of her court apparently refused to submit to the rule of her husband Přemysl and left Vyšehrad to found a colony on the other side of the river. In an effort to ensnare a young fearsome warrior named Ctirad the women tied one of their number (Šárka) naked to a tree in the expectation that he would take her to be in distress and attempt to rescue her. In her brief meeting v 'h Ctirad Šárka unfortunately fell in love with him and so devastated was she at what she had done to him she threw herself off a cliff down into the valley below.

South to Smíchov and Zbraslav

Smíchov is a nineteenth-century working class district and one of the liveliest of Prague's suburbs. It contains within its boundaries an eclectic bunch of anomalies that make it a little hard to pin down the precise character of the area, though industrial traditions remain strong here and Smíchov also plays host to the city's largest brewery (brewing the Staropramen brand). Factories and traffic vie with each other in the pollution stakes and the large minority of gypsies in the neighbourhood lend it a slightly exotic air, especially on sultry summer evenings though the other side of this is that if you head westwards you will soon find yourself in one of Prague's most exclusive villa quarters while to the north Smíchov actually takes in a large part of the Petřín wood together with much of the city's university accommodation and the Strahov stadium (actually the largest in the world).

The best place to head for to begin a tour of Smíchov is the metro station Anděl, blessed with the latest of the city's McDonald's restaurants. The nearby náměstí 14 října is dominated by the neo-Renaissance church of St Wenceslas (kostel sv. Václava) which was built in between 1881 and 1885 after a plan by A. Barvitius. Next door to this (technically on Matoušova) is the baroque Portheim Summer Palace built in 1725 by K. I. Dientzenhofer for his family. From 1758 to the nineteenth century it belonged to the Buquoy family after which it passed into the hands of the Porges family of Portheim. The building is presently undergoing restoration.

A short walk west of the square along Mozartova is the Mozart Museum at **Bertramka**, a homestead dating from the latter half of the seventeenth century named after one-time owner Bertram. During visits to Prague in 1786, 1787 and 1791 Mozart stayed here as a guest of the then owner composer F. X. Dušek and his singing wife Josefina (with whom Mozart was rumoured to be on intimate terms for a while). It was during his visit here in 1787 that Mozart composed his opera *Don Giovanni* which was premiered at the Estates Theatre in Central Prague, with Mozart (the conductor on the opening night) actually handing the just-composed overture to the orchestra to play through without rehersal, the ink on the scores barely dry. Though substantially damaged by fire in 1871 this was one of the few gentry villas to survive the nineteenth century industrialization of Smíchov and in the mid-1950s the house was fully restored. Today the interiors are furnished in the style of Mozart's time — exhibits include a piano which Mozart is said to have played and thirteen of his intimate bodily hairs. At the far end of the garden is a stone table over which Mozart is said to have mulled and mused. Regular concerts take place here during the summer.

Nearby and well worth a visit, tucked between the two main roads Plzeňská and Vrchlického, is the **Malá Strana Cemetery**, founded after the 1680 epidemic and in use until 1884. It is a hugely atmospheric combination of ivy and disintegrating late baroque and neo-Classical sculpture. Dušek and his wife are probably the two most famous names to be found here though one may be interested to know that the sculptor J. Malínský designed his own tombstone. Standing in the cemetery is the Empire-style church of the Holiest Trinity (1831-7). A small chapel dating back to 1680 stands by the cemetery gate.

From outside the cemetery one could catch a tram a couple of stops up along Plzeňská to the **Klamovka Park**, originally laid out in the mid-eighteenth century. On display in the park is a neo-Classical Temple of Night (dating from around 1790), a neo-Gothic pavilion (dating from around 1820) and a rococo garden pavilion dating from the end of the eighteenth century. Buses lead from outside the Klamovka park up the hill (along Podbělohorská Pod stadiony and then Vaníčková) to outside the enormous **Strahov Stadium** dating from 1926. Since 1955 it has been the scene of all the national Spartakiads. Covering an area of some 15 acres (6 hectares) and with a capacity for 220,000 spectators and 40,000 performing

Bertramka, the ornate villa in Prague where Mozart composed Don Giovanni

gymnasts it is actually the biggest staduim in the world.

Opposite the stadium are several large rows of sixties university accommodation blocks which serve as very cheap but very noisy tourist student accommodation during the summer months. The end of the road Jezdecká that leads through them takes one to the back of the **Petřín Wood**. A short walk downhill to the right from here is located the church of St Michael, an eighteenth-century wooden orthodox church moved here from Medvědovce (in the Ukraine) in 1929. This may provide a 'raster' for those planning to seek out similar such edifices to be found in the very north-easternmost part of Slovakia. Still more to the right a little bit further down the hill is the Empire-style Kinský Villa (1827-31). It used to house a collection of folk costumes and art gathered together as part of the 1891 exhibition but at present it lies forlorn and empty (though pregnant with possibilities).

Exit Petřín Wood via náměsti Kinských. Between the flagpoles here used to stand the Soviet tank T23, probably better known as the Pink Tank following events that took place in 1991. T23 was reputedly the first Soviet tank to enter Prague during its liberation on 9 May 1945. Following the collapse of the Communist regime the tank somehow managed to remain in place as the city authorities pondered over whether it was a monument to the war or to Communism before in 1991 Situationist artist David Černy finally decided to take matters into his own hands, painted it bright bubble-gum pink and stuck a large papier-mach penis on top of it. Černy was promptly arrested for 'crimes against the state' and the tank was repainted green, only for a group of twelve outraged MPs, using their special immunity from prosecution, to repaint it pink. After a couple of weeks Černy was released and the tank was finally removed; it is now situated in the Museum of Aeronautics and Cosmonautics just off Mladoboleslavská in Prague 9.

Surprizingly, one of Prague's finest art museums is situated in the village of **Zbraslav**, some 6 miles (10km) south of the main town though still within city limits — it is about a 30-minute journey by public transport, take bus 129, 241, 243 or 255 from outside Smíchovské nádraží (on metro line B). The National Gallery's collection of modern Czech sculpture is currently laid out in the courtyard and gardens of a baroque former Cistercian monastery (which was originally Přemyslid King Otakar II's hunting lodge) situated at the confluence of the rivers Vltava and Berounka. The present day appearance of the building dates from the reconstruction of the early eighteenth century. Among the pieces on display are outstanding works by Josef Václav Myslbek who made the St Wenceslas monument currently standing in Wenceslas square, Ladislav Šaloun (responsible for the Hus monument in Staroměstské náměsti), Stanislav Sucharda and Otto Gutfreund as well as *The Motorcyclist* the only surviving work by Otakar Švec who was responsible for the Stalin monument which used to stand on the Letná plain. There is a special section of the exhibition for the visually impaired and blind comprising some twenty copies of the exhibits on show; braille catalogues are available.

Further Information
— Prague —

Places to Visit In and Around Prague

East of the Centre Žižkov and Vinohrady

Military Museum
U památníku 2
☎ 27 29 65
Open: April to October 9.30am-4.30pm, closed Mondays. November to March 8.30am-5pm Monday to Friday only.

Žižkov Tower
Mahlerovy sady
Open: 9am-10pm daily.

New Jewish Cemetery
Jana Želivského
Open: April to August 8am-5pm, September to March 8am-4pm, closed Friday and Saturday.

Olšany Cemetery
Vinohradská
Open: daily, November to February 9am-4pm, March to April 8am-6pm, May to September 8am-7pm, October 8am-6pm.

North of the Centre Holešovice, Bubeneč and Troja

Museum of Technology
Kostelní 42
☎ 37 36 51
Open: 9am-5pm, closed Mondays.

Planetarium
Stromovka park
Open: 8am-12noon and 1-6pm, Monday to Thursday.

Maroldova Panoráma
Výstaviště
Open: 9am-5pm daily.

Troja Château
U trojského zámku
Open: April to September 10am-5pm, closed Mondays.

City Zoo
U trojského zámku
Open: daily, April 7am-5pm, May 7am-6pm, June to September 7am-7pm, October to March 7am-4pm.

The Western Suburbs

Hvězda Château
Hvězda park
☎ 36 79 38
Open: 10am-5pm, closed Mondays.

South to Smíchov and Zbraslav

Bertramka Mozart Museum
Mozartova 169
☎ 54 38 93
Open: daily 9.30am-5pm.

Malá Strana Cemetery
Plzeňská
Open: May to September 9am-7pm.

Czech Sculpture Museum
Zbraslav Monastery
Open: April to November 10am-6pm, closed Mondays.

Useful Information: Prague

Bicycle Rental
Cyklo Centrum
27-9 Karlovo náměstí
Nové Město

Car Rental

Avis
Opletalova 33
☎ 34 10 97

Budget
Národní 17
☎ 232 29 16

Hertz
Hotel Palace
Panská 12
☎ 236 16 37

Car Repair
24-hour breakdown service at
Limuzská 12
(☎ 77 34 55)

Chemist
24-hour service at Na příkopě 7
(☎ 22 00 81)

Cinema
Look in either *Prague Post* or
Prognosis for a complete listing of
films shown in English. NB *české
titulky* means Czech subtitles.

Currency Exchange
Banking hours are 7.30am-12noon
and 1.30-3.30pm Monday to Friday,
otherwise there are numerous
exchange outlets in the centre of town
open to 8pm or later.

Dentist
Emergency service at Vladislavova 22
(☎ 26 13 74) 7am-7pm.

Emergency
Police ☎ 158
Ambulance ☎ 155
Fire brigade ☎ 150

Filling Stations
24-hour service at:
Karlínské náměstí (Prague 3)
Olšanká (Prague 3)
Plzeňská (Prague 5)

Strakonická (Prague 5)
Evropská (Prague 6)
Argentinská (Prague 7)

Hospital
Záchranná služba
Dukelských hrdinů 21
Holešovice
☎ 155 (emergency)

Lost Property
Bolzanova 5
☎ 24 84 30

Police
Central police station is at Konviktská
14 (emergency ☎ 158).

Post Office
Main post office is at Jindřišská 14
(☎ 26 48 41). Letters sent poste
restante will arrive here.

Taxi
24-hour minicab service ☎ 20 29 51-9
English is usually understood.

Theatre, Ballet, Opera and Music
Look for the current listings guide in
either *Prague Post* or *Prognosis* or
pick up the leaflet *The Month in
Prague* from the PIS (Prague Information Service) on Na příkopě. The most
important venues have their own box
offices or there are ticket agencies
springing up in the centre of town (eg
Sluna in the Alfa arcade on Wenceslas
square). The PIS sells tickets for most
main events. Often standby tickets are
available on the night from the venue.

Tourist Information Office
Prague Information Service
Na příkopě 20
Nové Město
☎ 54 44 44
Open: Monday to Friday 8am-8pm,
Saturday 8am-3.30pm.

2 • North from Prague
The Elbe Valley

Nature has undeniably endowed North Bohemia with an abundance of scenic charms, but unfortunately the place has become more renowned as an ecological disaster area due to the presence of numerous brown coal-burning power stations and a huge open-cast brown coal mine. Already by the end of the nineteenth century factories and mines were very much a part of the region's landscape and with the collapse of the Habsburg empire at the end of the Great War the newly-formed Czechoslovak Republic actually became the world's tenth most industrialised state.

Historically the region has been part of Bohemia since the first Přemyslid princes, though large numbers of Germans from neighbouring Saxony have always drifted over the border into this area. The incorporation of this part of Bohemia into the new Czechoslovak Republic in 1918 was a bitter blow for the German speaking population, which had already set up an independent political regime of its own in this region on the breakup of the Austro-Hungarian Empire. It was decided however, at the Versailles Peace Conference, that without the natural resources contained here the newly-formed Czechoslovak state would lack economic viability and so the German claims were ignored and the area was declared part of Czechoslovakia. The virtual collapse of the industrial economy during the early 1930s (as a result of the worldwide economic depression) unfortunately only served to ferment problems between the Germans and the Czechs and in the parliamentary elections of May 1935 the Sudeten German Party, which called for the uniting of the Sudetenland with Germany, gained almost two thirds of the German Sudeten vote and ended up sending the second largest bloc of representatives to the Czechoslovak parliament. It is worth stating here that the Sudetenland was a political and not a geographical entity; it covered sections of North Bohemia and Moravia located in the vicinity of the Sudeten mountains and was identified by the presence of a predominantly German speaking population (the German minority in Czechoslovakia numbered some 3.2 million in 1930). When the protests of the Sudetenlanders became more violent, they convinced Britain and France that the Czechoslovak government should be forced to be more conciliatory towards them;

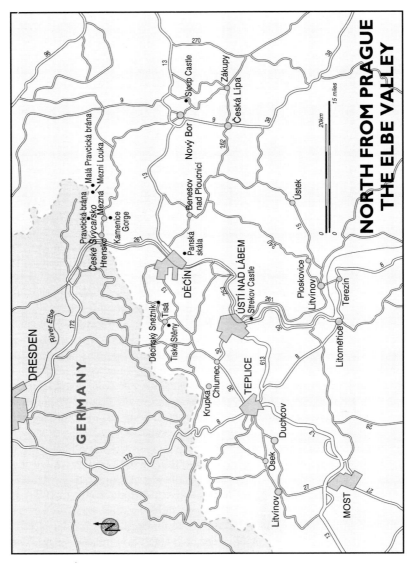

eventually this included full autonomy for the Sudetenland and the adoption
of a pro-German foreign policy but still no accommodation was reached and
in September 1938 France and Great Britain met with Germany and Italy in
Munich where they agreed to issue an ultimatum to Czechoslovakia to cede
the Sudetenland to Germany within 10 days. Explaining the Munich
Agreement Neville Chamberlain pronounced, 'How terrible, fantastic,
incredible it is that we should be digging trenches and trying on gas masks

Colourful Bohemian folk costumes

The River Elbe at Deččín (Chapter 2)

The church at Bilá Hora, near the site of the Battle of the White Mountain, in Prague (Chapter 1)

here because of a quarrel in a far-away country between people of whom we know nothing'. The region suffered very badly during the latter stages of World War II when it became the target of sustained allied bombing raids, and at the end of the war the German population was forcibly expelled and its houses were given to Czechs.

The area covered in this chapter is divided in two by the River Elbe. The best base for exploring the region is probably the uninviting river port of Děčín from where it is easiest to begin walks in the České Švýcarsko (Bohemian Switzerland) which features weird and wonderful sandstone rock formations, a couple of ruined castles and one of the largest natural rock arches in the world. The regional capital is Ústí nad Lábem, a little further south along the Elbe (or Labe); heavily bombed during World War II, its most attractive feature is undoubtedly the dramatically poised Střekov Castle, probably best viewed from the main railway line that runs alongside the river. Teplice is a wonderful antidote to the spa towns in Western Bohemia; its centre is under reconstruction, and will no doubt one day look very nice, but nothing can alter its position in the middle of a black industrial heartland — dramatically illustrated by the vast open cast brown coal mine between Duchcov and Most. Litoměřice is another good base for exploring the region and is certainly more attractive than Děčín; 2 miles (3km) to the south of Litoměřice is the fortress town of Terezín which was transformed into a transit camp for Jews on their way to Poland during the last war. A Gestapo prison camp was situated in a smaller fortress next door. The area to the east of the Labe is full of treats on a smaller scale with a good selection of châteaux and ruined castles, some more walking possibilities and a number of attractive glass-making towns.

Děčín

No one would deny that Děčín has a very attractive situation, straddling as it does the Elbe at the gateway to Bohemia; as a town however its attractions are limited, although it is by far the best base for exploring the region, especially if one wants to pay a visit to the nearby sandstone formations that make up the České Švýcarsko. Děčín actually came into existence in its present day form in 1948 with the amalgamation of two towns, Děčín and Podmokly, situated opposite each other on either side of the river. The oldest of these towns is Děčín (or 'Tetschen', as it was known to German speakers) on the east bank. In 1128 there is mention of a castle here and around this a settlement grew up, which in 1283 was granted the privileges of a town. The town was fortified in the second half of the sixteenth century when an estimated 2,500 people lived here. Děčín was devastated during the Thirty Years War by Saxon and Swedish troops and in 1779 the defensive function of the town ceased with the construction of the fortress at Terezín — the

The River Elbe at Děčín

castle was consequently rebuilt as a château and the town walls were knocked down. Nazi troops occupied the town on 3 October 1938, the Soviet army 'liberated' it on 9 May 1945.

The main rail and bus stations are in the former town of **Podmokly** which developed in the nineteenth century from a small village into the second biggest trans-shipment centre for coal and industrial goods into Germany after Ústí nad Lábem. The main square in Podmokly (Benešovo náměstí) is situated next to the railway station and is dominated by the Grand Hotel. Just beyond the Sever Hotel, on Mládeže, is the **Town Museum** which is housed in a former hunting lodge — it is mainly a mixture of art and shipping but also features a very good exhibition on the lives of the 450,000 Czechs deported to Germany during World War II as forced labour. From here continue down Mládeže, walk under the railway and continue on up Labské nábřeži until you come to a lift (*výtah*) to take you to the top of the 492ft (150m) high Pastyřská Stěna (Shepherd's Rock) — pay for the journey in the lift. At the top there is a restaurant, a small zoo and a stunning view over the river to the old town of Děčín. There is also a path up to the top of Pastyřská Stěna — starting a little further on along the road.

Děčín, on the other side of the river, is dominated by its **château** standing tall upon a 164ft (50m) high sandstone cliff overlooking the Elbe. The late eighteenth-century baroque château was built on the site of a former Gothic castle that was destroyed by fire; Chopin was a guest here in 1835. It is accessible by a 984ft (300m) long path called the Dlouhá Jízda (Long Ride), which was hewn in to the rock in 1670. The building used to house a Soviet army barracks and is presently not open to the public though one can visit its terraced baroque **Rose Garden** which was laid out in the last quarter of the seventeenth century — it is said to derive its name from the terrace and columns made of rosy sandstone. From the gardens one has a good view of the big red baroque Church of the Holy Cross (1687) whose wall paintings date back to 1792. One other point of interest is the late Gothic bridge (1540) featuring baroque sculptures by J.M. Brokoff that spans the River Ploučnice south of the château.

Walking in the České Švýcarsko

The main reason people stay in Děčín, other than to break a journey, is to visit the interesting scenery of the Elbe Sandstone Region nearby with its fascinating rock features, gorges and streams which lie amidst the steep, thickly-forested hills which stretch to the north and west of the town. The landscape features of this area were developed in the Cretaceous geological period, that began 135 million years ago, and result from the fact that sandstone is a very soft rock, easily eroded by the actions of wind and water, which over hundreds of millenia have moulded the rocks into their present form. The fast flowing streams and rivers of the area have also carved out steep-sided valleys and gorges, the sides of which are covered with dense forests of spruce and pine trees.

There are two principal areas of interest around the village of Hřensko, to the north of Děčín, and around the village of Tisá, to the west. A map called *České Švýcarsko* which shows all the walking tracks and features described in this section can be bought from bookshops. Visitors who want to appreciate the full benefits of this region should be prepared for a lot of walking since most of the places of interest are not accessible by road. The area is known as the České Švýcarsko (Bohemian Switzerland) after two Swiss painters who came here in the eighteenth century and never returned home, preferring instead the 'new Switzerland' that they felt they had discovered.

Hřensko is a pretty village 7 miles (12km) north of Děčín on the main road between Děčín and Dresden. It is from here that one can walk to the main places of interest in the Elbe sandstone region, the most important attraction being the fantastic rock arch Pravčická brána, the highest natural arch in Europe. Buses run from Děčín to Hřensko (a 25 minute journey), or alternatively one could take a boat along the Elbe. Boats run from mid-April to the end of September and while on the subject, an easy day excursion from Děčín could also be made to Dresden by boat, if the service — discontinued in the early 1990s — starts up again. (Dresden is also easily accessible by train from Děčín).

Hřensko itself was developed as a centre for the production of timber, which was cut in the sawmills in the village before being sent in boats down the Elbe. The land across the river from Hřensko is actually in Germany and the river here is narrow enough to be able to read the large sign boards of the railway station opposite which serves the village of Schöna. In the nineteenth century Schöna and Hrěnsko were linked by a steam-powered ferry, but today there are no means at all of crossing the river at this point. There are a couple of hotels and restaurants in Hřensko to cater for the large number of German day trippers who flock to the village in the summer months.

From Hřensko it is a 3 mile (5km) walk (initially along the minor road running alongside the river Kamenice) to the **Pravčická brána** rock bridge. The last part through thick, unrelenting forest is quite steep, but the paths are well-made and used by many walkers (in fact it is worth avoiding at weekends). The bridge itself is 98ft (30m) long and 69ft (21m) high, only two other natural rock bridges in the world are bigger, both are in Utah. It is not actually free to get to the very top but the views more than compensate for the minimal expense incurred. The wild surrounding scenery of jagged, highly weathered sandstone rocks poking out from a thick covering of fir trees, lends a surreal air to the whole area, particularly if cloud or mist collects in isolated pockets between the rugged cliffs in the area i nmediately below and surrounding the arch. A restaurant built under the arch, which dates from the nineteenth century, provides walkers with much-needed refreshment.

It is about another hour and a quarter walk from the bridge to **Mezní Louka** (buses run to and from Děčín from here) where there is a hotel and campsite with bungalows for rent. From Mezní Louka one can walk 1 mile (2km) south-east to the unassuming village of Mezná from where a green-marked path plunges one down to the River Kamenice. A little wooden bridge takes one over the river from where it is about $^{1}/_{2}$ mile (1km) walk in the direction of Hřensko to a landing stage. Boatmen then take you 1 mile $1^{1}/_{2}$km down the **Kamenice gorge** to a landing stage about 1 mile (2km) east of Hřensko. These boat trips (9am-5pm May to September, though do check ahead in Děčín) have been operating since the 1890s and are justifiably popular so be prepared to wait. One must walk from the second stage, back to Hřensko.

Alternatively from Mezní Louka one could follow the much less busy red-marked path 9 miles (14km) on to Jetřichovice passing a smaller rock bridge, the **Malá Pravčická brána**, and a castle ruin (Loupežnický hrádek), featuring very little actual castle but a good view. Much of the walk is through dark, dank woodland that features a wide array of funghi and those of a sensitive disposition should avert their eyes from the infamous stinkhorn, considered too shocking a sight to sully the pages of Victorian journals (the

Spectacular rock formations in the Elbe Sandstone Region, near Děčín

smell is designed to attract flies and other insects which assist in the dispersing of the spores). Jetřichovice itself has a bit of charm provided by the huge wooden farmsteads typical of the region but not much else; buses run from here back to Děčín. Hiking country to the north of Jetřichovice is pretty deserted, it is good walking territory with a couple of ruined castles to head for but getting back might cause problems.

Possibly less interesting, though still rewarding, is a trip west of Děčín to the rock town of **Tiské Stěny**, situated next to the village of Tisá. At present there is no direct bus here from Děčín so one may well have to catch a bus or train to Libouchec and then walk 1 $^1/_2$ miles (2 $^1/_2$km) north. A system of well-marked paths leads around the rocks and once here much less energy is expelled than over the water. It is a 20km walk from Tiské Stěny back to Děčín on the red trail, though one can shorten this by avoiding the village of Ostrov and walking along the road instead. The path goes past the **Děčínský Sněžník** 2,388ft (728m), a giant rock plateau where there is a lookout tower which is sometimes open. The view from the top of the tower is said to be very good though there is a good enough one at the bottom too. Unfortunately the surrounding woodland is a little unhealthy in places, having been damaged by acid rain and other forms of pollution.

Ústí nad Lábem to Most via Teplice

The route described in this section begins at Ústí nad Lábem, a town on the Elbe to the south of Děčín, and a port and industrial centre, and then heads west from there away from the Elbe Valley, through the spa town of Teplice to towns in the North Bohemian coal basin.

Ústí nad Lábem is the regional capital of North Bohemia. It is the second largest port on the Elbe after Hamburg and most noted now for its chemical industry. It was a solidly German port until the end of World War II when its German citizens were expelled and most recently hit the headlines in 1993 when its local beauty queen suggested that the same fate should befall the local gypsy community (the audience applauded). The first recorded mention of Ústí is in AD993, as a customs station on the Elbe on the trade route between Prague and Meissen (Germany); in 1260 it was granted its town charter. The town was largely destroyed during one of the biggest battles of the Hussite Wars in 1426 (commemorated by a monument at Na běhání 3 miles/5km to the west) and only really began to expand to anything like its present size during the mid-nineteenth century. Ústí was once again reduced to rubble during air raids in April 1945, when more than 3,000 people were killed and one fifth of the houses and almost all of the town's factories were destroyed. The steeple of the fourteenth-century Gothic Church of the Assumption of Our Lady on Hradiště in the town centre leans almost 7ft (2m) as a consequence of the bombing — it is the most inclined tower north of the Alps. Just along Hradiště towards the railway station is the eighteenth-century baroque monasterial Church of St Adalbert, now a concert and exhibition hall. Most of the buildings in the town centre and the housing estates on the outskirts date from the recon-structions of the 1960s and are not especially pleasing to the eye, though an interesting mosaic may be found on the building belonging to the North Bohemian Regional National Committee on the town's main square, Mírové náměstí, which depicts ten events in the history of North Bohemia (with a predictably Marxist slant). Other buildings of note around the centre are the neo-Romanesque Church of St Paul on Bratislavská, the Art Nouveau building of the State Theatre on Fučikova and the former villa of the banker and coal-magnate Petschek on Vladimírská. There is also a zoo a short distance east of the town centre, just around the cliff.

One mile (2km) south of Ústí, dramatically poised above the Elbe on an 279ft (85m) high volcanic rock, is the picturesque **Střekov Castle**, built in 1319 by King John of Luxembourg. The castle was restored in Renaissance style in the mid-sixteenth century by Wenzel von Lobkowicz and destroyed at the end of the eighteenth century — though it remained in the hands of the Lobkowicz family until 1945 (the castle is today in the process of restitution proceedings). The most famous visitor to the castle is Richard Wagner who came here in 1842 and derived sufficient inspiration from his visit to begin work on his opera *Tannhäuse*r; 'I obtained a tiny room in which a bed of straw was made up for me to sleep on at night.

Daily ascent of Wostrai, the highest peak in the area, revived me in such a way that, on one moonlit night, I clambered around the ruins of the castle wrapped only in a sheet, thereby hoping to provide myself with the ghost that was otherwise lacking, and delighting myself with the thought that some nearby wanderer might see me and be terrified'. Although the keep has been partially restored the castle today is pretty ruinous and the entrance charge is just a little bit cheeky — though on the positive side there is no guided tour and the views are predictably superb. It is about a 40-minute walk from Ústí nad Lábem's main railway station, but a local bus from the main square will get you most of the way — buy a ticket from one of the automatic machines.

The broad, undulating countryside around **Chlumec** (5 miles/8km north-west of Ústí nad Lábem) has often been the scene of military conflict. The most famous battle took place on 29 August 1813 when the combined Prussian, Russian and Austrian forces trapped the French army under Marshal Dominique-Réné who was forced to surrender with 10,000 men. This paved the way for the more decisive allied victory at Leipzig 6 weeks later which opened up the way to France. The battle is commemorated by several monuments.

Anyone remotely interested in a view could travel the 3 miles (5km) south-west from Chlumec to the old mining town of **Krupka**, founded in the fourteenth century, where there is a magnificent baroque pilgrimage church. Signs from the church lead to the bottom station of a chairlift which takes one on a satisfyingly long journey up to the summit of the hill Komáří Vizka (2,654ft/809m), on the eastern limb of the Krušné Hory mountains which stretch from here to Karlovy Vary. From the top there is a fantastic view over some frankly uninspiring scenery. In the valleys on the other side of the hill one can see the villages of Saxony, only a mile or so away across the German border. A blue-marked walking track, which does not follow the route of the chairlift, links the top and bottom stations.

Wagner described the spa town of **Teplice**, 2 miles (3km) to the south of Krupka, as the most 'beautiful place' he knew. Times change. Situated slap-bang in the middle of a vast and ugly industrial heartland the former beauty and charm of Teplice has been sadly eroded by time. According to legend the spa waters here were discovered by accident by a swineherd in AD763 but coins found in the Primeval Spring (Pravřídlo) and the Giant Spring (Obří pramen) testify to the fact that the local curative springs were known to the Celts and Romans. In 1156 a convent of Benedictine nuns was founded here by Queen Judith, the wife of Vladislav II at the time the Benedictine sisters were the only religious order expressly permitted to take

A chairlift at Krupka in the Krûsně Hory mountains

baths. The convent was destroyed in 1426 by the Hussites and the site was converted into a small stronghold which in the sixteenth century was rebuilt into a Renaissance château. The building has since been renovated in both baroque and Empire styles and today functions as a museum. The spa resort itself developed from a village called Teplitz (from 'teply', warm) around the convent. It began to prosper in the sixteenth century but only really developed into a major centre after it had been completely rebuilt in simple, elegant Empire style following the great fire of 1793. In the early nineteenth century Teplice became one of Europe's major social centres with visits from Chopin, Wagner, Liszt, Ibsen, Goethe and Beethoven amongst others and it was in the château on 9 September 1813, just prior to the battle of Leipzig, that Tsar Alexander I of Russia, Emperor Francis I of Austria and King Frederick William of Prussia concluded the 'Holy Alliance' against Napoleon. Unfortunately in the 1880s the flooding of the nearby Dollinger mine badly affected the flow of the spring waters and for many years the waters had to be pumped to the surface — it is only recently with the construction of wells over 3,280ft (1,000m) deep that their supply has become plentiful again. What has probably done more to deter visitors however is the rapid industrial growth of Teplice and the surrounding region, which has rather tended to snuff out the charm of all but the innermost crevices of the town. The waters are said to be good for treatment of the motor organs and the circulatory system but anyone with respiratory problems is advised to avoid Teplice especially in winter when a lignite-tinged smog settles on the town and sulphur dioxide levels reach twenty-five times the World Health Organization recommended maximum.

The centre of the old spa town is Zámecké náměstí which is dominated by a 65ft (20m) high Plague Column (1718-9), the work of Matthias Braun. The castle on the square has housed the regional museum since 1897 and features archaeological, historical and natural history collections as well as memorial rooms devoted to Beethoven and Pushkin. Its enormous gardens behind are now a large park. Adjoining the north side of the château is the Renaissance church of the Exaltation of the Cross, remodelled in neo-Gothic style in the late nineteenth century. The baroque parish Church of St John the Baptist adjacent dates between 1700 and 1703. On the other side of Zámecké náměstí there are some interestingly reconstructed shops, part of a wider reconstruction of the town centre continued on the narrow street Lázeňská leading off from the square where you will find the yellow Zlatá harfa house (with a plaque commemorating Beethoven's stay in 1811) and the blue Městské Lázně, a reconstruction of the municipal baths of 1838-9. The park at the end of Lázeňská is dominated by the big white Dům kultury and the greenhouse-style New Colonnade (this is Bohemia after all). There is a bit more spa to the east of this along Lipová in the once separate village of Šanov (linked to Teplice in 1894) which is overlooked by a large red brick Protestant church on Zeyerovo náměstí. It basically just consists of a collection of pleasant but peeling villas and spa pensions and there is not actually a great deal to do here. A crazy golf next to the Art Nouveau Thermal Baths on V. Hálke might occupy some time if you have forgotten your bathing suit, alternatively one could walk along Pod Doubravkou to the top of Doubravská hora where are situated the ruins of Doubravská Castle which was built between 1478 and 1486 and destroyed in 1644 — in the nineteenth century the castle was restored and the keep was transformed into an observation tower.

Perhaps more interesting is the château in the small mining town of **Duchcov**, 5 miles (8km) to the west of Teplice. The original castle at Duchcov (formerly known as Dux) was a late sixteenth-century structure belonging to the Lobkovic family and acquired by the Wallensteins in 1642 in whose hands it remained until 1921. Between 1675 and 1685 the property was rebuilt and extended by the French architect J.B. Mathey and in 1722 the gardens were laid out in baroque style. Six years later a large hospice containing frescoes by V.V. Reiner was built in the garden's western half and between 1735 and 1738 Matthias Braun created almost sixty sculptures for the garden. Between 1812 and 1818 the château was remodelled and the gardens relaid in English style which led to the selling off of much of the statuary, more of the statues were destroyed during a fire in May 1945 and in 1959 the hospice was pulled down to make way for an open-cast coal mine (there is a good view of the mine from inside the château). In 1988 many of the most important paintings in the château's collection were unfortunately stolen.

The château's forecourt, facing the town's main square, contains the surviving Braun statues. Adjacent to the main building is the chapel, rebuilt after fire damage sustained in 1945. The 45-minute tour guides you around the remains of the Wallenstein picture gallery via some porcelain and furniture on loan from the Fine Arts Museum in Prague though the bare interiors do little to kindle the spirit of a house which once played host to such luminaries as Schiller, Goethe, Beethoven, Chopin and Tsar Alexander I. Another famous name associated with Duchcov château is that of Giacomo Casanova who lived out the last 13 years of his life here working as a librarian (though he was principally employed by the Count Wallenstein to amuse his guests after dinner). To help while away the time Casanova wrote his memoirs *The History of my Life* (along with various other unpickupable treaties on history and philosophy) and he described his writing as 'the only thing which has kept me from going mad, or dying of grief in the midst of the discomfort and pettifogging annoyances daily caused me by the envious wretches who live with me in this castle'. He was also known to complain about the weather. Casanova died in the château on 4 June 1798 in the room dedicated to his memory. On his deathbed he is reputed to have said 'I have lived as a philosopher and die as a Christian'. Unfortunately there is no grave as the cemetery in which he was buried has long since been incorporated into the park. In the gardens there is a pavilion housing the frescoes of Reiner that used to decorate the dome of the destroyed hospice. A monument near the château park commemorates the hunger-march of the unemployed on 4 February 1931 when four participants were shot by gendarmes at the Duchcov railway viaduct. Be slightly warned that the railway station is a good 20-minute walk from the town centre.

From Duchcov one could head south to Bílina, where there is a seventeenth-century castle and a late Gothic parish church, or 3 miles (5km) north-west to the important baroque monastery of **Osek** — the Cistercian community at Osek was founded in 1198. The earliest surviving part of the building is the chapter house (around 1230) which is joined by steps to a cloister dating from the first half of the fourteenth century. The baroque abbey Church of the Assumption was built in 1712 though the basic form of the original three-aisled Romanesque structure is apparent inside. It has a profusely decorated façade, the work of Ottavio Broggio. Since 1950, when it was taken over by the state, part of the complex has been used as a retirement home for nuns. Along the red trail 1¹/₂ miles (2¹/₂km) above the town are the ruins of a thirteenth-century Gothic castle; on the way there is a monument commemorating 142 miners killed in an accident in the Nelson III shaft in 1934.

Litvínov, a little further west of Osek, has a reasonably pleasant if somewhat unremarkable town centre. It also has a huge chemical plant just to the south and special lights which instruct motorists to switch off their engines when chemical levels in the atmosphere are deemed to be too high, though that does not make it so special in these parts. From Litvínov it is 4 miles (6km) south to **Most**. Anyone looking at a map of North Bohemia will find that there is a large blank gap around the town of Most. Actually come here, and you will see that this is because there is a big hole in the ground at this location, for Most has the dubious privilege of standing right at the edge of a huge open-cast brown coal mine. Brown coal is one of the first stages of coalification, being formed from peat that has been only moderately compressed. On a world scale it is quite plentiful but it is generally not exploited unless there is a local fuel problem as it is prone to disintegration and spontaneous combustion which makes storage and transportation difficult. Problems with storage and transportation mean that to be economical the fuel must be used by industrial and domestic consumers close to the mining area, and unfortunately the effect of this has been to produce a suffocating smog that descends upon the region every winter. The town of

Most is actually so polluted that local schoolchildren have to be provided with respiratory masks.

Both the road and rail networks were shifted south to accommodate the mining and around one hundred villages and towns have been lost including the former town of Most which was gradually demolished during the 1970s. The town today is a completely new settlement (consisting of a series of concrete boxes) and the only part of the original settlement that survives is the valuable early sixteenth-century Gothic Parish Church of the Assumption of the Virgin Mary which was shifted to its present site during September 1975 — an extraordinary technical feat the church (102ft/31m high, 98ft/30m wide and 197ft/60m long) was encased in a giant steel corset and then moved a total of 2,758ft/841m on top of 53 railway wagons at a speed of 120cm per hour. Stabilizing work lasted until the autumn of 1988 when it was finally opened to the public. The plain exterior of the church, designed by Jakob Heilmann, in no way prepares one for the great richness of the artistic treasures contained within the gracious and airy interior, essentially comprising an exhibition of North Bohemian art from the fourteenth to the eighteenth centuries culled from a number of local churches and museums. The church is about ½ mile (1km) walk north from Most's main railway station.

Thankfully alternative sources of energy for the region are now being sought but this will of course lead to further unemployment in the region which can only heighten the resentment between the Czech and Romany communities. Estimates of Romany unemployment are over 50 per cent in the Czech republic and over 70 per cent in the Slovak republic. One of the major problems the Romany community faces in the increasingly competitive employment market is a major lack of education; only 2.5 per cent of Romany children even enter secondary school and the transfer rate of Romany children to special schools for the mentally backward is an astonishing twenty-eight times higher than for Czech and Slovak children — the transfers carried out less with regards to intelligence than language difficulties and cultural differences. Often Romany parents, themselves illiterate, prefer their children to be educated with other Romany children rather than be ignored by pupils and teachers in normal schools, and consequently in an increasingly computer literate society many Romany children do not even possess basic reading and writing skills. There are virtually no Romanies in parliament, the media or the professions and so most Czechs and Slovaks know as little about the Romanies living in their midst as the average visitor and dark stereotypes gain all too familiar currency. Holocaust researchers estimate that over 90 per cent of the Czech Romanies were murdered during World War II, a very real attempted genocide that few people know about and even fewer seem to care about —

an opinion pole published just after the 1989 revolution revealed that only 11 per cent of the population considered there to be no problems in maintaining good relations with the Romanies. The Communists did seriously attempt to integrate the Romanies into mainstream society by dispersing families, banning their language in schools and passing laws to curtail their traditionally migratory lifestyle, but the Romanies would be the first to admit that their culture and way of life is at best different to the rest of society and almost that of a semi-nomadic tribe — in fact the Romanies were originally a low-caste Indian tribe who made their way into central Europe via Persia back in the fifteenth century (though nobody knows exactly why).

Estimates of the numbers of Romanies in both republics are about half a million; these are estimates because many Romanies have not bothered to apply for citizenship of either republic which merely creates further problems and tensions when they attempt to claim social benefits — proof of citizenship is a necessary pre-requisite. When the problems of unemployment fail to be adequately met by social provisions the inevitable rise in crime, begging, black marketeering and alcoholism merely adds credence to the stereotype. Racist attacks have markedly risen during the past few years and the police seem powerless (or reluctant) to intervene.

Litoměřice and Terezín

Back in the valley of the River Elbe, the industrial town of **Litoměřice**, situated at the confluence of the Ohře and Elbe rivers, was once the third largest town in Bohemia and archaeological evidence suggests that Cathedral Hill was occupied back in Celtic times. The Celts were followed by the Marcomanni who in turn were followed by the Slavic Ludoměřic tribe after whom the town is named. In the ninth century a castle was built on the hill and in 1057 the Přemyslid duke Spitihněv II founded the collegiate chapter of St Stephen. From the early twelfth century German craftsmen and merchants migrated here in large numbers and the economic importance of the settlement is underlined by the establishment in 1200 of a mint — in 1227 the settlement was granted a town charter. Much of the medieval town was destroyed during the Thirty Years War and most of the older buildings standing today date from the baroque reconstruction begun in 1655 when a Catholic bishopric was founded here. The architects who most left their mark on the town were Giovanni Broggio and his son Ottavio Broggio. The former was an Italian immigrant who settled in Litoměřice in 1668, the latter was his son who was born here the same year. In 1945 the town suffered a great upheaval when virtually its entire, predominantly German, population was forcibly expelled.

The main bus station and the smaller railway station are a short distance from the centre up Dlouhá. It is about a 5-minute walk from the main railway

The cathedral in Litoměřice, a small town on the River Elbe

station (connecting with the Prague-Děčín line) to the centre. There is at present only one functioning hotel in town, at Vrchlického 10 (to the north-east of the town centre), but there is Čedok on Dlouhá and a couple of agencies on the main square which can help find a private room in town or a hotel out of town for those with their own transport.

Most of the originally Gothic houses around the town's large main square, Mírové náměstí, were destroyed either during the Thirty Years War or the great fire of 1712. Thus, with a few exceptions, most of the houses around the square today date from the eighteenth century. The most interesting house on the square is the Mrázovský dům on the south side at number 15 which has a huge wooden chalice on its roof (1581) — it is a little odd that it is been left there as it is a symbol of the Hussite movement. In the centre of the square is a Plague Column erected by grateful citizens after the plague of 1681. The regional museum is housed in the arcaded Renaissance former Town Hall (1537-9), which is covered in *sgraffito* decoration, at the east end of the square. The museum houses various bits of armour, ecclesiastical treasures, prehistoric remains and illuminated manuscripts though the most interesting part is the panelled council hall dating from 1542. At the south-east corner of the main square is the Church of All Saints, a late Gothic foundation remodelled in Baroque style by Ottavio Broggio in 1718 (though it still boasts the only Gothic spire on the skyline). The highlight of a look inside is the late-fifteenth-century panel painting of the *Agony in the Garden* by the Master of Litoměřice. The street Jezuitska leads from here to the large red Jesuit Church of Our Lady (1704-31) also by Ottavio Broggio. This church was actually used as a storehouse by the local brewery for 40 years after the suppression of the Jesuit Order in 1773. Along the street heading off the north-east corner of the main square, Velké Dominikánska, is Ottavio Broggio's baroque Church of St James.

Exiting the square along Michalská (at the south-western corner) one will come to the town's very worthwhile Art Gallery. On the ground floor is the museum's greatest treasure, the six remaining panels of the so-called Litoměřice Altarpiece painted around 1500. The painter of the piece is not actually known and is always referred to as the Master of Litoměřice. He was almost certainly a court painter to Vladislav Jagiello and the altarpiece was probably executed for the All Saint's Church attached to the Royal Palace in Prague Castle, from where it is likely to have been removed in 1541 when the Palace was destroyed by fire. The rest of the museum consists of a good representative selection of Czech art from the fifteenth to the twentieth centuries including an extensive collection of naïve art.

If you turn north at the end of Michalská you will eventually come to the scant ruins of the town castle, converted in the nineteenth century into a brewery and now being made into a cultural centre, turn south at the end of

Michalská and you will walk up Dómské to the cathedral, passing, a little way down Svatováclavská, the small Church of St Wenceslas (1714-16) built by Ottavio Broggio. The episcopal Church of St Stephen was founded in 1057 and rebuilt after 1655 to the designs of J.D. Orsi and Giovanni Broggio. The light interior contains two paintings by Cranach and a splended high altar by K. Škréta depicting the stoning of St Stephen. Adjoining the cathedral is the late seventeenth-century bishop's residence whilst also in the vicinity is a free-standing bell tower. A short distance away at Máchova 10 is a small memorial room dedicated to the popular Romantic poet Karel Hynek Mácha (1810-36) who lived and died (of consumption) here. In 1938, when this part of Bohemia was seized by the Germans, Mácha's tomb was moved from Litoměřice to Prague's Vyšehrad cemetery. Walking back to the main square along Máchovy schody one will pass some of the original medieval town fortifications. One final attraction of the town are the 'Garden of Bohemia' fruit and vegetable and flower shows held here every September and October.

Two miles (3km) south of Litoměřice, on the west bank of the Elbe and reached by crossing over it via a modern road bridge, stands the town of **Terezín**. This stern and imposing late baroque fortress town was built in 1780 in order to halt the advance of the Prussians into Bohemia. Austrian Emperor Joseph II personally laid the foundation stone and named the settlement 'Theresienstadt' after his mother, the Empress Maria Theresa. The streets are set out on a very rigid grid pattern; the park in the centre of the town was the parade ground. Eight miles (13km) of underground tunnels linked the defences and the so-called Little Fortress about $1/2$ mile (1km) east of the town. In 1784 building was completed, 5,000 civilians were moved into the houses and they shared the town with a garrison of 16,000 soldiers. An Empire-style church of the Resurrection was built on the main square between 1805 and 1810, it is the only building to exceed the height of the surrounding fortification walls. Theresienstadt was the biggest and most modern fortress of the century but it was never actually tested in battle and in 1886 it was closed, though the Little Fortress continued to be used as a prison and it was there in 1914 that the Serb Gavrilo Princip was imprisoned after assassinating Archduke Franz Ferdinand in Sarajevo. Sentenced to 20 years imprisonment he died of tuberculosis in 1918 (he always maintained that the Germans would have started World War I without him anyway).

In 1941 the SS removed the population of Theresienstadt (about 3,500 people) and turned it into a Jewish ghetto. Within a year nearly 60,000 Jews were interned here. Although many died here essentially this was a transit camp and in October 1942 the first transport left for Auschwitz. Terezín was a little different to the other Jewish ghettos though in that it was also used as a cover for the extermination process; there was a degree of self-government, schools were opened and theatrical and operatic performances took place (the scores of at least fifty musical pieces composed here have survived), civilian clothes were allowed to be worn and there were even some mixed barracks. Most importantly reassuring letters were allowed to be sent by internees back home to relatives. When, towards the end of 1943, the International Red Cross asked to inspect one of the Nazi camps the whole place was decked out as a spa town; streets were given names instead of numbers, cafés and shops were opened and a bandstand and benches were put on the main square, Marktplatz, which had previously been fenced off. The Red Cross visited Terezín twice, in June 1943 and April 1945, and were successfully duped both times. On 8 May 1945 Terezín was finally liberated by the Soviet army, but the first days of freedom were marred by a new tragedy — during the last days of the war thousands of people had been transported to Terezín from the evacuated concentration camps in Poland and they brought with them an epidemic of spotted fever which quickly spread throughout the town. By the end of the war out of the 140,000 Jews transported to Terezín from all over Europe more than 33,000 died here and about 87,000 were taken to their deaths elsewhere.

The main fortress today is still a dour garrison town largely populated by soldiers and military police. There is a very empty feel to it and the only place to visit as such is the Ghetto Museum on Komenského, finally opened in 1991 after nearly 50 years of Communist ignorance of the Jewish perspective. Inside there is a permanent exhibition displaying the ghetto's history, a display of pictures painted by inmates and the children's drawings from the Terezín school, next to which is printed the fate of each child. A documentary film is also shown including clips from the Nazi propaganda film shot in Terezín *Hitler gives the Jews a Town*. Many booklets are available and free with the ticket is a map of the town which points out the uses put to the various buildings during the ghetto years. The museum building itself is a former school.

The Communists preferred instead to concentrate attention on the events that took place in the Lesser Fortress during World War II when it was used as a prison by the Prague Gestapo. The Lesser Fortress is outside the main town, a little way along the road to Prague. Essentially this was a political prison used principally to house members of various resistance movements and not a concentration camp though the famous refrain 'Arbeit Macht Frei' may be seen above the entrance gate to one of the yards and the conditions that the inmates were kept in were certainly appalling; one cell intended for forty people was crammed with over one hundred and in cells originally designed for one person up to twelve men would be forced to sleep standing up. Out of the 32,000 people (including 5,000 women) who were imprisoned here during World War II an estimated 2,500 died of bad jailing conditions and disease. In front of this fortress is a vast grave of 29,172 Jews and other victims of Nazism who died at Terezín. Again a map is given free with the entrance ticket so one can walk around at one's own pace, though guides are available if required (often ex-internees). The main exhibition is housed in the eighteenth-century mansion which was home to the Commandant Heinrich Jockel (who was hanged in Litoměřice after the war) and the most important SS officers. A cinema constructed in 1942 for the officers' entertainment shows a documentary film about the prison though a significant number of people would have to turn up here for it to be shown. There is also an exhibition concerning the history of Terezín from 1780 to 1939 in a room by the entrance gate.

A few kilometres west of Terezín is the town of **Lovošice**, a centre of wine production and fruit-growing. The town has a nice enough central marketplace surrounded by Empire-style burghers' houses and dominated by the baroque Church of St Wenceslas. The early baroque castle was built by the Schwarzenbergs on the site of an earlier one. From here it is possible to begin a walk to the highest point in the Central Bohemian Highlands, Mount Milešovka at 2,745ft (837m).

Litoměřice to Děčín via Zákupy

Four miles (7km) north-east of Litoměřice, and accessible by bus or train, is the large country house at **Ploskovice**. The building was designed by Octavian Broggio — who built most of Litoměřice — in 1720 for Anna Maria Francesca, the Grand Duchess of Tuscany, though the bold and enthusiastic interior decoration largely dates from the nineteenth century when it was converted into the summer residence of the Emperor Ferdinand V. The pleasant gardens were laid out in 1850. The short guided tour lasts only about half an hour, but even so some of the exhibits (eg 'Portrait of an unknown noble woman by unknown artist, probably eighteenth century') scrape the barrel somewhat.

Situated a further 7 miles (12km) east is the town of **Úštěk**, standing by the shores of the Chmelař recreational lake. The town grew up on the trade route between Litoměřice and Česká Lípa, and its medieval core has been very well preserved (indeed the town as a whole is stuck in a bit of a time-warp). The broad main street is lined by a set of attractive late Gothic houses rebuilt after the great fire of 1765. Standing at the middle of the broadest point is the parish Church of St Peter and St Paul built by the Jesuits between 1765 and 1769, the altarpiece inside is by Karel Škréta. Opposite the Town Hall (1773) stands the unobtrusive former castle, remodelled into a Renaissance château, which was occupied by the Jesuits after the Thirty Years War and by a brewery at the end of the eighteenth century. Surviving from the original fortifications is the so-called Picard's Bastion, named after the refugees who came here from northern France in the late sixteenth century to escape religious persecution. In the western part of town along Kamenna are a number of picturesque wooden houses (called *ptačí domky*, bird's houses) perched on a steep rock constructed by Italian workers who built the railway here in the mid-nineteenth century.

Two miles (4km) along the yellow-marked trail from the town is the ruined castle Hrádek, founded in the thirteenth century, which has a huge and very well preserved tower and walls of up to 39ft (12m) in height. Folk architecture may be admired in the nearby village of Ostré and also in Kravaře where there is a folk museum exhibition. A 1 mile (1¹/₂km) walk along the green trail from Kravaře (or 6 miles/9km on the red from Úštěk) will bring one to the ruin of Ronov castle, a splendid observation point (1,814ft/553m).

The district town of **Česká Lípa** is a busy and boring industrial centre and one is only likely to spend time here waiting for a bus or train. The most interesting building here is the Červený dum (Red House), a small, *sgraffitied* Renaissance palace which served as a hunting lodge. The oldest church in the town is the Church of St Mary Magdalene, built by the Cistercians in 1200 though altered in the sixteenth, seventeenth and eighteenth centuries. The Church of the Holy Cross (1381) has been similarly altered but retains its Gothic portal. The baroque church of St Mary dates from 1714.

About 4 miles (7km) east of Česká Lípa stands the château at **Zákupy**. The original Renaissance building was built in the middle of the sixteenth century on the site of a medieval yeoman's seat, though its present baroque appearance dates from the end of the seventeenth century. Napoleon's son was made Duke of Zákupy in 1818 but never actually bothered to visit the place. Between 1850 and 1853 the château was adapted as a residence for the former Austrian Emperor and Czech King Ferdinand V. The château unfortunately suffered great damage from a recent fire but is still popular and may be visited on a guided tour.

Seven miles (11km) north-west of Zákupy are the romantic ruins of **Sloup Castle** built on (and into) a huge 98ft (30m) high and 328ft (100m) long sandstone rock with almost vertically sloping sides. The castle was built in the fourteenth century by Vinzenz of Oybin and in medieval times the top of the rock was completely without vegetation — wooden buildings formed the nucleus of the castle. It came out of use in the sixteenth century when the local feudal lord, Adam Berka, built a manor house in the town below and from 1690 to 1785 the rock was inhabited by hermits. Since the mid-nineteenth century it has been open to the public. An information sheet in English is available at the entrance.

Two miles (3km) north-west is the town of **Nový Bor**, an important centre of the Bohemian glass industry since medieval times (by the mid-eighteenth century glass manufacture was even included in the curriculum of the local Piarist grammar school). On the town's main square is a particularly fine Glass Museum, founded in 1892, which also sells souvenirs. An information sheet in English is provided. The town also boasts a baroque church.

Three miles (5km) further west, 984ft (300m) to the south of the main road just beyond the village of Prachen, is the basalt, organ-like rock formation known as the **Panská skála** which reaches up to a height of 39ft (12m), basically a smaller version of the Giant's Causeway in Ulster, Ireland. It is about another 2 miles (4km) north-west from here to the town of Ceská Kamenice which could conceivably make an alternative base for exploring the České Švýcarsko for those with their own transport. It is certainly a lot more pleasant than Děčín and there is the bonus of a sixteenth-century château. The town's one hotel is on the main square.

About 7 miles (11km) south-west of here, a mere 5 miles (8km) east of Děčín, is smoky **Benešov nad Ploučnicí.** The town's castle essentially consists of two buildings, both on the odd sloping main square and both built by Friedrich de Salhausen in the early sixteenth century. The 'lower' of the two, intended for Friedrich's only son, is the only one visitable at the moment (the 'upper' one is being renovated); inside are collections of armoury from the Thirty Years War, some sixteenth- and seventeeth-century furniture and an exhibition of (mainly Empire) clocks.

Further Information
— North from Prague: the Elbe Valley —

Places to Visit

Děčín
Town Museum
Mládeže
Open: 9am-12noon and 1-5pm, closed Mondays.

Zoo
Shepherd's Rock
Open: March to September 8am-6pm, October to February 8am-4pm.

Rose Garden
Dlouhá Jízda
Open: May to October 10am-5pm.

Litoměřice
Town Museum
Old Town Hall
Mírové náměstí
10am-12noon and 1-5pm closed Mondays.

Art Gallery
Michalská
Open: 9am-5pm, closed Mondays.

Mácha Museum
Máchova 3
Open: 10am-5pm, closed Mondays.

Litoměřice to Děčín via Zákupy

Ploskovice Château
☎ 0416 8692
Open: May to September 8am-5pm,
closed Mondays. April and October
9am-4pm weekends only.

Zákupy Château
☎ 0425 97278
Open: May to September 9am-5pm,
closed Mondays. April and October
9am-4pm weekends only.

Sloup Castle
☎ 0424 6338
Open: May to September 9am-5pm,
closed Mondays. April and October 9am-
4pm weekends only.

Nový Bor
Glass Museum
Main Square
Open: 9am-12noon and 1-4pm, closed
Mondays.

Benešov nad Ploučnicí Château
Main Square
☎ 0412 94575
Open May to August 8am-5pm,
September 9am-4pm, closed Mondays. April and October 9am-4pm
weekends and holidays only.

Terezín

Museum of the Ghetto
Komenského
☎ 0416 92 576-7
Open: 9am-6pm.

Small Fortress
☎ 0416 922 25
Open: April 8am-5.30pm, May to
September 8am-6.30pm, October to
March 8am-4.30pm.

Ústí nad Lábem (and the area to
the west)

Střekov Castle
☎ 047 31553
Open: May to September 9am-5pm,
closed Mondays. April and October

9am-4pm weekends and holidays
only.

Teplice Château
Zámecké náměstí
Open: 9am-12noon and 1-5pm, closed
Mondays.

Duchcov Château
Main Square
☎ 0417 935301
Open: May to September 9am-6pm,
closed Mondays. April and October
9am-4pm, weekends and holidays
only.

Osek Monastery
☎ 0417 937 393
Open: May to September 9am-6pm,
closed Mondays. April and October
9am-4pm weekends and holidays
only.

The Moved Church at Most
Open: May to September 9am-6pm,
April and October 9am-4pm, closed
Mondays.

Tourist Information Offices

Děčín
Čedok
Prokopá Holého 8
Podmokly
☎ 0412 28653

Litoměřice
Čedok
Dlouhá ul. 194
☎ 2588

Teplice
Čedok
Krupska 33

Ústí nad Lábem
Čedok
Hrnčířská 93
☎ 262 51

CKM
Masarykova 57
☎ 275 92

3 • North-Eastern Bohemia and the Krkonoše Mountains

Český Ráj

The Český Ráj (Bohemian Paradise) is the name given to the great swathe of sandstone rocks and densely wooded hills that cover the area between Mnichovo Hradiště, Železný Brod and Jičín which is punctuated by castles, châteaux, churches, small villages and even the occasional lake. Most famous are the 'sandstone cities' formed during the early Mesozoic era when sand and calcium clay were deposited here by the sea. When the water receded there remained chalk tables that were later eroded by rain water to form the shapes one sees today. Unsurprisingly adored by the nineteenth-century Romantics it is the oldest Protected Landscape Region in the country (created as such in 1955). One could get around it easily by car but the distances are so relatively small that it would be a pity to miss out on some walking.

Turnov is probably the best base for exploring the Český Ráj. The town is rather awkwardly divided into two by the River Jizera; the main railway station is on the west bank while the old town centre, such as it is, is situated on the east bank. Most buses leave from outside the main railway station. Turnov is one of the oldest towns in the region, being founded in 1272 by two brothers Havel Markvart of Lemberk and Jaroslav of Hruštice, but as a result of numerous fires over the centuries there are very few old buildings still standing and consequently despite its superb location and the beauty of its surroundings the town itself is rather drab. Turnov does however possess a long tradition in the processing of precious stones, many of which have been found locally. In 1884 the first school specialising in stone-cutting was founded in the town and the tradition is slowly being revived with the death of the Communist regime. Near the old town square at number 71 Skálova is the Museum of the Bohemian Paradise which was founded in 1866. Inside there are archaeological, mineralogical and historical rooms, an exhibition documenting the processing of precious stones in Turnov, an ethnographic room detailing the popular culture of the Jizera region and an art gallery which holds temporary exhibitions of the work of local artists. On the way from the old town centre to the Turnov město railway station is an unusually placed Jewish cemetery (it is under a flyover) with some valuable baroque and Classicist tombstones — the earliest legible stone dates to the late seventeenth century. The town's synagogue is on Krajířova inside a block of houses. Services were held in this simple baroque structure from the early eighteenth century until World War II after which it was used as a storehouse. Out on the west bank at the northern end of Turnov is the château of Hrubý Rohozec. Originally a Gothic castle dating from 1280 it was remodelled in Renaissance and then Empire style (1822). An hour long guided tour flits through twenty-three handsome rooms decked out with paintings, arms and Bohemian cut-glass.

With an early start it is quite possible to walk all the way from Turnov to Jičín (15^1/$_2$ miles/25km) in one day. Regular buses and trains pass between the two towns so it is possible to arrange any route to suit. Just under 1 mile (2km) south of Turnov město railway station (to the right of the D35 road as one drives towards Jičín), is the Gothic **Valdštejn Castle**, originally founded by the Markvartices in the thirteenth century, which is impressively stationed on the edge of a sandstone rock plateau. Occupied by the Hussites in the fifteenth century, the castle was ruined by the late sixteenth century and then revived in the eighteenth century by the Valdštejn family who built a chapel here dedicated to St John Nepomuk (1722) as well as the stone bridge, flanked by baroque statues of various Czech saints sculptured by Jelínek of Kosmonosy, leading up to it — previous to this castle could only be entered via steps chiselled into the sandstone rock. Further reconstruction followed in the eighteenth and nineteenth centuries before the castle was finally abandoned in the mid-nineteenth century.

Another 2 miles (3km) south-east, passing an arboretum on the way, is the first (and best) of the Český Ráj's 'sandstone cities', **Hrubá skála** — not to be confused with the nearby village of the same name. It is basically a collection of giant sandstone rocks that have been weathered into bizarre shapes. They are undeniably dramatic and there are several good vantage points. To get to them by car, pass through the village of Hrubá Skála and then leave the D35 road and take the turning to the right signposted Vyskeř. The nearby nineteenth-century château is closed to the public. Two miles (3km) south-west of Hrubá skála are the spectacular remains of the castle of **Trosky** (meaning 'ruins'), one of the most romantic sites in the whole of Bohemia. Two towers stand dramatically atop bare basalt cones dating from the tertiary period; the taller of the rocks is known as 'Věž Bába' (Grand-mother Rock) and the smaller is known as 'Věž Panna' (Girl Rock). The castle itself was built around 1380 by Honoratus of Vartenberg, the inner castle of residential buildings was founded upon the ridge between the two watchtowers. The castle fell out of use in the late fifteenth century and

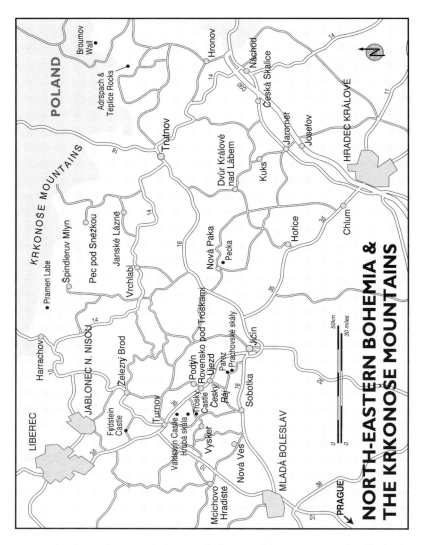

restoration has only recently begun. Only one of the towers may be climbed; the view from the top is predictably quite magnificent. Access to the castle is from a car park on the road linking the D35 with the hamlet of Troskovice. There is a steep path up to the castle, through thick forest. At the base there is a hotel and restaurant complex.

Not far from here, though a little out of thw way if one is travelling around on foot, is the picturesque small town of **Rovensko pod Troskami**, situated on the River Veselka. The first recorded mention of the town is in 1371. Of particular interest is the ancient belfry dating from 1630, the three bells held within are known as the 'rebel bells' because their peals once began a peasant uprising during the period of forced re-Catholicisation. One should also pay a visit to the important Gothic Church of St Václav at **Podtýn** which is ornamented with attractive medieval stone decorations. In the town park there is a monument to the poet Svatopluk Čech who spent his summers here.

Back at Trosky, it is about another 6 miles (9km) south-east on the red trail to the fourteenth-century ruined castle at **Pařez** which was adapted round and hewn into a large sandstone rock. The ruins stand at the very edge of the **Prachovské skály**, the largest of the sandstone cities, popular with both walkers and climbers, whose name derives from the sand, or 'dust' (*prach*), that covers the forest floor. Archaeological evidence suggests that the site was inhabited in prehistoric times and that there was a Slav settlement here. From the Prachovské skály it is a mere 6km to Jičín. To reach Prachovské skály by car, take the road from ˚jezd to Mladějov, and then the first side road on the left.

Jičín is undoubtedly a more attractive place to stay than Turnov though possibly slightly less convenient. The first written mention of the town is in 1293 when it is described as the property of Queen Jitka, the wife of Wenceslas II, after whom (it is assumed) the town is named. Unscathed during the Hussite Wars, the town is very closely associated with Albrecht von Waldstein (or Wallenstein), who confiscated Jičín during the Thirty Years War and chose it to be the capital of his very own little empire, ʰhe Duchy of Friedland. In the 1620s he rebuilt the town's main square (which is now named after him), one side of which is dominated by his late Renaissance château which today houses the town museum and art gallery. It was in the château's (newly-opened) great conference hall that the three emperors of Austria, Russia and Prussia signed the Holy Alliance against Napoleon in 1813. A covered passage connects the château with the towerless early baroque Church of St James (1627) next door; both château and church were designed by the Italian Nicolo Sebregondi. On the corner of the main square is the 171ft (52m) high late Gothic Valdická Gate (1568-70), part of the original town fortifications, which may be ascended for a view over the town. In the middle of the square is a baroque Plague Column dating to 1702. Wallenstein was also responsible for the lípova alej, an avenue stretching for over 1 mile (2km) that was planted by his rigorously drilled soldiers with 1,200 lime trees (each man was issued with a tree and a shovel). At the end of the avenue is Wallenstein's once-princely Libosad pleasure lodge, designed by Sebregondi in 1632, near to which, in Valdice, is a large seventeenth-century Carthusian monastery, designed by Sebregondi and Spezza, which functions as a prison. Wallenstein was murdered in 1634 in Cheb (Western Bohemia) by four English mercenaries at the behest of a justifiably wary Emperor Ferdinand II, in whose service he was employed. His body rested in Valdice until 1785 when it was moved to its present resting place beside his first wife in the castle church of Mnichovo Hradiště. Schiller later wrote about his life in his epic poem, *Wallenstein*. Wallenstein's death signalled the end of Jičín's brief foray into the historical spotlight, though in 1866 one of the biggest battles of the Prussian-Austrian War was fought near here — some 7,500 soldiers lost their lives.

Sobotka is situated about 8 miles (13km) from both Jičín and Turnov. It is accessible by regular bus or train from Jičín and an occasional bus from Turnov. The main point of interest is the early baroque Humprecht Hunting Lodge (1666-1680), inspired by the Galata Tower in Constantinople, which was designed by the Italian architect Carlo Lurago for Earl Humprecht Jan Černín of Chudenice (who was also responsible for the awful Černín Palace in Prague). Černín was a foreign ambassador for King Leopold I and the château houses a literary museum and an exhibition devoted to the Černín family, but is best remembered for its 52ft (16m) high windowless central hall which has the acoustics of a cathedral.

Two miles (4km) north-west along the road from the château, in the small settlement of Podkost, is the brilliantly preserved castle **Kost**. The castle was built in the late fourteenth century by the lords of Wartenberg on a large sandstone rock at the intersection of three valleys. It has been reconstructed several times since. The original Gothic parts of the castle include the large tower, the Old Palace and the Chapel of St Anne. An exhibition of late Gothic art has been installed in the castle, though one can only see it by joining the obligatory tour (50 minutes). The castle was first opened for tourists at the end of the nineteenth century.

Two miles (4km) north-west is the Komárovský lake besides which is the tiny village of **Nová Ves**. From here a multitude of paths travel around the volcanic basalt peak of Mužský (1,519ft/463m) which offers a good view. At Příhrazy there is a hotel and campsite from where one can ascend to the Příhrazy rocks which encompass the scant remains of a small medieval castle (Staré Hrady). There was a Slavonic settlement at Hrada from the six to the tenth centuries and an even more ancient settlement at Klamorna dating back to 3000BC. The Drábské Světničky (Small Rooms) sandstone rocks, transformed into a fortified stronghold in medieval times, provided a shelter for refugees during the Thirty Years War; the caves in which they hid are accessible via stairs and metal bridges. The ruins of the fourteenth-century castle of Valečov lie less than 2 miles (4km) from Mnichovo Hradiště. Much of the castle was chiselled out of the existing sandstone with the rest of the construction being made out of wood. The tower dates from the sixteenth century. The castle was abandoned in 1652, though inhabited by vagrants on an informal basis until the end of the nineteenth century.

Lakeside tranquillity in the Bohemian Paradise

The town museum in **Mcichovo Hradiště** is housed on the second floor of the town's eighteenth-century baroque château. It houses archaeological and ethnographical collections as well as an art gallery devoted to local talent and a collection of beetles and butterflies. The body of Albrech von Wallenstein lies in the precinct of a former monastery of the Capuchins (in the seventeenth-century baroque Chapel of St Anne) a little to the north of the château — Wallenstein once owned the château, along with over fifty castles and villages in the region. From Mnichovo Hradiště there are trains or buses back to Turnov. The walk from Sobotka to Mnichovo Hradiště, taking in all of the above, could certainly be made in a good day's hiking.

Finally, there is some interesting walking countryside north of Turnov. From Turnov it is 2 miles (3km) north to Dolánky u Turnova, noted for its wooden folk buildings (Dlask's farmstead, Abel's flourmill and Rakouš' log-cabin), and a further 4 miles (6km) to the summer resort of Malá Skála. Apart from the Pantheon (converted from a Gothic castle) overlooking Malá Skála, the village is unremarkable but from it one has the choice of three routes into the surrounding countryside. The first takes one on a 1 mile (2km) hike north-west to the ruined fourteenth-century **Frýdstein Castle**, partially carved from the sandstone rock. Abandoned in the sixteenth century the ruin was first opened to the public at the end of the nineteenth century. From here one could veer south-west to the town of **Sychrov** (though there is no actual walking trail) where there is a château surrounded by a beautiful English park. The château was originally built in baroque style between 1690 and

1693 though it was substantially remodelled in Pseudo-Gothic style in 1847-62 by the Rohan family. Most of the interior decoration also dates to the nineteenth century. The château houses a very good selection of French portrait art.

If this does not appeal one could walk from Malá Skála 2 miles (3km) south-east along the red-marked trail to the Suché skály (Silent Rocks) which feature a number of rock caves used by persecuted Protestants during the Counter Reformation. From here one could then walk 4 miles (7km) eastwards along the green trail to **Železný Brod**, a glass making town since 1866 with a real mish-mash of a main square consisting of a large faceless 1950s hotel, an equally nondescript modern supermarket, a newly refurbished nineteenth-century town hall and a small late eighteenth-century timber framed museum devoted to glass making and folk art — the Železný Brod region is especially well-known for its tradition in making Christmas cribs. Glass and folk art products may be purchased in the museum. The rest of the town consists of factories and blocks of flats which spread along the river and half-timbered cottages which pepper the hills above 6 miles (10km) east of Železný Brod are the Božkov Stalactite Caves.

Alternatively from Suché skály one could walk south-east along the red trail to the peak of Kozákov (2,440ft/744m), a famous finding place of semiprecious stones (agates, chalcedonies and jaspers), and then continue along to Lomnice nad Popelkou, renowned for its biscuit production, whose town museum features some more folk furniture (including one Christmas crib that took 11 years to complete) and an art gallery displaying the works of local artists. A little to the south of the town is the peak of Tábor (2,253ft/687m) which has an observation tower. Kozákov and Tábor are the two highest points in the Český Ráj.

The Krkonoše Mountains

The Krkonoše Mountains (also known as the Giant Mountains) which straddle the border between the Czech Republic and Poland offer visitors the finest mountain scenery in Bohemia. The main ridge of the mountains stretches round in a broad arch from Tanvald to Trutnov, and the main Krkonoše resorts — Pec pod Sněžkou, Špindleruv Mlyn and Harrachov — nestle in steeply wooded valleys overlooked by the typically rounded but nonetheless impressive bare peaks of the central part of the range. The highest point in the Krkonoše is Mount Sněžka (5,255ft/1,602m), the highest mountain in the Czech Republic, situated on the border. Its rounded dominant peak overlooks the resort of Pec pod Sněžkou, from where there is a chairlift to the summit. Another principal resort, Špindleruv Mlyn, is the first settlement on the River Elbe, whose source lies high up in the central plateau of the Krkonoše. In summer, there are many opportunities for walking in these mountains, for those who can bear the notoriously unpredictable weather or whose visit fortunately coincides with a dry spell. During winter the mountains are given over to skiers. Owing to their position, less than 99 miles (160km) from Prague and close to the major towns of Liberec and Děčín, the Krkonoše are very popular, especially at weekends, but a dense network of marked walking paths and cross country skiing tracks can take the more adventurous visitor, who is in possession of a detailed map, away from the crowds and deep into the mountains.

Like many mountain areas, the Krkonoše have always been sparsely populated. Until medieval times the only people who ventured into the mountains were hunters who gained access to the game-rich forests of the lower slopes of the Krkonoše along mountain rivers. A few limited trading routes were established over the mountain passes. In the Middle Ages the natural wealth of the Krkonoše was discovered and settlers from Bohemia and from many other parts of Europe began to prospect for gold and to establish glass and timber works. Many of these mineral prospectors came from Italy, and with typical Mediterranean exaggeration they began to describe wild and supernatural occurrences in these mountains. It was during this period that the legend of the 'Krakonoš' first began to enter the popular culture of the area; Krakonoš was thought to be a giant (hence — 'Giant Mountains') who lived in the hills and wrought thunderstorms, tempests and snow storms on those who dared to settle and farm in the mountains. The legend was not enough to stop the gradual development of the area however, and by the seventeenth century miners, wood cutters and herdsmen began to build *boudas* (wooden huts) high up in the mountains. The Krkonoše have been popular with tourists for over two centuries; the first travellers in the area sought accommodation in the local *boudas*, and soon *boudas* were built especially for walkers and tourists. Nowadays a *bouda* in the Krkonoše is anything from a luxury hotel to a timber-built hut, but in the true tradition of mountain huts, they are only accessible on skis or on foot, never by road.

Partly to protect the mountains from overutilisation from walkers and skiers, and also to help counter the increasing damage caused by pollution, the area was proclaimed a National Park (known as KRNAP) in 1963 and is now the largest protected area in Central Europe. The KRNAP has sought to protect the unique natural environment of the mountains, including the conservation of 1,000-year-old peat bogs and of the many alpine plants and animals which are native to the region. Many species have become extinct in the Krkonoše because of the development of the mountains by man; the last bear was shot in 1736 and wolves, lynx and wild cats all disappeared from the Krkonoše in the nineteenth century. The Krkonoše is one of the areas of Europe most affected by acid rain, which has been gradually killing off many trees and harming water life, thereby destroying in a few decades ecosystems which have been established in these mountains for thousands of years. KRNAP compliments a similar National Park set up on the Polish side of the Krkonoše in 1959. On the instructions of the KRNAP some of the walking tracks have been closed and many roads cannot be used by private motorists. Many of the resorts have large car parks (with relatively hefty parking fees) to keep their streets relatively free of traffic. However, the limited efforts to alleviate the damage caused by the mismanagement of the environment are mostly too little, too late. Protection of the environment is one of the top priorities of the new regime in the Czech Republic, but many now believe that no amount of money or expense can revitalise the ecology of this once wild and undeveloped area.

The Krkonoše mountains are excellent walking country. Some walks are described below, but those who buy the walking map of the area (and everyone is strongly advised to) can easily plan their own. A number of maps are available; most bookshops in the area will stock a choice of two or three. KRNAP regulations require visitors to keep to the marked and obvious paths, the total length of which is 620 miles (1,000km). Routes along ridges are colour coded red, those in valleys are blue and those along the side of a mountain, running along the contours, are coded green. Shorter yellow marked paths connect these tracks. Walkers should be aware of the notorious weather in these mountains; it rains or snows one day out of every two. Weather conditions can change very rapidly. Many of the mountain peaks are flat and are very high and exposed and the walker may find himself suddenly caught out in heavy snow or rain storms, strong winds or thick fog which can descend very quickly. Warm clothing and something to protect from the rain should be taken on all hikes. The summits have an average annual temperature of about freezing point. Walking in these mountains can be rewarding but needs the same care and proper planning as walking in mountain ranges which are much higher: near Vrbatova bouda, in the western part of the range, is a memorial — serving now as a salutary reminder to today's walkers and skiers — to two champion Czech skiers, Václav Vrbata and Bohumil Hanč, killed here in 1913 while cross-country skiing in adverse weather conditions.

Most walking tracks in the mountains are closed in winter. There is snow on the ground in the Krkonoše for 6 months of the year; the first snow falls in November. The snow and skiing season here is the longest and most reliable of any of the mountains in either republic, accommodation and ski passes are cheap but the mountains are very popular and there are long queues. Renting skiing equipment is also relatively difficult. The winter map of the area shows the degree of difficulty of the runs, graded by colour coding from black (hardest) through red to blue (the easiest). There are also many cross country skiing tracks, marked with poles, and there are ski jumps at Harrachov.

While not resorts in themselves, Vrchlabí and Trutnov are the main towns in the area and most people visiting the Krkonoše will have cause at least to pass through them, if not actually to find accommodation in them. **Vrchlabí**, a pleasant little town on the River Elbe, is the principal gateway to the Krkonoše. The main Čedok office in the Krkonoše, which deals directly with all the hotels in the area, is on the main street of the town which opens up into a square lined with Renaissance buildings. Hotel accommodation in the Krkonoše may be hard to find at the height of summer, but the cheap and abundant private rooms that have sprung up all over the region have made life much easier. On one side of the main town square is a Renaissance château (1546-1614), with its four towers, symbolizing the four seasons, topped by copper-coloured onion domes. Its twelve gates symbolize the months in the year and its fifty-two rooms, the weeks. The château houses the main administration offices of the Krkonoše National Park, and its interiors are inaccessible to the public. Behind the château there is a nice park with a lake and a small zoo. Further along the main street, up from the square, a picturesque wooden building houses both the Krkonoše Museum and an information office where there is a supply of information in English. Part of the Krkonoše Museum (with exhibits relating to nature conservation in the Krkonoše) is housed in a former Augustinian monastery, which was founded in 1705 by Count Maximilian Morzin, on the edge of the aforementioned park. There are a number of hotels in Vrchlabí, including a Čedok interhotel, and the town is the main centre for public transport in the Krkonoše.

Trutnov is an industrial town built on textiles and an important rail and road junction. A number of Renaissance and baroque buildings line the town's impressive main square, including a church (1755-82) with a notable 207ft (63m) high tower. In the square there is a fountain dedicated to Krakonoš and 36ft (11m) high column of the Holy Trinity (1704). The town museum is in an Empire style building occupying the site of the former castle, within are historical, art and ethnographical collections. For a while in the early 1970s Václav Havel used to work in the local brewery, his experiences providing material for his play *Audience*. The beer he helped produce, Krakonoš, is very good. Trutnov is a good base from which to see the Krkonoše (though it is not quite as central as Vrchlabí); Trutnov, Pec pod Sněžkou, Špindleruv Mlyn and Harrachov are all linked to Prague by express bus services which run several times a day (they are very busy, reservations are advised). The main resorts in the Krkonoše lie in the valleys of the rivers Elbe, Úpa and Jezira, which run parallel to one another in a north-south direction. There is little or no road access between the valleys

The resort of Špindleruv Mlyn in the Krkonoše Mountains

themselves, only walking paths run over the ridges. Road access between the valleys is normally via the towns of Trutnov or Vrchlabí, to the south.

From Vrchlabí a road runs north along the Elbe Valley for 9 miles (14km) to the resort of **Špindleruv Mlyn** (2,788ft/850m), the most important resort in the Krkonoše. The road along the Elbe is set in the river's deep, steep-sided valley that is typical of the Krkonoše. Just before entering the town the road passes by a small dam and lake on the river. Cars are not allowed in the resort itself and have to be left in the carpark on the southern edge of the town: try to check in advance with hotels in the centre of town as to whether you can drive a car up to their front door, if you are planning to be resident at one. Špindleruv Mlyn itself is very pleasant, set in a sharp bend of the River Elbe, where a smaller river, the Dlouchy, joins it. The town is named after one of the first settlers in the mountains, a man named Špindler who constructed a mill (*mlyn*) on the river Dlouchy near the present day settlement. Tourism began after the completion of the road up from Vrchlabí in 1871. Modern accommodation buildings built up the sides of both river valleys blend in well with the smaller wooden hotels located nearer the river, many of which were built in the nineteenth century. Two chairlifts run from near the town; $^1/_2$ mile (1km) up the Dlouchy Valley is a chairlift up to the summit of Mount Plan (3,923ft/1,196m), while the other chairlift, a short way along the Elbe Valley, rises up to Mount Medvědín (4,051ft/1,235m). There are also many ski lifts and tows in and around Špindleruv Mlyn and on the slopes of Mount Plan and Mount Medvědín.

Špindleruv Mlyn is the first settlement on the River Elbe, which here is little more than a mountain stream flowing in a rocky, boulder-strewn bed. A popular walk in the Krkonoše is to follow the river from Špindleruv Mlyn all the way up to its source at **Pramen Labe**, 6 miles (9km) along the blue-marked track called the Harrach Path, which was built in 1879 by Count Harrach who also established the first nature conservation area near here in 1904. The walk follows the Elbe all the way; from Špindleruv Mlyn it runs along the Labsky Dul Valley, getting gradually steeper and steeper until after about 8km it winds its way very steeply up past waterfalls, including the 148ft (45m) high Labská Waterfall, to Labská Bouda, an isolated mountain hotel (the road up to the hotel from Horní Mísečky is closed). From here it is about $^1/_2$ mile (1km) across a broad, high plateau to the source itself, Pramen Labe at 4,540ft (1,384m). A plaque nearby displays the coats of arms of all the towns along the River Elbe, up to and including the North German port of Hamburg, where the river enters the North Sea. The spot is set in the middle of a flat, marshy bog (there is no distinct spring, as such) and is the somewhat unexciting destination of an otherwise pleasurable walk. From Pramen Labe one can return to Špindleruv Mlyn back the way one came or via Horní Mísečky and Mount Medvědín, taking the chairlift down from Medvědín to Špindleruv Mlyn. Whichever route you take this expedition is an all day affair. The area offers numerous other opportunities for walks; for instance from Labská Bouda one could walk a short distance along the red-marked track towards towards Horní Mísečky to see another high waterfall on the River Pančava. Those who prefer to see their scenery from the road could take a bus along the road from Špindleruv Mlyn to Špindlerova Bouda (3,929ft/1,198m) set at the summit of a mountain pass into Poland and reached by a number of twisty hairpin bends. This road is only open to buses in winter; in summer you must get a special permit to drive a car up (which is difficult, as there is not much reason to do so — bus services from Špindleruv Mlyn are frequent and convenient all year round).

The Úpa Valley runs parallel with the Elbe Valley to the east of it. The only access by road between the two valleys is at the southern end, via Janské Lázně and Vrchlabí. Another scenic road in the Krkonoše runs from a junction on the Vrchlabí-Trutnov road at Čistá through the village of Černy Dul and then to the small spa town of **Janské Lázně** which is tucked away at the bottom of a deep valley. The main road along the valley here bypasses the town and runs above it rather than through it. Janské Lázně is a charming place with a park and a notable Art Nouveau Colonnade (1893). The warm mineral springs of the spa were discovered in the fifteenth century and the town was founded in 1677. Many people still come here to seek out the curative effects of the spring waters, and the spa is especially noted for its treatment of polio and children's diseases. A cable car runs up from the town to the summit of Černá Hora 4,261ft (1,299m). The first cableway up to Černá Hora was built in 1928 making it the oldest lift in the republic, though the original lift was dismantled in 1980 when the present one was installed. There is a lookout tower at the top of the mountain and a red-marked path takes walkers back down the valley sides to Janské Lázně.

Less than a mile beyond Janské Lázně the road meets the Úpa Valley at Svoboda nad Úpou, from where one can continue north for 7 miles (12km) to **Pec pod Sněžkou**, another important Krkonoše resort. A short distance before Pec pod Sněžkou is a short chairlift running up the mountainside to Portašovy Bouda. The name Pec pod Sněžkou means 'Furnace beneath Mount Sněžka', recalling the medieval metal ore mining and smelting that went on in the area. The town is spread out along the Úpa Valley and its tributary the Zeleny, and the parts of the town further up along the banks of the Úpa are indeed overlooked by the rounded peak Mount Sněžka. This is the highest mountain in Bohemia and the summit can be reached by a well patronised two-stage chairlift from Pec pod Sněžkou.

A road leads west from Vrchlabí to **Harrachov**, 18 miles (29km) away. Harachov is set in the valley of the River Mumlava, though for most of its length the road runs along beside the River Jizera, another important river that rises in the Krkonoše. Harrachov is the main centre of the western part of the Krkonoše and beyond the town is a road crossing into Poland. There is a strong local tradition of glass making in the town. The local glassworks was founded in the eighteenth century by Lord Harrach, the local feudal landlord, and the factory is still producing cut, painted and etched glass under the Crystalex trade mark. There is a small museum and shop in the centre of the town where one can buy the factory's products. In the local Church of St Wenceslas there is a glass chandelier and altar. Less than 1 mile (2km) from the town is a 33ft (10m) high waterfall (Mumlavska Vodopadé) on the River Mumlava. From here one can continue on along the blue-marked track for 6 miles (10km) to Pramen Labe, the source of the Elbe (see under Špindleruv Mlyn above). Many other walks are possible, such as to Vosecká bouda, which is on the Path of Czech-Polish Friendship, which runs along the main ridge of the Krkonoše, going in and out of Czech and Polish territory. There is a chairlift from the town up to Čertova Hora (1,346ft/1,020m) and on the slopes of this mountain there are five ski jumps of various lengths and heights. There are dozens of ski lifts around the town, and in the smaller winter resort of Rokytnice nad Jizerou, which is situated in the valley of the Jizera a short distance to the south of Harrachov.

Trutnov to Hradec Králové, and back to Jičín

As if the possibilities in the Krkonoše were not enough, there is more fine walking countryside to the east of Trutnov, around Broumov and the area near the Polish border. A detailed map is needed by all those who want to explore this region — the *Teplicko-Adršpašské skály/Broumovské stěny* map shows all the walking tracks in the region.

The **Adršpach** and **Teplice Rocks**, 9 miles (15km) east of Trutnov, are some more unusual sandstone rock formations on the same lines as the Český Ráj, ideal for a spot of gentle hiking. The rocks have been popular with tourists and climbers since the nineteenth century and are devided into two separate 'sandstone cities'; one just south of the village of Adršpach and the other 1 mile (2km) south near the village of Teplice nad Metují. The existence of the Teplice rocks only actually came to light in 1824 following a large forest fire. They have been a popular destination ever since the but Adršpach rocks are probably better value, comprising of about sixty listed rock formations up to 230ft (70m) tall (many with exotic names such as Crocodile, Cossak and Krakonoš's Tooth) as well as a beautiful rock lake and a waterfall where children gather to shout 'Krakonoš' three times and be greeted with a thunderous cascade of water — a tourist trick well over a century old. At the 'Goethova deska' rock there is a plaque to commemorate Goethe's visit here. Anyone feeling the urge to be loud should head for Echo Point ('Ozveňna'). Both 'rock cities' have been protected areas since 1933. There are a couple of hotels in Teplice nad Metují and every year in early September an annual festival of rockclimbing is held here when demonstrations are performed on the local rocks, and which attracts interest from all over Europe. Incidentally, there is a very scenic rail journey from Trutnov to Teplice nad Metují though the bus is generally more useful in this part of the world.

The so-called **Broumov Wall** (Broumovské stěny) is a high sandstone precipice from which there are fine views over the East Bohemian countryside and on into Poland. It is possible to walk along it in most places. The highest point of the Broumov walls is the Božanovský Špičák (2,404ft/733m) near the Polish border, where there are also many stunning rock formations; to get here take the bus from Police nad Metují to Machov and walk the final 2 miles (4km) or, if approaching from Broumov, head for Božanov and then walk from there (about the same distance).

To the north is Dientzenhofer's chapel of Panna Marie Sněžna, hidden amongst boulders 2 miles (4km) east of Police nad Metují railway station; there are also superlative views from here. There is one hotel in Police nad Metují on the main square but probably a better bet would be the formerly predominantly German populated **Broumov** which features an unusual wooded Silesian church on the outskirts (on the road to Křinice), two hotels

The resort of Pec pod Sněžkou in the Krkonoše Mountains, overlooked by the snowcapped Mount Sněžka

near the main square and an impressive baroque Benedictine monastery with an extraordinary courtyard by Kilian Ignaz Dientzenhofer (1726-38). The buildings are occupied by several orders of nuns but the monastery church is visitable. Dientzenhofer is also responsible for churches in the nearby villages of Verneřovice, Hermankovice, Ruprechtice and Vižnov as well as the small convent church in Police nad Metují — all commissioned by the monastery's abbot, Othmar Zinke, in an effort to promote the Catholic church in traditionally Protestant Silesia.

About 12 miles (20km) south-east of Bouzov is **Hronov** where there is a wooden cottage that was the birthplace in 1851 of the writer Alois Jirásek. He is commemorated in Hronov by a statue outside the house and an annual drama festival held in his honour. Continuing south, **Náchod** is situated right on the Polish border and is graced by a large Renaissance castle built for the Smiřický family. Following forfeiture after the battle of the White Mountain in 1620 it came into the hands of the Piccolominis who built an extension and laid out a formal French garden. Inside are collections of baroque and Empire furniture, some Dutch tapestries and a bit of art courtesy of the Duke of Kurland who bought the castle in 1792. The main square has been recently renovated, it features an attractive fourteenth-century Church of St Lawrence and a stunning Art Nouveau hotel. Náchod is the birthplace of one of the most popular modern Czech writers, Josef Škvorecký, who lived here from his birth in 1924 until just after World War II. During the war he worked at the local Messerschmitt factory where, in an attempt to impress one of the factory girls, he once tried to sabotage one of the planes (luckily for him this was interpreted as an example of mere incompetence). Škvorecky's most famous work is *The Cowards* (published briefly in 1958, banned and then republished in 1962), a humorous and largely autobiographical story set in the last days of World War II in a small Czech town (referred to as Kostelec but which is actually Náchod) with its main character named Danny Smiřický (see above). Directly autobiographical memories of the town are included in the essay 'I was born at Náchod' in Škvorecký's *Talkin' Moscow Blues* collection (1988). Škvorecky's critical reputation was hugely enhanced by the experimental novella *The Bass Saxophone* (1967), in which the prose-style emulates the rhythms of jazz, but he is probably best known and most widely read now for his series of books featuring the mournful detective Lieutenant Boruvka. Many of his works have been translated into English and are published in the UK by Faber. A reception camp was set up in Náchod in 1946 where Jewish refugees from Poland were given temporary shelter. An estimated 32,000 people passed through this camp and the similar one at Broumov.

Two miles (3km) south-east of Náchod there is an observation tower on top of the hill **Dobrošov** (2,047ft/624m). On the slopes of the hill is a chain of bunkers built from July 1937 to September 1938 as part of a fortification line against potential German aggression on the model of the French Maginot line.

From Náchod follow the main road 6 miles (10km) south-west to the small town and health resort of **Česká Skalice**, renowned principally for its association with the writer Božena Němcová (1820-62), Bohemia's first important woman writer and a household name still today, who went to school here between 1824 and 1830. In 1837 she was forced by her father to marry a customs officer twice her age at the Golden Lion Inn in the town which is now a museum dedicated to her; outside there is a statue of her by M. Kucova-Uchytilova. Next door to the building is a textile museum while just off the main square on B. Němcové the writer's, much altered, old school house also houses a memorial to her memory. Němcová was actually brought up in the tiny valley to the north of the town now named 'Grandmother's Valley' (Babiččino údolí) after her most famous novel *The Grandmother*, a romantic vision of country life recognizably set in the valley. In the baroque mansion of Ratibořice (rebuilt in Empire style around 1800) there is another small museum dedicated to her life. The mansion used to belong to the Duchess of Zahan who employed Němcovás parents as domestic servants. North of the château, in front of an old mill, is a modern sandstone statue group called *Němcová's Grandmother* (1922) by Otto Gutfreund.

Six miles (10km) south-west of Česká Skalice is **Jaroměř**, a quite uninteresting town with one museum housing sculptures by Otakar Španiel and Josef Wagner and paintings by Josef Šima — all local artists. The museum is actually placed in a former department store on the busy main road (Route 33) now called Husova. It was designed by cubist architect Gočár in 1911 and features an unusual neo-Classical top floor. The only other attraction of the town is a fifteenth-century church with a baroque belfry. One mile (2km) south from Jaroměř (on the yellow trail from the station) is the fortress town of **Josefov** which is going to seem horribly familiar to anyone who has visited Terezín. In the 1780s Habsburg Emperor Josef II created three fortified towns to protect the region against a Prussian assault; Hradec Králové (which has now lost its walls), Terezín and Josefov. The last two were built entirely from scratch and share almost identical plans. Both have been similarly preserved. Like Terezín, Josefov has two fortresses (one big and one small) and, also like Terezín, the town today is still packed with soldiers. There is an Empire church on the main square but most people who come here will want to pay a visit to the underground tunnels running through the walls — signs will direct you to their entrance as you enter the town from Jaroměř. Incidentally, the fortress never actually had to withstand a single siege.

Three miles (5km) north of Jaroměř is the once-grand spa of **Kuks**. The Kuks spa was created by Count Anton Graf von Šporck who inherited his father's estate in 1679 at the age of 17. In the early 1690s a mineral spring was discovered locally and Šporck determined to turn the place into a spa with a grandeur to rival that of Karlovy Vary. A number of spa buildings and guest houses and a new family mansion were immediately constructed on the left bank of the Labe (now occupied by the village of Kuks) and after 1707 construction work was extended to the right bank where was laid out a race course, a summer house and garden (with maze and fountains), a chapel and hospice, and another garden. Architect of the mansion and chapel was the much sought after Italian Giovanni Battista Alliprandi. In 1712 Šporck enlisted the services of sculptor Matthias Braun, who had sculptured the group of St Luitgard for the Charles Bridge in Prague, who produced twenty-four allegorical figures of Vices and Virtues for the terrace in front of the Hospice Chapel and some odd figures of dwarfs to surround the racetrack. During Šporck's lifetime Kuks became the thriving social and cultural centre he meant it to be; festivals, hunts, concerts and theatrical performances followed each other in quick succession and luminaries such as the lyric poet Matthias Gunther and J.S. Bach were attracted here. Šporck died in 1738 and 2 years later the town, already in decline, was hit by an even worse tragedy when on the night of the 22 December 1740 the Elbe broke its banks, destroying not only most of the spa buildings but also the spring waters. The following centuries record only neglect and decay. Šporck's mansion was finally pulled down in 1901 and today all that survives of the original spa on the left bank is a large stairway leading nowhere (it formerly led to the mansion), a village school (which functioned as an inn) and, on the outskirts of the village, one of the timber-roofed cottages built for the craftsmen and servants (this one belonged to the engraver M.J. Rentz). Still standing on the other bank is the Hospice and Chapel which is slowly being restored. At present only a small part of the interior may be visited (on an obligatory guided tour); the oval Chapel and Apothecary are the most interesting parts though look out for the fascinating paintings which depict Kuks in its heyday. Outside are the twenty four remarkable Vices and Virtues statues by Braun which splendidly illustrate the emotional intensity and apparent freedom of movement which is typical of the baroque sculptural style. They are all copies — the originals being on display within.

A visit to Kuks is best rounded off with a trip to the nearby **Bethlehem Wood** (Betlém) 2 miles (3km) away. Here Šporck commissioned Braun to design a series of chapels, statuary and hermitages as a form of outdoor sculpture park. It was completed in 1733 along with a clearly defined walking path from Kuks — the path has long since gone but the walk is still quite pleasant. After the destruction of Kuks the park was left to decay (some of the stone was even used in the late eighteenth century to build the fortress of Josefov) and all that remains today are a few heavily worn carvings chiselled out of the boulders of the forest, a little odd, a little decadent and a little pathetic. All the pieces have a strongly religious flavour, the best are the ones of the Egyptian hermit Garinus emerging from his cave with a terrified expression (there was once a sculpture of a large and fearsome dog opposite), and the excellently preserved reliefs of the Nativity, after which the place is named, and the Journey of the Magi.

Five miles (8km) north-east of Kuks in **Dvůr Králové nad Lábem** there is a zoo pretending to be a safari park. It was founded in 1946 by the African explorer Josef Vagner and has all the usual favourites. The zoo is $^1/_2$ mile (1km) west of town and is well signposted. In the centre of the town is an early fifteenth-century hall church (ie the aisles are the same height as the nave) and a former town hall, originally dating to 1572 but remodelled several times since, which now serves as a restaurant. There is one hotel on the main square. The bus station is two blocks from the main square, and the railway station is 1 mile (2km) south-west of the town centre.

Situated at the confluence of the Elbe and Orlice rivers, **Hradec Králové** is the administrative, cultural and economic centre of East Bohemia as well as being one of the oldest towns in the region — there was already a fortified settlement here before the founding of the Czech state in the tenth century. In 1225 Hradec Králové became one of the first Bohemian communities to receive a town charter. Badly damaged during the Thirty Years War the town was extensively rebuilt during the baroque period. Heavy fortifications were built around the town between 1766 and 1789 but these were destroyed shortly after the Austrian defeat at the hands of the Prussian army at nearby Chlum in 1866. During the early twentieth century the town was considerably enlarged, with leading Czech Functionalist architects such as Jan Kotěra and his pupil Josef Gočar heavily involved. One is deposited by bus or train in the midst of the new town; to reach the old town centre walk down Gočarova, the main shopping street, and cross the river. Accommodation, unfortunately, is not cheap and not that easy to come across in Hradec Králové (even the high-rise luxury Hotel Alessandria is often full) so do pay a visit to Čedok at number 63 Gočarova (the main street) beforehand.

The old town of Hradec Králove stands on the high ground between the Labe and Orlice rivers. At the centre is the vast Žižkovo náměstí, in the middle of which is a 62ft (19m) high baroque Plague Column which commemorates the epidemic of 1714. At the western end of the square is the Town Hall which dates back to the Gothic period though it was remodelled firstly in Renaissance style and then again in 1850. Next to this is the sandstone White Tower (1574-80), containing the second biggest bell in Bohemia 7ft (2m) in diameter, and the brick Cathedral of the Holy Spirit which was founded by the Dowager Queen Elizabeth, the widow of Wenceslas II, in 1307 and adapted in neo-Gothic style in the nineteenth century. On the southern side of the square is the eighteenth-century former bishop's palace which houses the Regional Gallery containing a collection of modern Czech art including works by Mucha and Filla. Adjoining this is an early eighteenth-century former Jesuit College which is attached to the early baroque Jesuit Church of the Assumption of Our Lady (1654-66). The eastern end of the square opens up onto Husovo náměstí with a fountain of St John of Nepomuk (1718) and some fine burghers' houses, originally Gothic but remodelled during the Renaissance (numbers 10-14). A short walk east from here along Pospíšilova is the town's Art Nouveau Synagogue (1904-5) which houses a scientific library. Exiting Žižkovo náměstí to the north-west along Kopečku one will eventually come face to face with the grimy Hotel Bystrica, a work by Jan Kotěra with an attractively decorated restaurant with stained-glass by František Kysela and murals by Jan Preisler. Walk across the road and straight on along Palackého and one will arrive at the Regional Museum, another work by Kotěra (1909-11). The distinctly odd figures that flank the entrance are allegories of History and Industry, and the interior contains collections of applied art from the nineteenth and twentieth centuries. The Jiráskovy sady park, to the south-west of the old town square, has a very nice rose garden and a sixteenth-century wooden Uniate church brought here in 1935 from the Trans-Carpathian Ukraine. On the other side of the Elbe is the new town (nové město) featuring numerous Functionalist blocks, the largest of which is Gočar's Statní Gymnazium, on V. lípach opposite from which is a Protestant church also designed by Gočar.

Five miles (8km) north-west of Hradec Králové is **Chlum** where there is a museum dedicated to the Prussian-Austrian War. The decisive battle of the war (known as the Battle of Königgrätz) took place here over 7 hours on 3 July 1866 with the Austrian army suffering a heavy defeat; 24,000 Austrians were either killed or wounded and 13,000 were taken prisoner. The war was actually a brief struggle (named the Seven Weeks War) that took place in June and July 1866, the result of disputes over the states of Schleswig and Holstein which had been taken by Austria and Prussia from Denmark in 1864. Each side had then accused the other of violating the Treaty of Gastein (1865) by which the futured of the districts had been regulated. The net result of the Austrian loss was the Prussian annexation of Schleswig-Holstein, Electoral Hesse, Nassau and Frankfurt am Main with the increase by 4.5 million of the Prussian population. The war's wider significance was that it eventually provoked France into a war with Prussia in 1870-1. Prussian victory in this led to the foundation of the modern German state (or second German Reich) when William I of Prussia, due to the machinations of his prime minister Otto von Bismarck, was made German Emperor.

The town of **Hořice**, about another 6 miles (10km) north-west, is famous for its School of Masonry and Sculpture founded in 1884. As a result the town boasts an incredibly rich selection of sculpture and plays host to the International Symposium of Contemporary Sculpture. There are works literally all over the town though the place to head for is the Gallery of Modern Sculpture on Janderova to the east of the town centre. All the famous Czech sculptors are represented including Šaloun, who built the Jan Hus monument in Prague, and Bílek — even though neither actually studied here. The gallery also puts on various temporary exhibitions. The town museum on the main square holds some more works as does the Smetanovy sady gardens to the west of the town centre. The Hussite church on Tovární is actually a former synagogue, built in 1767, extended in 1860 and then rebuilt in neo-Romanesque style. There is one hotel in the town just off the main square, the train station is ¹/₂ mile (1km) south of the town down Husova.

Completely out of the way, about 7 miles (12km) almost directly north of Hořice, is the fourteenth-century Gothic castle of **Pecka**, remodelled in the sixteenth century into a Renaissance château. In 1621 its owner Kryštof Harant was publicly executed for his part in an anti-Habsburg revolt and in 1627 the castle became the property of the monastery in Valdice. In 1830 a fire heavily damaged the castle which very soon after fell into ruins. Reconstruction started in 1921 and continues on to this day — at present one is able to inspect a reconstructed medieval kitchen and muse over an exhibition devoted to Harant. Four miles (6km) directly west of Pecka is **Nová Paka** which boasts a baroque church dating from the beginning of the eighteenth century and a *sgraffitied* neo-Renaissance Museum housing a large collection of agates, amethysts, jaspers and various fossils donated by private collectors. From Nová Paka it is about another 9 miles (15km) south-west to Jičín.

Further Information
— North-Eastern Bohemia and the Krkonoše Mountains —

Places to Visit

The Český Ráj

Frýdstein Castle
☎ 0428 96260
Open: May to September 9am-5pm,
April and October 9am-4pm, closed
Mondays.

Jičín
Town Museum
Château
Valdštejnovo náměstí
Open: 10am-6pm, closed Mondays.

Valdická Brána Observation Tower
Valdštejnovo náměstí
Open: 10am-6pm, closed Mondays.

Kost Castle
Podkost
☎ 0433 7144
Open: May to September 8am-5pm,
closed Mondays. April and October
9am-4pm weekends only.

Lomnice
Town Museum
Open: May to August Tuesdays and
Thursdays 2-4pm, Wednesdays and
Fridays 10am-12noon, Sundays 10am-
12noon and 1-4pm.

Mnichovo Hradiště
Château
☎ 0329 2198
Open: May to September 8am-5pm,
closed Mondays. April and October
9am-4pm weekends only.

Sobotka
Humprecht Château
☎ 0433 7283
Open: May to September 8am-5pm,

closed Mondays. April and October
9am-4pm weekends and holidays
only.

Trosky Castle
Open: May to September 8am-5pm,
closed Mondays. April and October
9am-4pm Saturdays and Sundays
only.

Turnov
Museum of the Bohemian Paradise
Skálova 71
☎ 0436 22106
Open: 9am-12noon and 1-4pm, closed
Mondays.

Hrubý Rohozec Château
☎ 0436 21012
Open: May to September 8am-5pm,
closed Mondays. April and October
9am-4pm Saturdays, Sundays and
holidays only.

Valdštejn Castle
☎ 0436 21384
Open: May to September 9am-
4.30pm, closed Mondays. April and
October weekends and holidays only
9am-4pm.

Sychrov Château
☎ 048 90843

The Krkonoše

Vrchlabí
Krkonoše Museum
Krkonošská
Open: daily except Mondays 9am-
12noon and 1-4pm.

Zoologicka Zahrada
In the park behind the palace on the
main square
Open: May to October 9am-5pm.

Trutnov to Jičín via Hradec Králové

Hradec Králové
Regional Gallery
Velke náměstí
Open: 9am-5pm, closed Mondays.

Regional Museum
Open: 9am-12noon and 1-5pm, closed Mondays.

Hořice
Town Museum
Open: 9am-12noon and 1-4pm, closed Mondays.

Jaroměř
Town Museum
Wenke Department Store
Open: Mondays to Fridays 9am-4pm, Saturdays and Sundays 9am-12noon.

Josefov
Underground Tunnels
Open: May to September 9am-12noon and 1-5pm, closed Mondays. April and October 9am-12noon and 1-5pm weekends only.

Kuks
Hospice and Chapel
☎ 0437 4761
Open: May to August 9am-6pm, September 9am-5pm, closed Mondays. April and October 9am-4pm weekends only.

Náchod Castle
☎ 0441 21201
Open: May to September 9am-5pm, closed Mondays. October 9am-4pm weekends only.

Pecka Castle
☎ 0434 9329
Open: May to August 8am-5pm, September 9am-4pm closed Mondays. April and October 9am-4pm weekends only.

Ratibořice Château
☎ 0441 52133
Open: May to September 9am-6pm, closed Mondays. April and October 9am-4pm weekends only.

Tourist Information Offices

Hradec Králové
Gočcarova 63
☎ 049 415 21

Jičín
Valdštejnovo náměstí 3
☎ 21977

Sobotka
Mír náměstí 6

Špindleruv Mlyn
Cědok
543 51 Špindleruv Mlyn
☎ 0438 93225

Turnov
Čechotour
5 Května 61
☎ 24604

Vrchlabí
Čedok
Krkonošská
Open: 9am-12noon and 1-4pm, closed Mondays and Sundays (and also Saturdays in winter).

4 • The Šumava Mountains

The Šumava Mountains are a rolling, heavily forested range of low mountains which stretch along Bohemia's borders with Germany and Austria. Lying in the heart of Central Europe, they are sparsely populated and, partly because they cover a comparatively large area, never seem overrun by visitors. A fair number of tourists come here from Germany and Austria; far fewer come from English-speaking countries, and those visitors that do come here rarely stray from the obvious tourist centres — old towns such as Český Krumlov and Domažlice, skiing areas around Churáňov and Železná Ruda, or the few resorts along Lake Lipno in the southern part of the area. This means that much of the Šumava, with its secluded, forested valleys and dusty timber-built villages, remains undiscovered. The road network is poor here; public transport seems often to be limited to a few sporadic rural buses, linking the remote hill villages with the nearest towns or with the few rail routes which run through the area. For decades much of this area was closed to visitors — whether Czech or foreign — as the area was the location of the old 'Iron Curtain' between Czechoslovakia and Germany, with dog patrols in the woods and military look-out towers poking above the tree tops, and where those who lived in villages near the border were once required to report the presence of a stranger in their village to the border police. This sensitivity has now gone — and a number of new border crossing points were opened in the early 1990s; but many parts of the area still have an end-of-the-road dilapidation about them, and the inhabitants of this frontier region remain poor and unused to large inward-surges of visitors. Within a few hours' travelling time of Prague and Nürnberg, this is an area of Central Europe unknown to most people, who prefer to speed through it en route to the more popular destinations in Bohemia.

The main ridge of the mountains stretches from Český Krumlov in the south-east to Domažlice in the north-west. The highest point is Mount Gross Arber (4,671ft/1,424m), which actually lies in German territory. German speakers know this area as the Bayerischer Wald — literally, the Bavarian Forest — and, over the border, the German part of the range has similar characteristics of isolated and comparatively poor villages, and forested

78

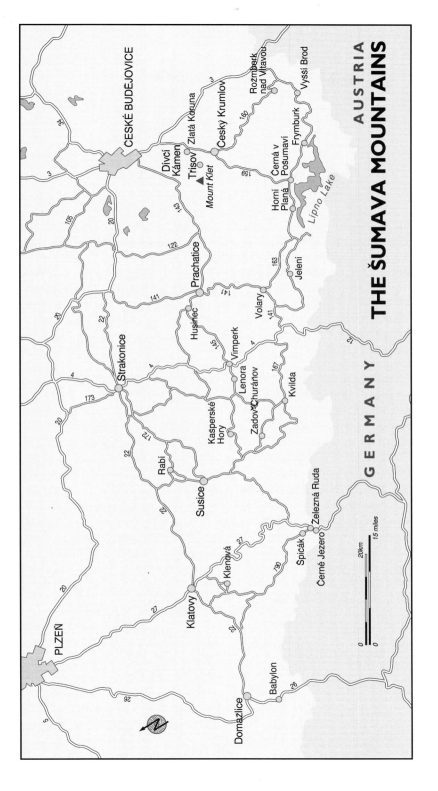

hillsides peppered with tracks through the woods cut for purposes of timber extraction. The highest point in the Bohemian part of the range is Mount Plechy (4,520ft/1,378m), on the Czech-Austrian border. Pine forests, some of the most extensive in the country, form the usual vegetation cover, and in fine weather the sweet smell of pine seems to thicken the air like a natural kind of incense. In many places, mature trees have been cut down for timber, and one can see large areas in the forests where new trees have been replanted to replace them. Many towns in the Šumava have saw mills and timber-working plants, and an extensive network of logging tracks runs through many parts of the Šumava forest. In contrast, many other parts of the Šumava are under stringent nature conservation measures. These include dozens of peat bogs, high in the hills, from where many streams rise, including the *Telpá Vltava*, the embryonic stage of the Vltava; and Boubínsky Prales, an area of virgin forest on the slopes of Mount Boubín, in the central part of the range, which has been closed to the public since 1858 to protect the unique forest ecosystems of the area. Some of the individual beech, spruce and fir trees in Boubínský Prales are several hundred years old.

The main activities here are relaxing, undemanding walking in summer, and equally undemanding (and fairly limited) skiing in winter: the snow season is short, and none of the runs long or hard — most skiers here are day-trippers from Prague or Plzeň, rather than foreigners. Ski and walking centres are Železná Ruda-Špičák, on the German border (the principal resort area in the mountains), and Zadov-Churáňov, in the interior of the range. The area around Lipno Lake, in the southern part of the range, is also good walking country, and the lake itself offers opportunities (again, limited) for swimming and water sports. Some walks are suggested in the pages that follow, and all those who anticipate getting away from the main towns and villages and deep into the hills — whether by car or on foot — should buy one of the large-scale walking maps of the region, such as *Šumava Prachaticko* (southern area) or *Šumava Klatovsko* (northern area), which show in detail the minor roads and colour-coded walking tracks which run through the hills. Virtually all visitors here will want to look round some of the interesting medieval towns in the region, including Domažlice, Prachatice and Český Krumlov, the latter being one of the most beautiful (and visited) ancient towns in the country.

Český Krumlov

'You can see all around picturesque, ancient beauty and historic glory', wrote Karel Čapek of Český Krumlov, and with one of the most spectacular settings of any small town in Europe, the place is firmly on the tourist trail, its narrow cobbled streets and lanes jammed with visitors on summer weekends. However, it would be daft to come to this area and not visit the

Boats along the River Vltava

Glassware is a popular souvenir to buy throughout Bohemia

The main square in Domažlice, with German-looking medieval arcades (Chapter 4)

*The medieval centre of Český Krumlov, a beautifully preserved town
on the River Vltava*

town, as it is not only well worth seeing in its own right, it also serves as a useful base from which to travel out to other much less well-known towns and villages in the surrounding picturesque countryside. Being so popular, the authorities actively discourage cars from coming right into the town centre, and there are car parks along the modern roads built around the historic centre. The bus station is in the eastern part of the town, and affords good views over it; the railway station, on the branch line from České Budějovice to Volary, is awkwardly situated in the modern part of town, a fair walk from the centre. The hotels here are usually full — there are not many, and it is a popular place to stay — but there are plenty of private rooms around.

The central part of the town lies tightly constrained within the core of a meander of the River Vltava above the river, on the northern side, rises the impressive castle — the largest in the country, outside Prague — in whose shadow the town grew. The town's name in German is Krummau (from Krumme Au — 'curved meadow', referring to the bend in the river), and once, like many towns in the region, its most important inhabitants were German-speaking aristocrats and merchants. The castle was founded by the House of Vitek (Witigon) in about the year 1240; during the thirteenth century, the town became fully established. The Rožmberk family, who took over the castle in 1302, were responsible for transforming the castle into a palatial residence, and for nearly 300 years the wealth of the town grew through the silver mines which were opened nearby. The later owners were the Austrian families of Eggenberg and then Schwarzenberg, the latter being landlords here from 1717 until 1947, during which time graceful baroque and rococo frontages were added to the medieval buildings and castle; the ancient groundplan of the town, with its narrow sloping streets and tiny squares, has been meticulously preserved and restored through the ages. The next few paragraphs give a step-by-step guide to the main points of interest in the town, but Český Krumlov is primarily a place in which to wander, with many unobtrusive delights — an oriel window, an elegantly decorated façade, an archway above a narrow lane — awaiting discovery by more alert and inquisitive visitors. The town has a strong cultural life — temporary exhibitions are held here, and concerts and plays are staged in churches or in the Castle. The Austrian painter Egon Schiele is a name to look out for, he lived here and painted many pictures of the town.

Although the Castle is the most obvious landmark here, the best place to start one's tour is the main central square, náměstí svornosti, whose cobbles slope upwards to a Marian Plague Column in one corner. On one side of the square is the **Town Hall**, whose façade is decorated with a Renaissance frieze and the coats of arms of Bohemia, Český Krumlov, and the Eggenberg and Schwarzenberg families. The cosy (and usually full) **Krumlov Hotel**

A view of the Castle, perched high on cliffs overlooking the medieval centre of Český Krumlov

lines the north-western side of the square; parts of the building date back to the thirteenth century, when it was owned by the monks of Zlatá Koruna (see below). Horní ulice runs east from the square; a short flight of stairs on the right takes one up to the entrance to **St Vitus' Church**, built in the early fifteenth century and designed by a German architect. The three-aisled church is airy and bright, with Gothic wall paintings along the side and an early baroque high altar. William of Rožmberk, who ruled over the town during one of its wealthiest periods, is buried here, in an ornate marble tomb. The church makes a good venue for concerts — visiting school and youth choral and instrumental groups from England have performed here in the past few years. Further up Horní ulice, on the left, is the **Town Museum**, with exhibitions of Gothic art, works of the local painter Adalbert Stifter, archaeological finds from the castle at Dívčí Kámen (see below) and an incredibly detailed model of Český Krumlov as it looked in 1800, constructed over a period of 7 years by a local architect and a ceramicist, and completed in 1985. There is also a reconstruction of a seventeenth-century shop.

The Latrán quarter of the town lies between the old centre and the castle. There is less to see here, but the beer halls are perhaps more authentic than the ones in the very centre of the town, and there are few sights to take in before heading up to the castle: **St Justus' Church** (kostel sv. Jost), by the bridge over the river, was originally a Gothic foundation, remodelled in the sixteenth century; the local brewery is in a medieval arsenal by the river, next door to two convents (of the Minorites and Poor Clares); and the České Budějovice Gate, at the end of Latrán ulice, is the only remaining medieval gateway into the town.

The **Castle** dominates the town. It was founded in the thirteenth century, but, like most buildings of its kind, has been extensively modified over the centuries. There are four courtyards within the massive complex, whose formidable walls seem almost to grow out from the near-vertical cliffs above the Vltava, on which it stands. The main entrance from the castle is through the Latrán gate (access from Latrán ulice); beyond the gate is the massive round castle tower, built between 1588 and 1590, 236ft (72m) high, and consisting of an elaborate sixteenth-century crowning-piece topping a solid-looking thirteenth-century base. There will be a good view from the gallery at the top — if the tower is ever re-opened to the public. Beyond this, a bridge spans a moat where bears have been kept since medieval times, and from the Third Courtyard access can be gained (only on guided tours) to the interior of parts of the castle, including lavishly decorated state rooms and porcelain and art collections which date from the eighteenth century, when this part of the castle was rebuilt as a sumptuous stately home for the Schwarzenberg family. Highlights are a coach, once used by an Eggenberg acting as an Austrian ambassador to the Vatican, many tapestries, and two chapels, one Gothic and one baroque. The Masquerade Hall is perhaps the most interesting room, with remarkable frescoes painted by an Austrian artist, Josef Lederer, in 1748, which depict spectators, musicians and masked figures at a Venetian ball; the artist himself appears on the fresco, drinking a cup of coffee.

Pressing on through the courtyards one reaches the castle viaduct, a remarkable structure built in 1764, consisting of arched covered ways which cross a narrow valley. Immediately beyond the viaduct is the remarkably well-preserved baroque theatre, still with its eighteenth-century Viennese stage scenery (and twelve original, movable backdrops) and stage machinery. The Castle Gardens, beyond here, are well-laid out ornamental gardens, complete with the Bellaria Summer House (1708) and Neptune Fountain (1745) and a modern open-air theatre, with a rotating auditorium capable of seating 500.

Near Český Krumlov

A road and railwayline run north-east from Český Krumlov to České Budějovice, the main urban centre of Southern Bohemia (and, from there, onto Prague). The countryside around this part of Southern Bohemia consists of rolling hills and woodland, occasionally interrupted by a steep gorge on the Vltava or another river, hidden from view in the forests. This is excellent walking country — full of gentle gradients and often surprising one with good views; a detailed map of the area will reveal all the possibilities, but the specific sights in the area are described below.

Taking the road from Český Krumlov back towards České Budějovice, after 4 miles (6km), at the village of Rájov, one should turn left on a more minor road which leads towards Zlatá Koruna and Křemže. **Zlatá Koruna** is the first village along this road. In the village is Zlatá Koruna monastery, founded in 1263 by King Otakar II, ostensibly to commemorate his victory over the Hungarian armies at the Battle of Kressenbrünn in Austria, but in reality the reasons for its foundation were the wishes of the king to strengthen royal power in this part of Southern Bohemia. Zlatá Koruna literally means 'golden crown'. The main period of building activity was between 1300 and 1370; then in 1420 the monastery was burned down by the Hussites, and it remained a ruin until the late seventeenth century, after which it was restored and rebuilt in baroque fashion. In the nineteenth century it was used as a factory; in the twentieth century it was again restored. The oldest part of the monastery is the chapel, a fourteenth-century building dedicated to St Mary; the vaulted chapter hall, dating from 1290, and the gilded and frescoed library, dating from 1770, can also be seen by visitors.

Typical south Bohemian countryside near Český Krumlov

At **Dívčí Kámen** are some of the most extensive castle ruins in Bohemia. The name means 'Maiden's Stone', and the castle was built in the fourteenth century. It is now completely in ruins, but these ruins are quite extensive, with clearly discernible rooms, storeys and outer defensive walls. Part of the castle's charm is its isolation, set on a high, steep bluff overlooking the River Vltava, and inaccessible by road. The nearest village to the castle is Třísov, which is 3 miles (5km) beyond Zlatá Koruna (in a northerly direction), along the road towards Křemže. The marked track leading to the castle starts from the railway station in Třísov, which is on the right as one enters the village from Zlatá Koruna, set back from the main road along a dusty side street. After crossing the railway lines, one comes to a small shrine next to a large tree; turn left here, then follow the markers, which are clearly shown. The walk is very pleasant, through a forest and then down over the River Křemžsky, which is crossed on a small bridge, and then up to the ruins. The distance from Třísov railway station is about 1 mile (2km).

Mount Klet (3,552ft/1,083m) is the highest point in the melancholy hills of this part of Southern Bohemia. On its summit are an observatory, a pub, a hotel, and an observation tower, built in 1825. It is sometimes possible to see the Austrian Alps from here. It is not possible to drive a car up. From Třísov, one can continue on to the next village, Holubov, and from here drive a further 2 miles (3km) through the village of Krasetín to the bottom station of a chairlift which runs up the mountain.

It is possible to see the three places mentioned above, by public transport. The following stations are on the railway line between Český Krumlov and České Budějovice: the monastery at Zlatá Koruna is about 1 mile (2km) from Zlatá Koruna station; Dívčí Kámen castle is conveniently approached from the station at Třísov (see text); and it is a 2 miles (3km) walk from the station at Holubov to the start of the chairlift up Klet. Some ideas for longer walks in the area: a green-marked track runs from the castle in Český Krumlov to the summit of Klet (2-3 hours' walking time, a distance of 5 miles/8km); Zlatá Koruna and Dívčí Kámen are 4 miles (7km) apart, on a red-marked track; Klet can also be climbed from Zlatá Koruna, on a red-marked track which runs past the monastery and the railway station. Klet can also be approached from the west; a red-marked walking track runs up from the village of Chvalšiny, on the Český Krumlov-Prachatice road (buses run along this road, linking the two towns).

The Southern Šumava

The Šumava proper begin South of Český Krumlov. A road runs south from the town, along the valley of the Vltava, to **Rožmberk nad Vltavou**, a small village dominated by its castle which rises above the Vltava, situated on a steep bluff of rock. The castle was founded in the thirteenth century by the Rožmberk family, who later moved their seat to the castle at Český Krumlov. The oldest part of the present-day castle is a round tower dating from the thirteenth century, which is situated at a higher level to the rest of the castle; other parts of the castle date from the nineteenth century, when it was used as a small country residence by the French noble family, the Buquoys, who filled the place with largely uninspiring neo-Gothic decorations. The interiors of the castle contain collections of weapons and paintings (the one by Jacob Grimer of the Feeding of the Five Thousand depicts King Ferdinand I of Austria, and his queen, amongst the throng!), and other rooms of the former Buquoy residence, including a sixteenth-century Dutch bed and chandelier, and an extravagantly frescoed Banqueting Hall. The figures representing the musicians, at one end of the hall, are gilded with real jewels. In the village itself, below the castle, there are Renaissance houses and a Gothic church.

Follow the road on from Rožmberk. After 2 miles (4km) there is a junction where one should turn right; after another 5km (3 miles) one reaches the town of **Vyšší Brod**. Just past the centre of this small town, on the left, is Vyšší Brod monastery, founded in 1259 by the lords of Rožmberk Castle who wanted to bolster their control of what at that time were sparsely populated borderland forests. The Rožmberk lords initially brought Cistercian monks over from the monastery at Wilhering in Austria to found the monastery, which grew to become wealthy and powerful under the patronage of the Rožmberks (it was dissolved as late as 1950). Its wealth and proximity to the Austrian border led to the construction of solid defensive walls around the complex (it successfully withstood two sieges by the Hussites). The monastery church is thirteenth century, with fourteenth-century vaulting which springs from the piers, and there are two side chapels, dedicated to St Roch and St Barbara, which contain late Gothic winged altarpieces (1525). The frescoes are copies of original medieval works which were damaged during shoddy restoration work carried out in the nineteenth century. One shows the founder of the monastery being miraculously rescued from the Vltava. Peter Vok, who died in 1611, was the last member of the Rožmberk family, governors of the castle at Rožmberk and Český Krumlov, and is buried here. When his coffin was lowered into the ground, a rose — the symbol of the family — was broken over it, marking the end of the family line. The Chapter House, dating from the 1280s, is the oldest part of the monastery; its vaulting is supported by a single central pillar and there is a nineteenth-century stained glass window. There is also a library, where 70,000 volumes (and the first official map of Bohemia) are displayed in gilded and frescoed eighteenth-century rooms; a picture gallery with paintings by seventeenth- and eighteenth-century Dutch masters; and a museum of postal history. Many other treasures, notably the remarkable painting of the Vyšší Brod Madonna (1420; a copy is in one of the side chapels of the church) have been moved to museums in Prague.

Beyond Vyšší Brod, the road heading west to the lake passes a small reservoir before once again hugging the banks of the Vltava. From a car park on the road side, a red-marked path leads a short way into the forest for the viewpoint over **Čertova Stěna** (Devil's Rocks), an interesting rock forma-tion where giant slabs of granite tumble down the valley sides into the Vltava. Further on, the road runs through the village of Loučovice before coming to the comparatively inconspicuous dam at the eastern end of **Lipno Lake**. This artificial lake — one of several created on the southern stretches of the Vltava — is the largest in the Czech Republic, situated at an altitude of 2,381ft (726m) and picturesquely surrounded by high, forested, rounded peaks that are typical of the Šumava. Often there is no water flowing in the river channel below the dam, as the bulk of it is piped through the hillside to the small reservoir near Vyšší Brod. The dam, and the hydro-electric plant under the ground nearby, were constructed in 1960. The lake itself is 25 miles (40km) in length, a long, irregularly shaped reservoir which is the dominant geographical feature of the Southern Šumava.

Despite its size and its interesting setting, the number of things to see and do around the lake are limited; isolation has meant that resort facilities have not developed beyond anything that could be described as 'rudimentary', and the towns and villages along the lakeside are not particularly interesting or pretty — most of the resorts are bland, featureless places, simply bases from which to enjoy the (comparatively few) recreation possibilities the lake offers, rather than places to look round or visit. There are few walking tracks in the region (the blue marked track along the lake's northern shore is not particularly exciting) — and there are better areas for walking in the Šumava than here. A number of more modern (and very ugly) resorts have also grown up along the north-eastern shore of the lake, along the road running from Vyšší Brod to Volary. There are plenty of opportunities for camping or taking private rooms in the area; most, however, will want to push on to the central or Northern Šumava — or, at least, only use Lipno as a base rather than a destination in itself.

The road along the northern shore passes through the villages in the following order: **Frymburk** is situated on a promontory which juts out into the lake, and boasts a Gothic church and a seventeenth-century fountain; further on, a road leads out to **Dolní Vltavice**, a small town with a grassy beach and a view over to the short stretch of shore opposite that lies in Austrian territory. Next, **Černá v Pošumaví** offers the best possibilities for hiring rowing boats, as does **Horní Planá**, the largest town on the lake shore. Here, the thirteenth-century Church of St Mary Magdalene is pretty enough, and the place celebrates its local artist, Adalbert Stifter, whose former house is a small memorial to his life and work; Stifter spent most of his life in Austria and there is a gallery of his paintings in Vienna. In summer, all these resorts are linked by tourist boats, and Lipno becomes popular with anglers and swimmers, and with users of boats of all types, including sailing vessels and rowing boats (look for the sign *lodí* — meaning 'boats'). There are passenger ferries from Frymburk, Dolní Vltavice and Horní Planá to the other side of the lake — but there is little or nothing to see or do along the south-western shore, and there are no real settlements or resorts here, only isolated farms linked by poor roads. The area here is right up against the Austrian border, and was once considered so sensitive that it was often not included on maps of the region.

Beyond Horní Planá, road and railway line (the latter the České Budějovice-Český Krumlov - Volary Vimperk line) continue along the broad valley of the Vltava to Volary, one of the main centres of the central Šumava.

The Central Šumava

Volary is a useful jumping-off point for the central part of the Šumava, with easy access (by road, rail and bus) to all the places listed in this section, and to the area around Lipno Lake, to the south. Cheap hotels and private rooms can be found in most of the places listed in this section — and Churáňov is a resort proper, with a number of possibilities of accommodation. A few of the houses in Volary, and in other villages in the central Šumava, are built in 'Alpine' style, constructed entirely of dark timber, with a wide, squat roof and an extensive balcony on the first floor.

Volary was known to German speakers as Wallern, and was founded by Austrians specifically as a rest-place on the Golden Way trading route between Bohemia and Bavaria (see below). Backed up by their royal patronage, the town's people used to force all merchants passing through Volary to spend the night and eat there; any merchant caught passing through the town, without sleeping or eating, was forced to pay a fine.

One of the most popular walks in the Šumava is to follow the yellow-marked path known as the Medvědí Stezka (the Bear Trail) from the railway station at Ovesná, near the north end of Lipno Lake, to the station at Černy Kříž, close to Volary — a distance of 9 miles (15km). From Ovesná, thick forest and boulders are encountered on the way up to the summit of Perník (3,441ft/1,049m), before the path drops down past a small, pretty lake, Jelení Jezírko, to the village of **Jelení**. Here one can see the few visible remains of the Schwarzenberg Canal, built 200 years ago to transport Šumava timber south to the Danube. Between Jelení and the end of the walk at Černy Kříž one can see the stone called Medvědí Kamen (Barenstein in German), which marks the spot where the last bear in the Šumava was shot, in 1856. There are now lynx and wildcats in the Šumava (the former were re-introduced into the area in 1985), but there are no longer any bears. This walk, if completed in its entirety, should take around 6 hours. A blue-marked path also leads westwards from the station at Černy Kříž, to the tiny mountain hamlet of České Žleby a short distance off this path is the summit of Stožecká Skála, (3,195ft/974m), with a good view and a tiny chapel at the top.

There is little to see in Volary itself; the town is an important road and rail junction, and like many Šumava towns, it is home to an important timber-working mill. A road and railwayline run north from Volary to Prachatice, 12 miles (18km) distant. A left turning off this road leads to **Křištanovicky Rybnik**, a small lake in the hills with a campsite on its shores. The road to Prachatice carries on over the pass Libínské sedlo, before dropping down to Prachatice around a number of hairpin bends. From the village of Libínské Sedlo, at the highest point in the road, a blue-marked walking track (1 mile/2km in length) leads up to the summit of Mount Libín (3,562ft/1,086m) where there is a lookout tower. This walk should take about 45 minutes up, 30 minutes down; a red-marked track also runs up from Prachatice to Libín, which takes about 90 minutes to go up, and an hour to descend.

The town of **Prachatice** has a charming medieval core — nothing as dramatic as Český Krumlov, but it is a pleasant enough place to spend a couple of hours in. The town developed on the medieval trading route known as the 'Golden Way', which linked Prachatice with Passau, in Bavaria. Cloth, spices, wines, armaments and especially salt came into Bohemia from Bavaria, and butter, honey and wax were sent the other way. From the eleventh century until 1692 Prachatice grew wealthy through its salt trading; in that year salt trading came under imperial control, and trading routes were altered, but the Saumerglocke — the pack-horse drivers' bell — is still rung in Prachatice at 10pm every evening, as it did in medieval days when it would be rung to direct merchants who had lost their way into the town.

The richly decorated buildings in the centre of the town testify to its former prosperity. The old merchants' houses around the main square have lavishly ornamental façades, decorated with sgraffiti and frescoes. Around the square are the Latin School, where Jan Hus was educated as a boy (see below); the Rumpal House, the principal building where salt was traded; and the Old Town Hall (1571), decorated with classical and biblical scenes. Just off the square is the Church of St James, with its steep timbered roof and twin towers, which dates from the fifteenth century; inside, decorations are late Gothic and baroque, including an elaborately carved oak door which opens onto the nave. Some of the town's fortifications still exist: just below the church is the Pisek Gate, the main point of entry into the old town from the ugly modern town square, and this again is decorated with frescoes — showing a member of the local Rožmberk family on horseback, with the rose that was the emblem of the family.

A short distance north of Prachatice is **Husinec**, the birthplace of the reformer Jan Hus (John Huss). Although Hus spent most of his life in Prague, Husinec is rather proud of its famous son, and a memorial stands outside the church in which he preached. The house in the village in which he was born is now a museum of his life and work, and of the history of the Hussite movement, which he founded.

The main road in the Šumava continues on from Volary. The next village along this road is **Lenora**, where there is a glass-making factory. In an orange-coloured building beside the road, above the factory, is a glass-making museum. Beyond Lenora the road meets road 4 (the main Prague-Passau road) and one can turn north to Vimperk. The road on to Vimperk passes through Kubova Huť. The railway station serving the village (it is next to the road) is situated at an altitude of 3,264ft (995m), and is the highest in Bohemia. Near Kubova Huť is Mount Boubín, with more possibilities for walking. From Kubova Huť, a blue-marked track takes one up to the summit of Boubín, 4,467ft (1,362m) — a walk of just over an hour. The view at the top is obscured by trees (this is, however, one of the highest parts of the Šumava). The blue-marked track continues down the other side, through a deer reserve (walkers should keep to the marked paths) and then down past

These buildings on the main square in Prachatice are covered in sgraffito *designs*

Boubínský Prales, an area of protected forest. The track markers take one around the protected forest area, rather than through it. Below Boubínský Prales, the blue markers bring one to a tiny lake, U Pralesa, and then a green-marked track takes one to two car parks on the road, and, after this, to z. Zátoň railway station. This walk, in its entirety, should take 4 to 5 hours.

From Kubova Huť the road descends to **Vimperk**, which is overlooked by an austere (and not particularly interesting) castle. The castle protected trading routes into Prachatice, and in the town itself, Bohemia's first printing press was established in 1484; the town still has a strong tradition of printing religious texts and prayer books, which are sent all over the world by the Steinbrenner Press. Having said this, there is little to detain one in Vimperk — although it is one of the principal centres of the central Šumava. There is also a railway from Volary to Vimperk, which passes through Lenora and Kubova Huť. Both road and rail travellers are treated to fine Šumava scenery on this route.

At Vimperk, motorists can join the main Prachatice — Klatovy road. North-west of Vimperk, heading in the direction of Klatovy, minor roads lead off from the main Vimperk-Klatovy road up to **Zadov-Churáňov**, the main resort in the central part of the Šumava, where there are a number of hotels. Primarily a ski resort, there are opportunities for walking here, too. Zadov is the lower settlement, linked to Churáňov by a chairlift and by a road which twists up the hillside. There are a couple of small ski-jumps at Churáňov, and ski-lifts for very limited downhill skiing; the place is more important as a starting point for cross-country skiing — there is a map available of the tracks.

The Vltava rises in the central part of the Šumava. The spring itself lies deep in the hills, on the German border; maps show that there is a dirt-track out to the spot (pramen Vltavy), but since the border is so close visitors are not encouraged to go there. The pretty hamlet of **Kvilda** is the first settlement on the Vltava (here called the Teplá Vltava). The river at this point is really no more than a mountain stream. The Vltava Valley east of Kvilda makes for a pleasant drive.

The area around Kvilda and Churáňov is good walking country. The hamlets of Srní, Modrava and Antigl, to the west, have new hotel developments grafted onto what were once very traditional mountain villages, with timber houses and a distinct Austrian flavour about them. The hills around here are wild and boggy; the network of paths is limited. Antigl is a good base from which to explore the Vydra River gorge, accessible on a red-marked track running north and south from the hamlet, but other specific sights are few — although opportunities for exploration and discovery are ample.

A road runs north from Vimperk to **Strakonice**, via Sudslavice, where there is a 600-year-old lime tree, one of the largest in the country. Strakonice is a sizeable town in the Šumava foothills. It grew up as an old gold-mining centre around a castle and monastery, which can still be seen, in a fairly good state of preservation, on an island in the middle of the Otava. The fourteenth-century Chapter House boasts early medieval wall paintings, while the church, dedicated to St Procopious, is a simple building with Romanesque origins. Part of the castle site is a museum devoted to motorbikes and fezzes, two of the town's manufactured exports. Nearby is a huge round tower, dating from around 1300, which once contained a winch for the raising of goods up to the top. The town also specializes in the manufacture of bagpipes, and there is a bagpipers' festival held in the castle grounds, every year.

The main road through the Šumava, running north-westwards from Vimperk towards Sušice and Klatovy, passes through **Kašperské Hory**, in whose central square is a colourful Renaissance Town Hall, embellished with eighteenth-century gables, a Gothic church, and part of the Šumava museum, with an excellent display of local glass and crystal products. Most of these were made by the local prize-winning craftsman Johann Loetz in the nineteenth century. Entering Kašperské Hory it is possible to see a castle on a hilltop, way above the town to the right, its two distinctive square towers poking up over the tree tops. This is Kašperk Castle (Hrad Kašperk), an extensive ruin situated at an altitude of 2,906ft (886m) above sea level. The castle was founded by Charles IV in 1356 to defend the local gold mines.

There is no road to it, but it can be reached by a number of marked tracks which lead up through the forest. The most convenient way to reach the castle is to take the green-marked track, which leads up to the castle from the village square, first over a hill and then through a docile Šumava Valley, and then up through the trees. This is a very agreeable 2 mile (3km) walk. The castle has been closed for many years for restoration, but even if it is impossible to get inside, a walk around its massive walls, looming silently amongst the trees, is interesting enough.

Continuing on beyond Kašperské Hory, **Sušice** is a tiny manufacturing town, famous for its match-making industry — once the biggest in Eastern Europe, exporting matches all over the world. On the main square, is a house sporting an interesting Renaissance façade with intricate gables, in which is the main part of the Šumava Museum, with collections of local glassware, and ethnographical, archaeological and historical items. North of Sušice, at **Rabí**, is one of the largest ruined castles in Bohemia. The Hussite commander Jan Žižka (see section on Huss) lost his second eye here, during a Hussite siege of the castle in 1421.

The next large town on the road beyond Sušice is Klatovy, one of the centres of the northern Šumava.

The Northern Šumava

Travellers often approach the northern part of the Šumava from the north — from Western Bohemia and the city of Plzeň — rather than from the south, which is the pattern described so far in this chapter. It has a different character to the rest of the mountains: slightly higher, slightly less bleak, and much more populated and accessible, by road and public transport. **Klatovy** in the north acts as the gateway to the region; it is a small town on the main road and railway which run from Prague, via the city of Plzeň, south to Bavaria (and eventually Munich). This road crosses the German border at Železná Ruda, the most important resort in the whole of the Šumava.

Klatovy was founded in the year 1260, as a settlement on the old trade routes running between Prague and Bavaria; now a road and rail junction with a couple of hotels, most travellers in the northern part of the Šumava will at least pass through here — if not stay in Klatovy, for all the places in this final section of the chapter can be visited easily and conveniently from here, whether by road or by public transport. The town has a few points of interest of its own: forming a distinctive position on the skyline of the town are the twin towers of the baroque Jesuit church, which is situated at one corner of the town's expansive square. The church dates primarily from the years 1703 to 1722, when the original seventeenth century structure was rebuilt by Kilian Ignaz Dientzenhofer, who built many of the splendid Baroque churches in Prague. More interesting, however, is the grisly collection of mummified bodies of Jesuit monks, which lie in the special air and temperature controlled catacombs beneath the church (entrance is via a side door to the church). The catacombs were used for burial between 1676 and 1783 and are part of a sizeable network of interconnected three-storey passages that run under the square and outside the old town walls, which were built to allow the medieval inhabitants of Klatovy to withstand medieval sieges; however, only the catacombs under the church are open to the public. The corpses are kept in carefully ventilated conditions, which allow for continuous circulation of dry air; there are forty bodies here (there were once over 200), mostly of people who taught in the Jesuit College attached to the church.

Another of Klatovy's oddities is an old Apothecary building (U Bílého Jednorožce — The White Unicorn), at number 149 on the square, with good and quite gruesome displays of the ancient medicines which were once made up and sold here (all labelled in Latin), and of other medical apparatus. The baroque carved centrepiece in the room, made in 1733 by a Bavarian woodcarver and cabinet maker, shows St Michael, the patron saint of pharmacists, trampling over the devil (who represents disease). Also on the square is Klatovy's Renaissance Town Hall (1559), and another landmark, the 249ft (76m) high Black Tower, topped by four clock faces and a spire. There is a good view over the Šumava from the outside gallery at the top. There are other Gothic and Renaissance buildings in the square and in the adjoining streets; set back a little from the square, on the opposite side of it to the Town Hall, is the Church of the Nativity of Our Lady (founded in 1260, rebuilt in 1560), and next to it is another tower, the White Tower (1758), which serves as a belfry of the church. Some of the fortifications around the town have survived.

Five miles (8km) to the south-west of Klatovy, in the village of **Klenová**, are the insubstantial ruins of a Gothic castle, which now contain an art gallery.

Two roads lead south from Klatovy to Železná Ruda, 25 miles (40km) to the south. The more interesting route is along the more minor of the two roads, which runs via Nýrsko. The main railwayline also follows this road, and both run along the scenic valley of the River Úhlava. After Nýrsko, road and railway enter the Šumava range, and begin to climb. They pass by a pretty lake in the valley, before reaching Hojsova Stráž (2,952ft/900m), an important winter resort, on the slopes of Mount Můstek. There are a couple of skilifts above the town, to the left of the road. Beyond Hojsova Stráž the road goes over the low pass, Spičácké Sedlo (3,191ft/973m), before descending into the resort of Spičák. At the top of the pass is a track signpost, which points the way to two pretty glacial lakes that lie near here, **Černé Jezero** (Black Lake), which is a 2 mile (4km) walk along the yellow-marked track, and the smaller lake **Čertovo Jezero**, a mile (2km) walk away along another yellow-marked track. A green-marked track runs between the lakes themselves. People swim in the lakes in summer, and in winter, when they freeze over, they are used for skating. The resort of **Špičák** stretches along the roadside from the top of the pass.

The main part of the resort is at the bottom of the pass, around the railway station, and it is from here that a two-stage chairlift runs up to the summit of Mount Pancíř (3,982ft/1,214m), via a middle station at Hofmanky Mesiztance, where there are a few more hotels. From the summit of Mount Pancíř there are good views over the northern part of the Šumava; the rounded, flattish mountain to the south, with the distinctive silhouettes of military installations and aircraft navigation towers on its summit, is Mount Gross Arber (4,779ft/1,457m), the highest peak in the Šumava, which lies over the border in Bavaria.

Just beyond Spičák is **Železná Ruda** (2,591ft/790m), situated at an important road junction. Although Železná Ruda is more important as a resort, the greatest opportunities for downhill skiing are actually at Spičák. Železná Ruda is bigger than Spičák, however, and has more character, with some older, wooden buildings, one of which, on the main street, houses a museum of the crafts and woodworking traditions of the people of the Šumava. Further up is the interesting twelve-sided Church of Our Lady the Helper (1732), topped by an onion-shaped cupola. A relatively easy blue-marked path links Železná Ruda with the summit of Mount Pancíř (see above).

Less than 1 mile (2km) south of Železná Ruda is a frontier crossing with Germany, at Železná Ruda-Bayerische Eisenstein on the main Prague-Munich road. Železná Ruda and Bayerische Eisenstein were once one settlement. Both names mean 'iron ore' in Czech and German (iron ore was once mined here in the Middle Ages), and Železná Ruda used to be called Markt Eisenstein. There used to be one station for the town, which was situated right on the German border; a line drawn down the centre of one of the benches on the station platform marked the boundary between Czech Bohemia and German Bavaria, but when the Iron Curtain was drawn across the Šumava, the village was split in two, and although the road crossing remained, the rail crossing was closed for 40 years. It re-opened in the summer of 1991, a result of the sudden desire for greater contact with the West that has come since the ending of Communism in 1989.

Twenty-three miles (37km) west of Klatovy along road 22 (the journey can also be done by achingly-slow branch-line trains), **Domažlice** is the centre of the **Chod** region. The Chod people were brought here to guard the ancient boundary between the Czechs and the Germans; their name derives from the verb *chodit*, meaning to walk about or patrol, and the eleven

Castle ruins at Dívčí Kámen near Český Krumlov (Chapter 4)

St Vitus' Church, Český Krumlov (Chapter 4)

*Images of
Bohemia;
chamber music
and cold beer*

villages in which they lived were granted many royal privileges (such as freedom from serfdom) in return for their frontier guarding duties — the earliest being made by King John of Luxembourg in 1325. The Chods were responsible for the road from here to Regensburg, in Bavaria, and would escort merchants who had to cross the nearby Scafhberg pass through the forest, protecting them carrying vicious Slavic fighting axes known as cakans. The Šumava forest, along which the ancient border runs, was a difficult obstacle for any attacker to pass, but the Chods were instrumental in defeating the Bavarians in 1040 and again in 1431. In 1695, a Chod leader, Jan Sladký (better known as Kozina), was hanged in Plzeň after he led a rebellion against the Habsburgs, who, after taking control of Bohemia, were suspicious of the independence of the Chod region and its people. Just before his execution, Kozina prophesied that his Habsburg adversary, Lammingen, would die a year and a day later; and, at a banquet to celebrate the first anniversary of the execution, Lammingen died from a stroke after scornfully mentioning this prophesy. But the people of the region remained defiantly loyal to their own customs and traditions throughout the Habsburg years, and their folklore and richly coloured traditional costumes have survived. The Chod festival is held every year in Domažlice (usually during the first weekend after 10 August), and is the most important folklore festival in Bohemia. During the festival, the villagers and townsfolk of the Chod region wear traditional Chod costumes (the women wear colourful cotton skirts, an apron, a short jacket, and red stockings and a shawl; men wear white shirts and wide-brimmed black hats). Chod music is also played during the festival, on traditional bagpipes (known as *dudy*), violins and clarinets. The festival normally takes place on a low hill called Svaty Vavrinecek, on the western edge of the town. Other Chod specialities include distinctive local ceramics, which are characterized by decorative designs which include cornflowers, wild poppies and daisies.

Outside festival times, Domažlice is a quiet sort of place, attractive enough to wander around for a while. In addition to many well-preserved medieval streets, the arcaded central square, called Náměstí Míru, is very picturesque, lined with buildings painted different pastel shades and adorned with a variety of gables. There is a solid-looking medieval gateway at one end, which dates from 1270 and which is the only remaining part of the town's medieval fortification walls. On the square is a thirteenth-century church tower, round and visibly leaning slightly from the vertical, which used to be a look-out post for those controlling this vulnerable region — and today, the view from the top over the surrounding countryside, is still a very commanding one. The church next to it has some baroque frescoes inside; opposite is the neo-Renaissance Town Hall, dating from 1891.

There are two museums in the town. The Castle Museum, in Chodský

Hrad, is housed in the rooms from where the Chods used to govern themselves; it traces the history of the town, and can be found close to the Augustinian Monastery at the north-west end of the square. Much better is the Jindřich Jindřich Museum, founded by a local writer, composer and Chod enthusiast, who spent a lifetime gathering ceramics, costumes, and musical instruments into an interesting museum; there is also a mock-up of a Chod cottage interior.

Four miles (7km) south of Domažlice, along the road to the German border at Furth-im-Wald, is a popular holiday resort called **Babylon**, where there are many opportunities for fishing, swimming and water sports.

Further Information
— The Šumava Mountains —

Places to Visit

Český Krumlov
Castle
Open: April and October, 9am-4pm; May to September, 8am (9am Sept)-5pm. Closed 12noon-1pm daily, all day Monday, and from November to March.

Town Museum
Horní ulice
Open: Tuesday to Saturday, 9am-4pm, Sunday 9am-12noon.

Near Český Krumlov
Dívčí Kámen
Ruins
Open: access to castle ruins at all times.

Zlatá Koruna
Monastery
Open: April to October only 9am-4pm. Closed daily 12noon-1pm, all day Mondays, and November to March.

Southern Šumava
Rožmberk Castle
Open: as for Český Krumlov Castle.

Vyšší Brod
Monastery
Open: as for Český Krumlov Castle.

Central Šumava
Husinec
Jan Hus Museum
Open: 8am-5pm daily. Closed Mondays and 12noon-1pm daily.

Lenora
Glass-Making Museum
Open: Tuesday to Saturday 9am-1pm, 2-4pm; Sunday, 9am-12noon.

Northern Šumava
Domažlice
Castle Museum
Open: mid-April to mid-October daily, except Monday, 8am-12noon, 1-4.30pm.

Jindřich Jindřich Museum
Open: daily except Mondays 8am-2.30pm.

Klatovy
Catacombs of Jesuit Church
Main Square
Open: daily, April, October, weekends only, 9am-12noon, 1-3pm: May to September, daily except Monday, 9am-12noon, 1-5pm.
Apothecary
Building on Main Square
Open: daily, except Monday, 8am-4pm April to October only.

Klenová
Art Gallery in Castle
Open: May to October daily, except Monday, 10am-12noon, 12.45-6pm.

Železná Ruda
Museum
Open: Wednesday to Sunday only 9am-5pm (12noon Sundays).

Tourist Information Offices

Tourist information offices in this region are few and far between. As everywhere, Čedok offices also handle accommodation; but there is also a fairly good provision of private rooms in this area. Čedok offices are as follows:

České Budějovice
Hroznová 21
☎ (038) 32381, 34050

Český Krumlov
Náměstí Svornosti 15
☎ (0337) 2189, 3444

Domažlice
Náměstí Míru 29
☎ (0189) 2266, 2713

Klatovy
☎ (0186) 37419

Prachatice
☎ (0388) 21864

Part Two
MORAVIA

Introduction

Moravia (Morava) is the smallest of the three provinces which make up the Czech and Slovak Republics. Sandwiched between Bohemia and Slovakia, it shares characteristics with both its larger neighbours. Fully a part of the Czech Republic, Czech is the language spoken here and Moravian desires for independence and self-government — though they exist — have never been as strong or as vociferous as those felt in Slovakia, yet calls for a certain degree of Moravian autonomy are growing, as people look back to the time between the wars when the province had much more of a say in its own affairs — an independence smothered by the Communists in 1948. Moravians are as conscious of having a unique culture and heritage as are the Slovaks: here, folklore customs and traditions are upheld with the same vigour as they are in Slovakia, and one of the most important cultural figures that the region has produced, the composer Leoš Janáček based much of his music on diligently collected Moravian folk songs and dances, and described the lives of rural Moravia in his operas. Moravia is also the birthplace of the philosopher Sigmund Freud, the British playwright Tom Stoppard, and the novelist Milan Kundera, the most widely translated and read of all modern Czech writers. Much of the region, however, is as urbanized and industrialized as parts of Bohemia; the area around Ostrava in the north-east of Moravia is the most important manufacturing area in the Czech Republic, so much so that severe environmental problems have occurred in this region caused by the pollution from outmoded factories which date from Communist times, when the need for economic growth transcended any concerns for the environment. Further south, Brno, the region's capital and the second largest city of the Czech Republic, is also an important manufacturing centre. On the periphery of the province, however, there are regions of fine scenery, such as the Beskydy Hills to the south of Ostrava, or the White Carpathians in the extreme south-east of the province.

The first chapter in this section looks at the city of Brno — the most obvious gateway to Moravia, an attractive place with a distinct buzz that is missing in many Czech provincial towns, and an ideal centre from which to explore South-Central Moravia: the karst scenery to the north, with fabulous underground caves and many walking opportunities, is an obvious destination to head for, but Pernštejn Castle and the site of the Battle of Austerlitz, fought on what is now productive farmland to the east of Brno, also have considerable appeal to visitors. South-eastern Moravia is an area of hill-top castles and concealed châteaux, and also the town of Zlín, home to some of the earliest experiments in modernist architecture. Olomouc, an industrial city in the heart of Moravia, is, like Brno, a place to see in its own right, and a good base for excursions into the surrounding countryside. Finally, the last chapter in the section shows Moravia at its most contrasting: the city of Ostrava is not everybody's idea of a holiday destination, although there are some things worth seeing there — and it is not as bad as other books might suggest. To the south of its polluted, grimy sprawl, are the Beskydy Hills, with arguably the best walking countryside in Moravia, amidst deserted forests and remote villages. Moravia is not instantly appealing as a destination for travellers, but here, there are lively cities, underground caves, hilltop castles, peaceful countryside and historic towns — all easily accessible, but experiencing much less of a tourist onslaught than those in Bohemia.

5 • Brno and its Surroundings

B rno is the most obvious focal point for anyone arriving in Moravia.
It is an underrated city; most people usually only stop here in order to
break a journey between Prague and Bratislava or Vienna. The city does not
raise one's spirits upon arrival, due to the ugly industry and forbidding tower
blocks that surround its heart — but then this ritual strangulation of the city
centre is a phenomenon true for all but a handful of Czech (or even East
European) towns. The centre of Brno can not be described as pretty, but it
is interesting enough, with a clutch of museums, churches and historic
buildings and some more off-beat sites as well. The city has a strong cultural
life, with many theatres and important annual fairs. The principal destination for day-trippers from the city are the limestone caves known as the
Moravský kras, to the north-east. A visit to one of these could easily be
combined with a bit of walking in the surrounding countryside away from
the crowds, maybe visiting one of the attractive, or more accurately unusual,
churches of the region. The fields to the south-east of Brno played host to
one of the most famous battles in history, the battle of Austerlitz. History
buffs can survey the battlefield at exactly the same point Napoleon did back
in 1805 before they visit the château of Slavkov (in which there is a museum
dedicated to him) where Napoleon signed the armistice. Other attractions of
the region include a beautiful ruined convent in Dolní Kounice, an astonishing art exhibition devoted to the Art Nouveau painter Alphonse Mucha held
in the château in Moravský Krumlov and the ever popular medieval castle
of Pernštejn. Add to this the usual plethora of châteaux and castles along
with one of the country's best preserved Jewish ghettos (in Boskovice) and
this is a region designed to cater for all tastes.

Brno

Brno is the second largest city in the Czech republic with a population of
over 400,000. Situated at the confluence of the Svratka and Svitava rivers
it is one of the most important industrial centres in the country and it is
probably the combination of heavy industry and the high-rise tenements on
the outskirts of the city which mean that, despite a reasonably attractive core

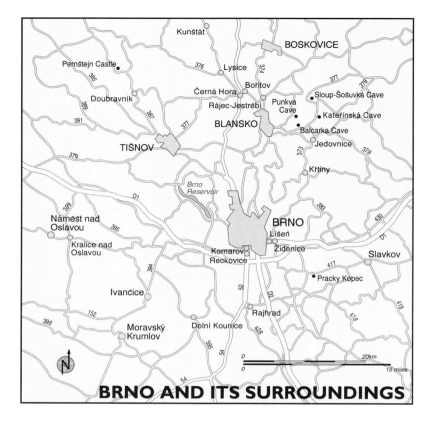

BRNO AND ITS SURROUNDINGS

and a number of really very good museums and galleries, Brno plays host to relatively few visitors outside of the trade fairs and the annual Motorcycle Grand Prix. The city's Art Nouveau railway station was renovated to mark the 150th anniversary of the arrival of the first train from Vienna to Brno in 1839 (the line is the oldest in the country). The city's main bus station is a 5-minute walk south of the train station; the old ČSAD station, opposite the Grand Hotel, is now used by the private bus company ČEBUS. Most of Brno's attractions are situated within easy walking distance of the centre but for anything a little out of the way one might prefer to use a tram. Tickets for these are bought at kiosks and yellow ticket machines and are validated by punching them once on board in one of the machines by the doors. There is a flat fare and the same tickets are valid for the town's buses and trolley buses, though these will generally be less useful. The red machines dispense day tickets. Trams identified by a red number on the tram stop run all through the night (usually hourly). Finding hotel accommodation in the city should present no problems though prices are relatively high due to the commercial importance of the city. Čedok at Divadelní 3 can arrange private rooms as can Accomodea on Rašínova which stays open until 8pm. It is possible to stay in student accommodation during July and August, for details see CKM on the corner of Skrytá and Česká — there is a reduction for IYHF card holders but non-members are also admitted. On a purely incidental note, Brno gave the first two letters to the Bren gun which was originally made here before production in Enfield in England.

The area of Brno had already been settled in by the Slavs in the fifth century. A seat of the apanage Přemyslid princes in the eleventh century, in 1243 Brno was raised to the status of a town, emerging as capital of Moravia in 1641. Brno managed to withstand two sieges during the Hussite Wars but after damage sustained from the Swedes (1645) and the Turks (1663) massive defences were built which successfully withstood an attack by Frederick the Great in 1742. On 2 December 1805 Napoleon stayed in Brno before the battle of Austerlitz, as indeed did his Russian counterpart General Kutuzov. Brno only really began to grow to anything like its present size during the late eighteenth century when the town's first cloth factory was built. By the end of the century there were another twenty, and the town soon became an industrial heartland of the Austrian Empire. The creation of the Salms ironworks in nearby Blansko and the completion of a railway line between here and Vienna in 1839 further boosted the town's economy and in 1860 the town walls were demolished. Between the wars many local industrialists decided that their town should reflect the spirit of their new republic and became patrons to some of the greatest figures of the European avant garde. Particularly important in the reshaping of the city was the Functionalist architect Bohuslav Fuchs (1895-1972), responsible for projects as diverse as the Hotel Avion on Česká, the boarding school on Lípova and the arcade off Jánska. Functionalism emerged during the 1920s principally as an antidote to the historical revivalism of the nineteenth and early twentieth centuries — Neo-this and Neo-thatism — its essential belief was that the form of a building should be determined entirely by practical considerations. Brno suffered badly from the dispersal of its Jewish community in the late 1930s and even more so by heavy American bombing during World War II (due to the presence of an arms and ammunition factory). After the war the city's German speakers (about 25 per cent of the population) were expelled to Vienna.

The largest of the old town squares is the sloping **Zelný trh** (where the fruit and vegetable market is situated) which has kept the shape of the original thirteenth-century market. In the centre is the splendid Parnassus Fountain (1693-5) designed by Johann Bernhard Fischer von Erlach; in days gone by live carp used to be sold from its waters at Christmas. The Trinity Column dates from 1729-33. The late eighteenth-century Reduta theatre at

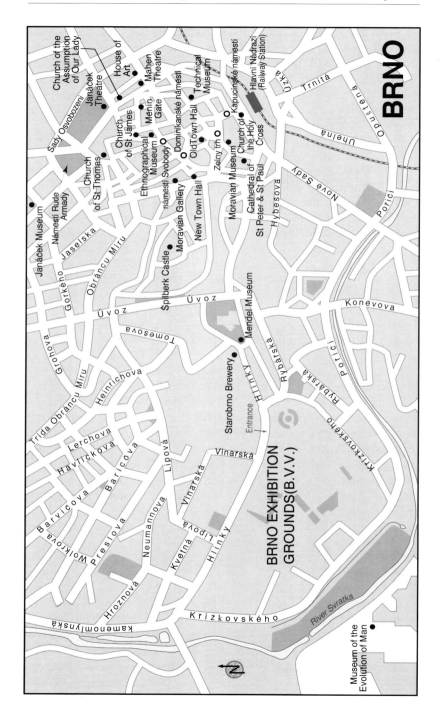

the south-east corner of the square is the oldest theatre in Brno; An 11-year old boy called Wolfgang Amadeus Mozart played here in 1767, just at the time when he was beginning to be hailed as a genius. Today it specializes in opera — tickets may be bought half an hour before the performance or, more expensively, there is a box office for all the city's venues at Dvořákova 11. To the south of the Reduta on Kapucínské náměstí, the former coal market, is the **Church of the Holy Cross** (1648-51) designed by the architect Otto Erna. The crypt of the church contains about fifty mummies of monks and benefactors — not embalmed but dried by the air. In the glass coffin is Baron Trenk (1711-49) who commanded a Dirty Dozen-esque troop of hardened ex-criminals while in the service of the Austrian state. He died after spending an unhealthy 2 years imprisonment in Brno's Špilberk Castle bequeathing an amount covering 600 masses to the Capuchins who buried him in the crypt out of gratitude. For anyone lacking an awareness of their own mortality signs in Czech proclaim 'What we are, they once were. What they are, we will be'. The south-western corner of Zelný trh is dominated by the **Moravian Museum**, founded in 1818 and housed in the much-restored seventeenth-century Dietrichstein Palace, the former residence of the Bishops of Olomouc in Brno. Inside are valuable archaeological and natural history collections including the 25,000-year-old *Venus of Vestonice* fertility idol (the world's oldest piece of ceramic) which was unearthed nearby, and the world's largest collection of cicadas. There is also a meaty section on the Great Moravian Empire for anyone particularly interested.

Petrská ulice leads from the square up to Petrov hill upon which is situated the very clean **Cathedral of St Peter and St Paul**, built in the fifteenth century on the foundations of a Romanesque church (1131). It was renovated in baroque style in the 1740s by the architect Mauritz Grimm after having been badly damaged in the Swedish siege during the Thirty Years War. At the beginning of the twentieth century it was re-Gothicized and two towers were added. The midday bell actually rings one hour early at 11am because of an event that took place during the Swedish siege in 1645. After several months of fruitless bombardment the Swedish commander Tortennson decided to make one last assault, ending the siege if the town had not been captured by 12noon the next day; the bellringers heard of this and rang the bells early when it seemed the Swedes might break through and ever since the midday bell has been rung at 11am. From the nearby Denisovy sady there is a great view over the plain towards Vienna, along with the remains of some medieval town walls and a white obelisk, erected in 1818, commemorating the end of the Napoleonic Wars — the bloody battle of Austerlitz took place nearby.

North of Zelný trh on Radnická ulice, is the **Old Town Hall**, the seat of the town council from the thirteenth century until 1945. The tower (1489) may be ascended for a view and the building sometimes houses temporary art exhibitions. The late Gothic superstructure above the main doorway was created in 1511 by the Austrian Master Anton Pilgram, the architect of St Stephen's Cathedral in Vienna. Look up and you will see that the toppermost pinnacle is bent. According to legend this is because Master Pilgram only spent part of his advance on materials, using most of it to buy wine, so it was not surprising when the pinnacles began to twist and turn. The town burghers were furious and refused to pay the rest of the fee and so Master Pilgram corrected the portal at his own expense. The council, however, still refused to pay and the angry artist then cursed the portal so that the middle pinnacle bent again — his curse is still supposed to strike anyone who dares straighten the pinnacle. Another tale tells how the notoriously belligerent Pilgram, considering himself underpaid for his efforts, destroyed the central pinnacle on his last night in the town and replaced it with a bent one to symbolize the fraudulent ways of the town burghers. This would not be out of character, for Pilgram also caricatured the leading members of the Viennese mason's guild in his sculptural decoration of the pulpit of St Stephen's Cathedral after another quarrel, but such perversity would also not be out of character for the late Gothic period. In the passage underneath the portal there hangs from the ceiling the 'Brno Dragon' (actually a stuffed female alligator). Legend relates how this once ravaged the country outside the Brno walls, eating livestock and children. The town was saved when a young journeyman mason filled a sack with unslaked lime, put it in the skin of a freshly killed goat and set it out as bait. The dragon ate it and when it went to quench its thirst in the Svratka river the water slaked the lime and the dragon burst. Guides point out the scar on the alligator's belly. Probably a more trustworthy history though relates how the gift was presented to Matthias Corvinus by a Turkish delegation passing through to Poland — Matthias then offloaded the gift onto the town in gratitude for its hospitality. Either way, a picture of the dragon appears on bottle labels of Brno beer. Also in the passageway is the 'Brno cart-wheel' made in 1636 by the young wheelwright Georg Birk who was bet a barrel of good wine that he could not in the space of 12 hours fell a tree, make a wheel from it and roll it all the way from Mikulov to Brno Town Hall (about 31 miles/50km). He won the bet but was considered by the town folk to be in collusion with the devil and so his business dropped off and he died in poverty. The wheel has since become a symbol of the town. Leaving the Old Town Hall along Mečová look for the small stone head sticking out of the wall between the windows. It is reputed to be the head of a councillor who was buried alive in the wall for attempting to betray the town and hand it over to the Hussites, though a different tale suggests that it might be a Turk.

Sculptures above the main doorway to the Old Town Hall in Brno; a popular legend relates why the central pinnacle is curved

Mečová leads to **Dominikanské náměstí**, the town's former fish market, and the Dominican Church of St Michael, a two-towered baroque building built in the late seventeenth century by J.K. Erna from a thirteenth-century Gothic church. The adjoining baroque Dominican friary is now the **New Town Hall**; all three sundials in the courtyard date from 1728, the modern fountain dates from the 1928 exhibition — newly-weds often have their photographs taken in front of it. A walk north along Panenská leads one to the Hotel International, adjacent to which is the **Moravian Gallery** which was built by a Jewish textile merchant in the 1880s as a museum of the applied arts. It contains works from all over Europe dating from the sixteenth century to the present day and the Art Nouveau section is particularly worthy of attention. Walk north up Husova to the nineteenth-century Besední dům, home of the Brno State Philharmonic Orchestra, then turn right into Solniční and then right again down the attractive pedestrianized shopping street Česká where the local youth hang out. Walk south down Česká to Svobody náměstí passing to your left the slimline Hotel Avion, brilliantly designed in 1927 by Functionalist Moravian architect Bohuslav Fuchs (at one point the building is only 7ft/2m wide), and to your right at number 5 the sgraffitied Stopka's Beer Hall (1919).

The large, triangular and drab **náměstí Svobody** is the oldest and second largest square in Brno and was the focal point of the town demonstrations during November 1989. From the early thirteenth century until 1870 when it was demolished a large church dedicated to St Nicholas stood in the centre of the square at the site of the present day tram stop. The only reminder of the church today are two statues taken from it and placed in the niches at the front of the Church of St Mary Magdalene at the bottom of Masarykova. The early baroque Marian column, designed by J.K. Erna, has stood in the square since 1680. The only survivor of the once-proud burghers' houses around the square is at number 13 in the south-western corner, the house belonged to merchant Karl Schwarz and was built between 1589 and 1596. The building was given *sgraffiti* decoration in 1938 and has an attractive arcaded courtyard. People have never been able to take the 'House of the four Caryatids' (number 10) opposite entirely seriously; it was built in 1901 by Germano Wanderley for a Jewish industrialist and quite openly rubbished by the predominant Functionalists during the inter-war period — though of course the Functionalists themselves are not so popular now. On the north-eastern corner of the square, just along Kobližná, is the **Ethnographical Museum** containing a large collection of Moravian folk costumes, ceramics, photos and the like. The building used to be a home for orphaned girls from aristocratic and burgher families.

To the north of náměstí Svobody along Rašinova is the **Church of St James,** the parish church of the town and the finest of the town's medieval monuments. The present late Gothic church was built in the early sixteenth century after its predecessor had been destroyed by fire. High on the south side of the tower is a rude figure believed for many years to have been waving his behind in the direction of the cathedral. Cleaners removing bird droppings from the roof in 1989 discovered two heads and four arms and presumed the sculpture to be even more rude than first imagined though a more recent investigation has concluded that the sculpture is in fact a Siamese twin (it only has one pair of legs) holding onto the window ledge so as not to fall down — probably a symbolic representation of the Catholic-Protestant split. The furnishings are all nineteenth-century neo-Gothic save for the late Gothic stone pulpit (1526) and the early baroque choir stalls (1707). At the end of Rašinova is the pale yellow Gothic **Church of St Thomas,** founded in 1350 and altered in baroque style around 1737. The picture of St Thomas above the high altar was painted in 1764 by Franz Anton Maulpertsch. Adjoining the church is the former Augustinian monastery which houses an exhibition of arts from the Middle Ages to the

The main square in Brno, náměstí Svobody

nineteenth century. It formerly housed an exhibition dedicated to the workers movement and (ironically) atheism.

From here turn right and right again down Rooseveltova třída which is dominated by the **Janáček Theatre** (1965), the country's largest opera house (it can hold 1,380 spectators). The first main turning on the right from here leads along Jezuitska to the baroque Jesuit **Church of the Assumption of Our Lady** (1666) which is lavishly decorated within. Back along Rooseveltova, further south down the street to the left is the **Mahen Theatre** (1881-2), the city's main drama theatre, built by the Viennese theatre architects Ferdinand Feller and Georg Helmer in a French Renaissance style. It was actually the first theatre in Europe with electric lighting and Thomas Edison himself supervised the installation of the wiring. The small, squat building 328ft (100m) east of this is the **House of Art** (1911) which houses temporary art exhibitions and which also puts on a bit of theatre and the occasional concert.

Clearly visible from the Mahen Theatre, looking back in the direction of the old town centre, is the Centrum department store built by the shoe magnate Tomáš Bata in the late 1920s. The original idea was to construct a massive 23-storey skyscraper but the city council put a stop to it when local residents complained about their loss of light, thus the building today stands a piffling third of its intended height. From in front of the Centrum store turn down Měnínská which leads to the **Měnín Gate**, the only remaining gate of the town's fortifications, which houses a small exhibition room. The house at number 16 Orli is the former Brno residence of the Pernštejn family. If one walks through to the yard one will find a stone sculpture of a half-naked girl. This relates to the story of a chambermaid accused of witchcraft after stirring the loins of the son of the Lord of Pernštejn. Fearful of being burned at the stake she jumped down a deep well in the yard (long since gone) and killed herself. Her lover was so distraught that he had her true image carved into stone and wept by it. At the corner of Orli and Minoritská is the **Technical Museum** housed in a former convent which displays literally everything from hunting weapons to computers. Along Minoritská is a fourteenth-century Minorite church which was given a richly decorated façade in 1716 by M. Grimm who was also responsible for the attached Loreto Chapel. Returning to náměstí Svobody along Jánská one will pass the Europa Hotel, scene of an unusual suicide in 1930 when two lovers blew themselves up with dynamite after spending a night here, taking half the hotel with them.

Špilberk Castle, a short walk to the west of the town centre, was originally built around 1270 by King Otakar II Přemysl. During the Thirty Years War the castle was converted into a mighty citadel to withstand the Swedish onslaught and in 1783 a prison was established here to house, in particular, those considered to be enemies of the Austro-Hungarian monarchy — mainly Italian, Hungarian and Polish revolutionaries. The most famous prisoner was the Italian poet Silvio Pellico who wrote a famous account of the conditions in Špilberk in 1832 called *My Prisons* which so shocked the Austrian bourgeoisie that many areas of the prison were immediately closed down (the poet's name is recalled today in one of the streets under the citadel). Špilberk prison was finally completely closed in 1855 though it was reopened by the SS during World War II when thousands of Czech patriots were murdered here. There is a modest museum in the castle dedicated to the history of Brno, much more worthwhile though is a visit to the Casemates in which were situated the prison cells. Dingily evocative if a little short on actual exhibits, the Casemates were first opened to the public in 1880 when a large number of horrific tales of torture were recounted and ever-increasingly embellished by the guides to the wide-eyed and curious. They have since become part of the folklore of the place though in actual fact there was never any need for torture in Špilberk as only already convicted criminals were ever sent here so no confessions had to be extracted. A strait-laced guide dispels the torture myths, but recounts them all for good measure.

At the south-western corner of the Citadel stands a former Cistercian convent founded in 1323 by Queen Eliška Rejčka. In 1784 the Cistercians were replaced here by the Augustinian monks and it was here that one of them, Gregor Johann Mendel (1822-84), deduced the laws of heredity from his experiments on peas, beans and bees (the Mendelian laws). Although Mendel never lost faith in his work it was only after his death that its importance was finally acknowledged by the scientific establishment. The small **Mendel Museum** commemorates him and an eighteenth-century library with unusual baroque shelving may also be visited. The Gothic abbey church of the Assumption next door was founded in the early fourteenth century (its bricks were originally plastered over). Behind the church, in the former convent cellar, there is a stylish wine bar.

Just along Mendlovo náměstí, on the way to the Exhibition Ground, is the **Starobrno Brewery**, founded in 1872 and a listed technical monument despite the fact that it is still fully operational and brews large quantities of beer. Just opposite from the Exhibition Ground entrance is the late eighteenth-century summer palace of the Counts Mittrowsky where Napoleon stayed the night before the battle of Austerlitz — the Russian general Kutuzov stayed in the Dietrichstein Palace on Zelný trh. Today the palace serves as temporary exhibition space. There is a small park at the back with a statue of Mars dating from 1789.

The **Výstaviště Exhibition Ground** was created in 1928 for a large exhibition celebrating Czechoslovak culture on the tenth anniversary of the

The old centre of Brno, looking towards the cathedral from the Capuchin monastery

founding of the republic. Exhibitions take place all through the year and members of the general public are admitted. The most important event held here is the September Engineering Trade Fair though perhaps more likely to be of general interest is the International Dog Show held every July which attracts up to 12,000 dogs. The main exhibition hall is a vast dome dating from 1960 though the grounds also contain several of the original 1928 buildings which are of architectural interest — in particular the pioneering white and glazed Hall A designed by the architects Kalous and Valenta and the stunning glass tower by Bohumír Čermák. If one continues past the exhibition grounds to Pisárky one will cross the Svratka river and reach a park with the **Museum of the Evolution of Man**. As well as bones the museum contains many paintings by Zdeněk Burian, a Czech painter who specialises in scientifically accurate portraits of Stone Age life.

Leoš Janáček (1854-1928) acquired the Classical mansion (1893) at the corner of Kounicova and Smetanova, just to the north of the town centre, in 1908 for the Brno School of Organists which he founded (in 1882) and where he was headmaster. Today it houses the music department of the Moravian Museum and has an extensive manuscript collection. Janáček lived with his wife in the small house in the garden, writing many of his best known works there, and today the house contains a museum dedicated to the composer which includes his piano. Born in Hukvaldy in northern Moravia, Janáček moved to Brno at the age of 11 where he became a young boy chorister, and he subsequently spent most of his life in the city. Overshadowed for much of this century by Smetana, whom the Communists revered, and Dvořák, who was popular in the West, Janáček's music has only recently received the attention that it thoroughly deserves. His music was strongly rooted in Moravian traditions and in its countryside: he collected and catalogued many hundreds of Moravian folk songs and dances, and set his most famous opera, *Jenufa*, in an isolated Moravian village. Another famous opera, *The Cunning Little Vixen*, features woodland animals as characters. The presentation of both operas outside Czechoslovakia since 1945 (most recently, by companies such as English National Opera in London) has helped to widen the interest in his music. For anyone with sufficient enthusiasm Janáček's body lies in Brno's municipal cemetery.

One final attraction within walking distance of the town centre is the **Tugendhat House** at number 45 Černopolní in the north-eastern suburb of Černá Pole, one of the most important works of the Modernist movement in architecture. The Tugendhats were a rich Jewish family who operated a number of the city's textile factories. In 1930 they commissioned the German modernist architect Mies van der Rohe to build a house for them with no financial limitations (he even designed all the furniture too). Built on the side of a hill, the building has three levels with the top one being at street level. It was designed to be as open-plan as possible, with a minimal use of walls and decorative details and with everything decked out in monochrome. The main living space of 2,528sq ft (235sq m) was conceived as a study and library; a place for resting and receiving guests. In 1938, on the eve of the Nazi invasion, the family fled (with most of the furniture) to Venezuela. The Nazis and the Communists both used the villa for important social functions and today the house is owned by the City of Brno with access being by appointment only (☎ 576 909). The few bits of surviving furniture are now housed in the Moravian Gallery in town.

The château in the eastern suburb of **Líšeň** dates from the first quarter of the eighteenth century; the Church of St Giles in Líšeň was reconstructed in the seventeenth century from an early fourteenth-century structure. Nearby, along the yellow trail, are the ruins of Staré zámky — evidence suggests there was a settlement here from the Neolithic Age through to the twelfth century and it is likely that this was in fact the military and administrative centre of the whole region before it was moved into the present day town centre. In the nearby suburb of **Židenice** is the Jewish cemetery, founded in 1852 and twice enlarged. It contains over 11,000 graves and over 9,000 tombstones. The oldest tombstones (brought here from various localities) date from the late seventeenth century. The neo-Romanesque Ceremonial Hall dates from 1900. The bereaved would gather here before a burial, as according to Judaic principles it is prohibited to leave the deceased's body in the house overnight. The Holocaust monument dates from 1950; an estimated 8,400 Jews from Brno perished during the Nazi occupation (in 1930 the Jewish population of the city was around 10,000).

In the southern suburb of **Komarov** is the Romanesque-Gothic Church of St Giles, the oldest church in the territory of greater Brno. To the south-east of here in the suburb of Tuřany is a miracle-inducing statue of the Holy Vigin (1280-90). The church was built by J.B. Erna between 1693 and 1697. The former farming village of Královo Pole is in the north of the city. It was given municipal rights in 1905 when a new Art Nouveau and Functionalist town centre was built around Slovanské náměstí. The former village green was at the present day Mojmírovo náměstí upon which is situated the Carthusian monastery and church of the Holy Trinity. The monastery was founded in 1375 by Margave Jan Jindřich of Luxembourg. The originally Gothic church has been baroquized, inside are frescoes by F.A. Maulbertsch, the outstanding Austrian decorative painter of the eighteenth century. A little further north in the suburb of **Reckovice** is the fourteenth-century Church of St Laurence which was almost completely reconstructed by M. Grimm between 1716 and 1718. The oldest part of the church is the tower with its stone 'helmet'.

Accessible by tram (#14, 18 or 21 from the centre) on the north-western

Brno Reservoir, with its giant sculpture of a matchstick

corner of the city, **Brno Reservoir** is the major recreational centre, ideal for lazing, eating ice-cream or playing crazy-golf — there is also a zoo nearby. Boats zig-zag all the way up the dam to Veverská Bityška passing the mid-thirteenth-century Veveří Castle (remodelled in the eighteenth and nineteenth centuries) which is not open to the public. One could walk to Veverská Bityška (7 miles/ 11km) along the side of the reservoir on the red-marked path though be warned that the path can no longer cross the dam by the castle and so one would have to continue on to Veverská Bityška on the yellow. This is worth bearing in mind if walking back from Veverská Bityška as, if starting out on the red rather than the yellow, one will end up walking a large amount of the way along the road (or having to catch a bus).

South-West from Brno

The former Benedictine abbey at **Rajhrad**, 7 miles (11km) south of Brno, was founded in 1048 making it the oldest in Moravia. The baroque abbey Church of St Peter and St Paul was built between 1722 and 1724 by Johann Santini-Aichel, his last work. The interior comprises three interconnected oval spaces, the domes of which are covered by illusionistic frescoes. A tablet on the left hand side of the church commemorates George James

Ogilvy who helped defend Brno against the Swedes in 1645. Three miles (5km) south of Rajhrad in **Židlochovice** is a former fourteenth-century fort that was converted into a stately home in two phases (1720-9 and 1844-5). It was used as a residence for the presidents of the Czechoslovak republic. The church in the town dates from 1724-30 and was designed by J.L. Hildebrandt.

About 6 miles (10km) west of Židlochovice is the pretty town of **Dolní Kounice** featuring the beautiful ruins of the High Gothic convent of Rosa Coeli (Celestial Rose). The convent was founded in 1180 for the women's Premonstratensian Order. It was burned down during the Hussite Wars was restored and then ruined again. A wine called Rosa Coeli is produced in the town reviving an old convent tradition; there is also a Renaissance château in the town. Six miles (9km) west, **Ivančice** is less worthy of attention, lying at the confluence of the Jihlava, Oslava and Rokytna rivers it is one of the industrial centres of the region though there are some interesting Renaissance houses on the main square (numbers 8, 9 and 35) and a museum in the late sixteenth-century château that also functions as the Town Hall. Ivančice is the birthplace of the Art Nouveau painter Alphonse Mucha (1860-1939) who became famous as the designer of posters, costumes, stage sets and jewellery for the actress Sarah Bernhardt during the 1890s and whose work is celebrated 7 miles (11km) south-west in Moravský Krumlov. Mucha's paintings are housed in the town's decaying Italianate Renaissance château, rebuilt from the original castle in 1560 by the Italian architect Leonard Garovi for Pertold of Lipá, marshal of the Kingdom of Bohemia. The works on display consist of twenty massive canvases devoted to Slavonic history commissioned by a Chicago industrialist Charles Richard Crane and executed between 1910 and 1928. A free information booklet in English (compensating some way towards the relatively hefty entrance fee) explains each scene. Although Mucha spent most of his life in France (where he shared a studio with Gauguin) and the USA Mucha in fact was quite a fervent nationalist and when the First Republic was declared in 1918 he busily designed stamps, banknotes and posters for it. The town itself was heavily damaged during an air-raid in 1945 and has not quite recovered yet. If arriving here by train note that the railway station is 1 mile (2km) east of the town though a bus is usually on hand to transport you to the centre.

Twelve miles (20km) north-west of here (as the crow flies) is **Náměšt nad Oslavou** which is dominated by its sixteenth-century Renaissance château. Inside is a collection of twenty four Renaissance and baroque tapestries, a Renaissance chapel and a wonderfully decorated library from the seventeenth century. The château is surrounded by an English-style park. The eighteenth-century stone bridge with statuary across the River Oslava is by Josef Winterhalter. The baroque Church of the Holy Cross features paintings by Paul Troger. Three miles (4km) east is **Kralice nad Oslavou**. The Kralice fortress served as the secret printing workshop of the Jednota bratrská (Union of Brothers) who were crushed during the Thirty Years War. Six volumes of the Bible were published here between 1579 and 1593 and in the Museum of the Bible of Kralice there are some reconstructed machines from the workshop. The Kralice Bible has a linguistic excellence very much on a par with the St James Bible in England and has since become the standard Czech translation.

North-West of Brno

At **Tišnov** 6 miles (10km) north-west of Brno there is a Cistercian convent founded in 1233 by Queen Constance. Of particular interest is the richly adorned Romanesque-Gothic early thirteenth-century west portal featuring statues of the twelve apostles. Its beauty and ostentation, quite contrary to the laws of the Cistercian Order, is undoubtedly the result of it having been built to the order of Queen Constance, the wife of Přemysl Otakar II, who is buried here. The interior of the church is baroque with frescoes and paintings by F.A. Maulbertsch and I. Raab.

Six miles (10km) north-west of Tišnov is **Doubravník** with an early sixteenth-century, hall-type late Gothic parish Church of the Holy Cross, originally designed to serve as a burial ground for the lords of Pernštejn. The white marble came from nearby Nedvědice. Another 4 miles (6km) north-west is the main attraction of the region, **Pernštejn Castle**. If approaching by train the nearest stop is Nedvědice from where it is a 20-minute walk along the yellow trail — the castle is clearly visible from the station. Buses wind their way up here from Brno much less frequently than trains. Pernštejn is one of the largest castles in Moravia and one of the most picturesque; first mentioned in 1285 it was extended and strengthened several times by the Pernštejns. At the core of the complex is the Romanesque Round Tower (Barborka); during the early sixteenth century William of Pernštejn converted the fortress into a grand family seat and the picturesque oriel windows were built. The castle chapel was constructed in 1570 and baroquized in the seventeenth century. The Pernštejn family held the building until 1596 when it was taken over by the Mitrovsky family who held it until 1945. It is they who are responsible for the incongruous rococo and Empire-style interior. The guided tour last an hour, information sheets in English are provided.

An alternative route directly north from Brno will lead you to **Černá Hora** 15¹/₂ miles (25km) north of the city with a famous brewery renowned for its dark beer (similar to bitter but sweeter) and its late Gothic castle reconstructed into a stately home between 1859 and 1867 which is not presently

Pernštejn Castle

open to the public. Half a mile (1km) north from here at **Bořitov** is the Romanesque Church of St George with a wall painting of St Christopher dating from about 1200. Three miles (5km) north-west in **Lysice** there is a Renaissance château, reconstructed in baroque and then Empire style, which has an attractive colonnade and a delightful garden (inside are various collections acquired from the Dubský family). In the pottery-making town of **Kunštát**, 6km (4 miles) to the north, there is a baroque château which is not presently open to the public and a square tower called Poděbradka, the only surviving remnant of the town castle.

Six miles (10km) east of Kunštát is **Boskovice** which has an Empire-style château (1819-26) built on an original monastery dating from the second half of the seventeenth century which was recently returned to the Mensdorff-Pouilly family after confiscation by the state in 1945. On a nearby hill are the ruins of the original town castle with a 315ft (96m) deep well. Boskovice used to be one of the major centres of the Jewish population in Moravia — in 1848 they comprised nearly 40 per cent of the town's population — but none survived World War II. The Jewish ghetto in Boskovice was situated to the south of the main square around Bílkova and Plačkova streets and was established in the fifteenth century. The concentration of Jews in a particular neighbourhood of a town (ie a ghetto) was obligatory from the Middle Ages and systematically enforced in the early eighteenth century under the Emperor Charles VI, when the rigorous segregation of communities was ensured by the forced exchange of houses between Jews and Christians. The reason for this was primarily religious — ghettos would be closed off (at least symbolically) with a chain on Saturdays, Sundays and religious holidays so that one community did not disturb the other's worship. As with most other urban ghettos, after the Jews were made equal before the law in the mid-nineteenth century the quarter was largely rebuilt and modernized. However, unlike most other urban ghettos the one in Boskovice is still largely intact and plans are afoot to refurbish the synagogue, rebuilt in neo-Gothic style in the nineteenth century from the original seventeenth-century structure. The large Jewish cemetery lies 229ft (750m) south-west of the synagogue, the oldest tombstones date from the late seventeenth century. It may be of interest to know that, due to the time it often took to carve them, tombstones in Jewish cemeteries were generally erected one year after burial (usually a short ceremony to consecrate the tombstone would take place on the first anniversary of the death).

About 9 miles (15km) south of Boskovice at **Rájec-Jestřebí** is a baroque-classicist French-style château (1763-9) housing a moderate quality picture gallery.

North from Brno: The Moravský Kras

The region of limestone caves and scenery of the Moravský kras (Moravian karst) is easily the most popular excursion from Brno. The boundary of the Moravský kras, designated a Protected Landscape Region, enclosed an area about 15^1/$_2$ miles (25km) long and 4 miles (6km) wide, stretching in a north-south direction immediately to the north-east of Brno. Its attractions include steep, forested valleys and ravines and hundreds of underground limestone caves, four of which have been opened to the public. Anyone wishing to see this area should hunt around Brno's bookshops for the map *Moravský kras*, which shows all the locations and attractions described here, as well as the walking tracks that link them.

All the caves are seen on guided tours. There are English translations of what the guide says, and other information in English, available at each cave. The caves are very popular; be prepared for long waits in summer and try to avoid visiting the caves at weekends. Make use of the fact that the caves open very early in the morning — an early start from Brno will avoid the worst of the queues. Also note that all the caves close quite early in the afternoon. The temperature inside the caves is a constant 7°C (45°F), so bring along a jumper.

The starting point for any visit to this relatively small area is the town of **Blansko**, accessible by bus or train from Brno. In the town's castle, remodelled in neo-Renaissance style in the late nineteenth century, there is a museum devoted to the Moravský kras and to the town's iron foundries. There are hotels here and around the area but the caves are easily, and probably most conveniently, seen on a day trip from Brno. The most important area of the Moravský kras is due east of Blansko, reached by a road (there is an hourly bus) that runs into the hills along the valley of the River Punkva. The roads and walking tracks in the area pass through steep sided limestone gorges, and in many places one can often see rivers coming out of the limestone cliff face, or the entrances to caves which have been closed off. The more specific attractions of the area are listed below:

The nearest cave to Blansko is the **Kateřinská Cave** (Kateřinská jeskyně) which is essentially a huge dome 315ft (96m) long and 66ft (20m) high with splendid acoustics (demonstrated by the guide) and some beautiful and bizarre limestone rock formations which have been given some equally bizarre names such as 'The Bamboo Forest' and 'The Witch'. The latter is lit by a ghostly red light and resembles, with a bit of imagination, a witch flying on a broomstick. There is no running water in the cave, the streams have long since taken a different route.

Around the corner from here are the **Punkva Caves** (Punkevní jeskyně), the largest caves in the country first opened to the public in 1914. They actually spread over 12 miles (20km) in length, though only 1^1/$_2$ miles

($2^{1}/_{2}$km) are open to the public. The first part of the tour takes one through fine stalactite and stalagmite features before coming out into the open air at the stunning Macocha Abyss; this enormous pit is 459ft (140m) deep with sheer, vertical walls formed by the collapse of the roof of a former cave — thus leaving the top of the pit, way above, open to the sky. One of the two tiny lakes at the bottom is 82ft (25m) deep! The entrances to more caves, many of them unexplored, open from the walls. The abyss has a unique climate which is unusually mild and allows many species of plants and insects to thrive there. The earliest recorded descent into the abyss was in 1723 when two monks lowered themselves down from the top on hoists. The name of the abyss (*macocha* means stepmother) comes from a sixteenth-century folk tale which tells of how a woman from the nearby village of Vilémovice attempted to kill her stepson by throwing him into the ravine after being told that her sick young son would die if she did not. The stepson, however, landed in some bushes on the ledge and survived. Angry villagers then decided to throw the stepmother into the ravine and so she is probably the first person to have reached the bottom of the abyss. The abyss can also be approached from the top where there is a stunning view down into this remarkable feature, there is a road to the top, which is signposted.

After the abyss the tour plunges back into the rock with an incredible trip by boat along the underground River Punkva, the boat barely narrow enough to navigate the twists and turns of the river, the rock ceiling never far above one's head — there is a break of journey along the way for some more stalactites. The boats emerge from the rock near the entrance to the caves. After seeing the cave it is not difficult to tell why it is so popular! Rising opposite the entrance to the caves are the ruins of Blansek castle which was destroyed by the Hussites between 1430 and 1431.

The **Sloup-Šošuvka Cave** (Sloupsko-Šošuvské jeskyně) is near the village of Sloup in the northern part of the area. This system consists of caves on two different levels which are connected by holes. Many archaeological finds have been made here including the skeletons of cave lions and bears and, in a cave nearby, the jaw bone of a Neanderthal Man. Concerts are sometimes held in the cave because the acoustics are so good.

The last cave in the region that may be visited is the **Balcarka Cave** (Balcarka jeskyně) just to the south of the village of Ostrov u Macochy, 1 mile (2km) east of the Macocha Abyss. If travelling here from Sloup one may care to detour to the ruined castle at Holštejn.

The physical geography of this region is a result of the actions of water flowing in underground streams which dissolves and then carries away in solution the carbonate minerals that make up limestone, a very soft sedimentary rock that is easily weathered. Moreover, limestone is geologically composed of many vertical and horizontal cracks which means that the surface streams can easily disappear into the ground through a 'swallow hole' (a vertical crack) that has been dissolved and widened by actions of water. In the rock itself, water flows along horizontal cracks, dissolving the rock and hollowing it out to form subterraneous tunnels and channels. Boats take tourists along such an underground waterway in the Punkva Caves. In this way cave systems are composed of several relatively level storeys that are linked by vertical or near-vertical shafts. Over time the water may take another route inside the rock, leaving previous channels and tunnels dry; there has been no water in Kateřinská cave for millions of years and the old underground channels through which the water once flowed can now be walked through by visitors. The limestone in this area is classified by geologists as being 'Devonian' limestone (ie it is about 350 million years old). The features seen take tens of millions of years to form and are in many cases still being altered and changed by the actions of water. The existence of some of the caves has been known about for centuries, other caves have only recently been discovered and many parts of the underground waterway are still waiting to be explored. During World War II the caves were used as a hiding place by members of the Czech resistance and an illegal printing press was even set up in one of them.

There are a number of other attractions that one might like to visit in the area of the Moravský kras to add a bit of variety to one's walking. From Macocha or Balcarka one could walk south-east to **Senetářov** which features an uncompromisingly modern concrete church, built in 1972 in the shape of a ship and containing a vivid blue altarpiece by Mikuláš Medek. In a thatched cottage opposite the church is a small folk museum displaying the contents of a typical Moravian home at the end of the nineteenth century.

Two miles (4km) west is the village of **Jedovnice**, set beside a pretty lake. The town itself is quite unremarkable but of particular interest is the late eighteenth-century village Church of St Peter and St Paul, the interior of which was completely redesigned during the 1960s in a strikingly modern fashion. The centrepiece is the altar painting, again by Mikuláš Medek; the blue cross symbolises hope, the red symbolises the chaos in the world. An English text is available from the priest who lives opposite — the address is posted on the outside of the church.

Four miles (6km) south of here is the small village of **Křtiny** which is, almost ridiculously, the home of an enormous (and partially unfinished) baroque pilgrimage Church of the Name of the Holy Virgin (1728-50) designed by Giovanni Santini. The doors are usually left open for one to admire the ceiling frescoes by Jan Jiří Entgens, Ignac Raab and Winterhalter. By the side of the church are the cloisters, only half of which were ever completed — they are filled with the gifts of pilgrims and bags of concrete. Walking east of Křtiny along the blue trail towards Adamov one can walk for 2 miles (3km) along a special nature trail around a mini-karst region of five caves, none of which is accessible to the public. The cave known as Býčí skála (Bull's Rock) was named after a small bronze figure of a bull that was found there along with numerous objects from the Stone Age. Trains back to Brno from Adamov are, alas, quite infrequent and Adamov is not the most attractive place to hang around in. Tower blocks rise out of the hills above the town like a grotesque cigarette commercial and the town's football ground (below the brick church) is in such a state of disrepair that it is almost worth a detour. It certainly sums up something. There is at present one restaurant in the town (up on the hillside), recommended only for those who like their popular culture (and cuisine) in thick slices.

Anyone with time or energy to spare could walk to Blansko from Adamov via Vranov and Kateřina; in Vranov there is an early seventeenth-century Mannerist church of the Nativity of the Holy Virgin with paintings by Kremserschmidt whilst Kateřina boasts a church dating from the fifteenth century.

East from Brno to Slavkov

Twelve miles (20km) east of Brno, the village of **Slavkov** is dominated by a baroque château built around 1700 for the Kaunitz family and designed by the Italian architect Domenico Martinelli. The interior houses a very good Napoleonic exhibition and a rather less good picture gallery. Sandstone baroque statuary by G. Giuliani litter the unkempt gardens. In 1805 one of Napoleon's most famous battles was fought on the plains to the east of Slavkov and named by the Emperor after the German name for the town, Austerlitz. The armistice was signed in the château on 6 December, 4 days after the battle. The battle was directed by Napoleon from the top of the hill Zuráň (near the town of **Šlapanice**) on which is a bronze plaque inscribed with a diagram of the respective positions of the troops. At the top of the Pracký kopec (Pratzen heights) a little to the south, where the worst fighting took place, there is a stone and bronze Art Nouveau monument created by J. Fanta in 1911 and paid for by the French, Austrian and Russian governments. The base contains a chapel dedicated to peace. A small museum adjoins the memorial with various mementoes of the battle that still continue to be dug up in the surrounding fields. Among the exhibited items is the table on which Napoleon played chess with his officers shortly before the battle.

The Battle of Austerlitz, also called the Battle of the Three Emperors, was fought between a French army of some 35,000 and the combined forces of the Russians and Austrians, totalling over 80,000. By the end of the battle the French had lost about 7,000 and the Alliance 35,000. The battle began on the 2 December 1805 at 7am when the allied forces began making their way from the Pratzen heights to Santon hill where they believed the majority of Napoleon's forces were gathered. Napoleon however, under cover of thick fog, had moved most of his troops to Zuráň hill which stood above the fog and from where he could watch the allied manoeuvres. At 7.30am, with the confused allied forces stretched right across the battlefield, Napoleon attacked and captured Pratzen heights before proceeding to defeat the remaining allied forces from the rear. It was one of his most perfect victories. The battle is vividly described in Tolstoy's *War and Peace* and anyone lucky enough to be here on the anniversary of the battle will be treated to a re-enactment by the Friends of the French Revolution.

Further Information
— Brno and its Surroundings —

Places to Visit

Brno
Art Gallery
Former Augustinian Monastery
Rašínova
Open: 9am-5pm, closed Mondays.

Brno-Líšeň Château
☎ 641 64
Open: 9am-4pm, closed Mondays.

Crypt of the Church of the Holy Cross
Kapucínské náměstí
Open: Tuesday to Saturday 9am-11.45am and 2-4.30pm, Sunday 11-11.45am and 2-4.30pm.

Ethnographical Museum
Kobližná 1
☎ 05 240 58
Open: Tuesday to Sunday 9am-6pm.

Exhibition Grounds
Výstaviště 1
☎ 31 41 111
Opening times vary according to exhibition.

House of Art
Malinovského náměstí
☎ 24226
Open: Tuesday to Sunday 10am-6pm.

Janáček Museum
Smetanova 14
☎ 05 750 540
Open: Monday to Friday 8am-12noon and 1-4pm.

Mendel Museum
Mendlovo náměstí 1
☎ 05 337 854
Open: Monday to Friday 9am-4pm.

Měnínská Brána Gate
Měnínská 7
☎ 277 27
Open: 9am-5.30pm daily.

Moravian Gallery
Husova 14
☎ 23726
Open: Tuesday to Sunday 10am-5pm.

Moravian Museum
Dietrichstein Palace
Zelný trh 8
☎ 05 222 41
Open: Tuesday to Sunday 9am-6pm.

Museum of the Evolution of Man
Anthropos Pavilion
Pisárky Park
☎ 05 33 77 19
Open: Tuesday to Sunday 8.30am-5pm.

Observation Tower
Old Town Hall
Radnická
Open: daily 9am-5pm.

Špilberk Castle
Špilberk Hill
☎ 27793
Open: Tuesday to Sunday 10am-5pm.

Technical Museum
Orli 20
☎ 27996
Open: Tuesday to Saturday 9am-6pm,
Sunday 9am-2pm.

Tugendhat House
Černopolní 45
☎ 576 909
By appointment only.

Limestone Caves
Punka Caves (Punkevní jeskyně)
Open: April to September 7am-
4.30pm, October to March 7.30am-
2.30pm. Open daily, 50-minute tours
run every 15 minutes.

Kateřinská Cave (Kateřinská jeskyně)
Open: April to September 7.30am-
3.30pm, October to March 8.30am-
3.30pm. Open daily, 30-minute tour.

Balcarka Cave (Balcarka jeskyně)
Open: April to September 7.30am-
3.30pm, October to March 8.30am-
3.30pm.

Sloup-Šošuvka Cave
(Sloupsko-šošuvské jeskyné)
Open: April to September 7.30am-
3.30pm, October to March 8.30am-
3.30pm.

Lysice
Château
☎ 0501 972235
Opening times as for Pernštejn Castle.

Moravský Krumlov
Mucha Gallery
☎ 0621 2789
Open: April to October only, Tuesday
to Sunday 9am-4pm.

Náměšt nad Oslavou
Château
☎ 0509 3319
Open: May to September; Tuesday to
Sunday 9am-5pm. April and October
9am-4pm weekends only.

Pernštejn Castle
☎ 0505 96101
Open: May to August 8am-5pm,
September 9am-4pm, closed Mondays. April and October 9am-4pm
weekends and holidays only.

Slavkov
Château
☎ 05 941 204
Open: May to August 8am-5pm,
April, September, October and
November 9am-4pm. Closed Mon-
days.

Austerlitz Monument
Pratzen Hill
Open: May to September 8am-5pm,
October to April 8.30am-3.30pm.
Closed Sundays.

Brno: Useful Information
Banks
Agrobanka Lidická 31 ☎ 75 80 00
Banka Bohemia, Malinovského
náměstí 26170
Investiční Banka, Rooseveltova
☎ 22 811
Komerční Banka, náměstí Svobody 21
☎ 2195
Živnobanka, Vídeňská 56
☎ 3179

Bicycle Rental
Tyršova 5, Královo pole

Car Rental
Brnocar, Solniční 6 ☎ 240 39
Novocar, Nám kpt Zajceva, Žebětín
☎ 57 21 20

Car Repairs
Autoservice and Pneuservice
Fáměrovo náměstí
☎ 536 377 (7am-7pm daily).

Chemists
All-night service at Kobližná 7
☎ 22275

Cinemas
Scala, Moravské náměstí 3
Capitol, Divadelní 3
Alfa, Postovská 8/10
Art, Cihlarska 19
Jalta, Dominikánské náměstí 2
Jadran, Palackého 78
Last programme usually begins
around 8pm.

Currency Exchange
Čedok at Divadelní 3 only accepts
cash. A better bet is the Komerční
bank at náměstí Svobody 21. 24-hour
exchange at the Taxatour snack bar
near the main rail station.

Dentist
Bratislavská 2
☎ 67 86 11

Emergencies
Police ☎ 158
Ambulance ☎ 155

Filling Stations
24-hour service at Opuštěná jih
☎ 33 78 24, alternatively down
Okružní Lesná, Výstaviště,
Merhautova or Královopolská (all
6am-9pm).

Hospital
Bratislavská 2
☎ 312 67 74 48

Lost Property Office
Malinovského náměstí 3
☎ 216415

Motorcycle Grand Prix
Held at the end of August at the
Masaryk track in the western suburb
of Žebětín. Special buses are laid on
during the competition or take bus #65
and walk for 5 minutes. The race
forms part of the World Championships.

Night Clubs
Avion, Česká 20 ☎ 276 06
Bolero, Česká 1 ☎ 245 53
Gourmand, Josefská 14 ☎ 232 84
Interclub, Husova 16 ☎ 264 11
Pavillon, Zelný trh 20 ☎ 220 82
Roxy, Divadelní 3 ☎ 253 01

Police
The main police station is at
Kounicova 46 which includes the
passport and visa division (☎ 448),
alternatively Běhounská 1 (☎ 24432)
or Bratislavská 68 (☎ 574480). Traffic
police Příční 31 (☎ 67 23 61).

Post Office
The main post office is next to the
railway station — 24-hour service
☎ 2192

Pubs
Plzeňka, Veselá ul
Stopkova pivince, Česká 5
Špalíček, Zelný trh 12
U Formana, Česká 19
U tří knížat, Minoritská 2

Taxi
Lidotaxi ☎ 22 009
Citytaxi ☎ 266 11
Ave taxi ☎ 25250

Theatres
Janáček's Opera House (opera, ballet)
Rooseveltova 1
☎ 263 11

Mahen's Theatre (drama)
Malinovského náměstí 1
☎ 263 11

Divadlo Reduta (opera, musicals)
Zelný trh 4
☎ 279 36
Advance booking office at
Dvořákova 11
Open: Monday to Friday 8.30am-
5.30pm and Saturday 9am-12noon,
☎ 233 67. Tickets available at the box
offices of the above theatres one hour
before performance.

Tourist Information Offices
City Information Office
Radnická 4 (by the Old Town Hall)
Open: Monday to Friday 8am-6pm,
Saturday 9am-6pm.

Čedok
Divadelní 3
☎ 254 66
Open: Monday to Friday 9am-6pm,
Saturday 9am-12noon.

CKM
Česká 11
☎ 236 41
Open: Monday to Friday 10am-
12noon and 1-5pm.

Travel Information
ČSAD (buses) ☎ 337226
ČSA (airlines) ☎ 671229
ČSD (trains) ☎ 27562
MHD (city transport) ☎ 334334

Wine Bars
Baroko, Orlí 17 ☎ 255 47
Muzeum, Lidicka 1 ☎ 74 70 74
Reduta, Kapucínské nám 4 ☎ 244 65
U formana, Česká 19 ☎ 254 46

6 • South-Eastern Moravia

Although the area around Brno sees many visitors, other parts of Moravia do not which is a shame, for there are many things to see in the province beyond its capital. South-eastern Moravia, is a warm, hilly (without ever being mountainous) region, stretching from Brno towards the Slovak and Austrian borders. Easily accessible from Brno, the places described in this chapter could also be visited by anyone travelling from Brno to Vienna or Bratislava.

Uherské Hradiště and the remains of the Great Moravian Empire

Uherské Hradiště is a convenient a base as any to explore this region, founded in 1257 by Přemysl Otakar II and retaining fragments of its medieval fortification. It possesses a pleasant main square, a bustling local market (by the bus station) and a number of hotels and restaurants to cater for all tastes and pockets. There is relatively little to see in the town itself though there are two churches of interest; the large early-baroque Jesuit church (1670-87) and the late Gothic Church of the Annunciation, which was founded in 1491 and given a baroque remodelling in the seventeenth century. On the main square is a pretty *sgraffitied* late baroque apothecary which still serves its original function. Next door to this is the town's oldest hotel, the Fojta, whose refurbished resplendent exterior conceals the town's cheapest beds and a restaurant with ambience (to put it mildly). A 5-minute walk to the east of the town centre, behind the cinema in the Smetanovy gardens, stands the Slovácké Museum featuring a large display of folk costumes and various local archaeological finds.

The main reason to pause for breath in Uherské Hradiště is to pay one's respects to the archaeological ruins, suspected by some to signify the site of the capital of the Great Moravian Empire, in that part of town known as Staré Město. The Great Moravian Empire was essentially born in AD833 when Moravian Prince Mojmir I united the principalities of Moravia and Western Slovakia under his rule in direct confrontation to the then presiding Franks. This policy was continued by his successor Rastislav who in AD855

SOUTH-EASTERN MORAVIA

repelled an attack from Louis the German, king of the East Franks. A further defeat in AD870 forced Louis to recognize a certain degree of autonomy for the Great Moravian Empire which by then had extended itself into Silesia and Hungary and as far north as Cracow. In AD894 however, after the death of King Svatopluk, the Bohemian princes decided to pay homage to Arnulf of Carinthia who had become king of the East Franks and after Bohemia was lost the empire began to break up. At the beginning of the tenth century Bavarian and Bohemian armies attacked Moravia. Bavaria and Moravia eventually made peace but their combined army was roundly defeated on 4 July AD907 by the Magyars at the Battle of Bratislava. Moravia then came increasingly under the control of the Bohemian princes while Slovakia was retained by the Hungarians until 1918.

Opinion is divided as to the exact whereabouts of Veligrad, the legendary capital of the Great Moravian Empire, between Nitra in Western Slovakia, Mikulčice on the Slovak border and Staré Město. The ruins at Staré Město can be reached from Uherské Hradiště town centre by local bus (presently bus #1, though do check beforehand) or it is about a half an hour walk — once over the bridge turn right down the main road to Olomouc, the ruins are then signposted to your left down a minor road. What you will find here is a museum based around the foundations of a church, dating back to the mid-ninth century and discovered in 1949, which turned out to be in the centre of a huge necropolis comprising over 2,000 graves.

On your way to the ruins you will pass the Church of St Michael in Staré Město, the site of a Great Moravian rotunda discovered in 1962. The exact position of the rotunda is marked in gold on the church floor (the door is usually left open). The rotunda dates from the mid-ninth century and was probably founded by one of the Great Moravian princes. A small part of the original church can be seen emanating from outside the back wall of the modern one. A little out of the way 1 mile (2km) to the south-east of Uherské Hradiště just before the settlement of Sady, are the remains of a Bishop's church from the first half of the ninth century, thought to have been based in the middle of an unfortified non-agrarian settlement and surrounded by a wall. Another church was discovered near the present day village of Modrá 2 miles (4km) north-west of Staré Město (a visit to which could be easily combined with a trip to Velehrad); it is situated on the top of a small hill by the junction where the Staré Město to Velehrad road turns off into Modrá. The church dates to AD830-40; next to it was unearthed a burial ground containing thirty-seven skeletons.

North-West from Uherské Hradiště: Velehrad, Buchlov and Buchlovice

Situated 6 miles (9km) from Uherské Hradiště and accessible by a regular bus service that takes about 20 minutes is the Cistercian monastery at **Velehrad**. The monastery's importance as a place of pilgrimage is based on the belief that it was the seat of the archbishopric of St Methodius and the place where he died on 5 July AD885 (the day is a national holiday). The saints Cyril and Methodius were brothers from a wealthy family in Constantinople sent as missionaries to the Great Moravian Empire in AD863 at the behest of the ruler Rastislav who was anxious to oppose German political and ecclesiastical influence. Faced by a hostile local clergy Cyril soon retreated to Rome and became a monk while Methodius was imprisoned for 2 years at the insistence of the German bishops. The Pope eventually had him released though and Methodius returned to Moravia where he taught until his death in AD885. The real significance of Cyril and Methodius is that they preached in the Slavonic tongue; Cyril in particular is credited as the father of the Slavonic language and his Glagolithic script is still used in the Eastern church — it is the origin of the Cyrillic alphabet that takes his name. After the death of Methodius his followers were chased out of the country and it was not until the fourteenth century that the common people were to hear the gospel preached in their own language again.

In 1985 on the 1100th anniversary of the saint's death an estimated 150,000 pilgrims gathered here; in April 1990 when Pope John Paul II gave the church a Golden Rose some half a million people came to witness the event. At most times though the church and the small village that it dominates are quite bereft of visitors and the atmosphere resembles something of a cross between a sacred, empty archaeological site and the morning after the last night of a funfair. The present appearance of the church dates from around 1700 after the original Romanesque construction, built in the 1240s, had been destroyed by a fire. A museum at the back of the church displays the remains of the original church but is not recommended for anyone over 5ft (1¹/₂m) tall. The baroque interior of the church has been basically preserved, in the 1930s all the interior was (very expensively) restored.

Anyone keen on a day's walking could then conceivably pay a visit to the castle of Buchlov and then descend to the château at Buchlovice before returning by bus to Uherské Hradiště. It is a 5 mile (8km) walk along a red trail from Velehrad to Buchlov castle, a pleasant stroll with a gentle but persistent incline until the final mile (2km) when it does get a bit steep and from where it is worth crossing onto the green trail in order to pass the **Chapel of St Barbara** which was built between 1672 and 1673 as the family vault of the Petřvald family who took over the running of the castle around that time (the most impressive tombstones though belong to the Berchtold family who took over the ownership of the castle in the late eighteenth century). The altar dates from the late seventeenth century and was taken from the church at Velehrad in 1783 which had been closed on the orders of the Austrian Emperor Joseph II. The church's original altar is presently housed in the parish church in Buchlovice.

The compulsory guided tour of **Buchlov Castle** lasts just under an hour; be sure to pick up a copy of an English text at the cashdesk. This darkly imposing castle originally dates from the mid-thirteenth century though the last period of reconstruction came in the second half of the seventeenth century. The second floor of the castle houses a museum, opened in 1856 and preserved almost as original, dedicated to the exotic travels and eclectic interests of Leopold and Bedřich Berchtold. The Berchtolds took over the running of the castle during the latter half of the eighteenth century and also owned the late seventeenth-century baroque château situated an easy 2 miles (4km) walk away in the village of **Buchlovice**, itself only 2 miles (4km) west of Velehrad. The 40-minute guided tour around the resplendently rococo interior is a real treat. Most of the furniture is original and was left behind by the Berchtold family when they fled to Austria in 1945. One unusual exhibit on display is a leaf from the tree under which Mary Queen of Scots was executed. The gardens are well laid out if a little unspectacular; the most endearing quality is provided by the families of peacocks that inhabit them.

Buchlavice Château

From Uherské Hradiště to Kroměříž

The small town of **Napajedla**, about 9 miles (15km) north of Uherské Hradiště, is probably most famous for its stud farm, founded in 1886 by the owner of the town, Ariste Baltazzi, which still breeds English thoroughbreds. The annual auction of one year olds held on the farm's premises is the highlight of the town's social calendar. A great deal more visible however, especially if arriving from the north, is the huge Fatra plant founded in 1935 and it is with either a palpable air of resignation or possibly a perverse sense of civic pride (it is hard to be sure which) that local tourist literature proclaims Napajedla to be 'a town with a long tradition in producing plastics on the Morava river.' If after seeing the Fatra works you have somehow managed to resist the temptation to press your foot hard down upon the accelerator you may wish to pay a visit to the town's run-down château (on the top of the hill) which dates from the 1760s. Local tourist literature suggests that there is a town museum within the château's walls, but you cannot believe everything you read in local tourist literature. The surrounding park borders the famous stud farm. Along the town's main street Masarykovo náměstí, opposite the Renaissance-style town hall, is a memorial to two US pilots R.W. Winters and J.W. Johnson who crashlanded here during World War II. They were found by Nazi secret agents and murdered near Uherské Hradiště.

A mile (2km) further north, beyond the turn-off to Zlín, stands the uncompromising settlement of **Otrokovice**. First mentioned in 1141 the town today betrays little of its history previous to 1929 when the Bat'a company (responsible for the Fatra works in Napajedla) bought land here and started constructing tanneries, paper mills and dye-works. Today the town's most famous factory belongs to the Moravan aircraft company which exports planes to thirty-seven countries worldwide. The town's only sight as such is the small parish Church of St Michael dating from 1769 which is situated beside the main road. All in all Otrokovice is a town probably best viewed from the main road (preferably at speed). From Otrokovice it is about 9 miles (15km) by road north-west to Kroměříz.

Kroměříž is undoubtedly the most attractive town in the region. The seat of the Bishops of Olomouc from 1110 until the nineteenth century, it was ravaged by the Swedish army during the Thirty Years War but resurrected on the orders of Prince-Bishop Karl von Liechtenstein-Kastelcorn, a member of one of the richest Moravian dynasties who came into the family fortunes in 1627 and whose motto was 'Money exists only that one may leave beautiful monuments to eternal and undying remembrance'. Much money was indeed spent upon the rebuilding of the town, the enriching of the château's art collection and the maintenance of an extravagant court, and because of the richness of the town's cultural and architectural heritage Kroměříž is sometimes referred to as the 'Athens of Haná', though it is not a particularly helpful analogy. In 1848, when Europe was gripped by revolutionary fever, the Austrian Imperial family and their parliament escaped to Kroměříž from their troublesome capital and a famous constitution was drafted declaring that 'all power comes from the people', though it was quickly repudiated. The town's Jewish population was exterminated during World War II and the German-speaking population was expelled soon afterwards. As with many Czech towns the hotel situation in Kroměříž is not so good, with the two cheapest hotels presently undergoing reconstruction, so one might prefer to base oneself elsewhere in the region and come here on a day trip. Bus and train stations lie east of the old town centre.

The centre of the old town is the large oblong former marketplace called Velké náměstí whose shape dates back to the 1260s. The baroque Marian Plague Column in the middle was erected after the plague epidemic of 1680; the date on the plinth (1716) refers to its restoration after another plague epidemic. The nearby fountain originally dates to 1655 though it was rebuilt in 1811. Most of the buildings around the square date from the baroque period, the main exception being the Town Hall which was originally constructed as a one-storey building with a 131ft (40m) high tower on an older core between the years 1550 and 1611. After the Thirty Years War it was repaired thanks to the contribution of Bishop Liechtenstein who is

The picturesque centre of Kroměříž

commemorated by a plaque in the hall (1668). The second floor was added in 1850 when the whole building was reconstructed in a Pseudo-Classical style. At number 38 on the square, in a former Jesuit college, is the Kroměříž Museum inside which is a collection of paintings by local born artist Max Švabinský (1873-1962) which are supplemented by numerous biographical items and photographs. The rest of the museum is taken up by various temporary exhibitions. The so-called 'Regent's House' at number 39 is decorated with some lovely *sgraffiti* dating from the end of the sixteenth century, though only rediscovered during reconstruction work in the 1950s (*sgraffiti* is a monochrome plaster decoration produced by the scraping of the top white layer to reveal the black one underneath). The 'Regent's House' arose from the joining and adaptation of two Renaissance houses, as did the 'Sheriff's House' at number 40 named after the sheriff Maxmilián Rudolf Řikovský of Dobrčice who owned the more northerly section during the first half of the seventeenth century. Completely out of place at number 104 is the Functionalist 'House of Footwear' erected for the Bata shoe company in 1930 (a valuable baroque house was sacrificed for this).

Just beyond the northern corner of the square on Sněmovní náměstí is the late seventeenth-century baroque Archbishop's Palace, built on the site of an earlier Gothic castle and resembling more a fortress than a palace though it is richly decorated within. High points of the obligatory guided tour of the palace are the richly stuccoed ground floor room (around 1700), the Sněmovní sál on the first floor (a vast rococo hall used for concerts), and the

Vassalage hall on the second floor with its vivid ceiling painting depicting the Apotheosis of the Bishops of Kroměříž, the work of F.A. Maulbertsch. The undoubted highlight of a visit here though is the most famous picture gallery in the country outside of Prague. The bulk of the collection was brought together by Prince-Bishop Karl von Liechtenstein-Kastelcorn and made up of private collections he had bought, this was then supplemented by paintings amassed by Bishop Egkla during the mid-eighteenth century. Standing pride of place is Titian's *Flaying of Marsyas* painted between 1570 and 1571 though there are also impressive works by Cranach, Veronese and Van Dyck. Incidentally, part of the film *Amadeus* was shot inside the château.

Next to the palace is the Mill Gate (1585, restored in 1830), the last remaining city gate, next to which is the Archbishop's Seminary dating back to 1856-8 though enlarged in 1911. Beyond the gate along Na Sladovnách can be found the baroque Bishop's Mint (1665) — from the Middle Ages until the mid-eighteenth century the Olomouc bishops were allowed to mint their own coins; examples are displayed in one of the palace libraries.

Behind the palace stand the Zámecká Zahrada gardens which cover a vast area, indeed twice that of the old town. The beginning of the gardens dates back at least to the Middle Ages though their present appearance dates to the revamp of the 1830s under the direction of the Chotek family who then held the archbishopric. Features include the so-called 'Angler's House' (1839), a lakeside Chinese pavilion (1839) and a Pompeian Colonnade (1846).

Leaving the main square at its eastern corner along Jánská, which was completely rebuilt in the late seventeenth century under the directions of Bishop Karl Liechtenstein, one will eventually find oneself in Masarykovo náměstí which is dominated by the Baroque Piarist Church of St John the Baptist dating from the mid-eighteenth century. Leaving Masarykovo náměstí at its most northern point along Pilařova will lead you to the originally Gothic Church of St Maurice. Founded in 1260, the last reconstruction of the church was in Pseudo-Gothic style between 1836 and 1848 after a very serious fire. Inside are the tombstones of many of the Bishops of Olomouc while in front of the church is a statue of St John Nepomuk (1704).

Across to the south-east of the main town square is Reiger náměstí, site of a former horse and then vegetable market, at the end of which is the Church of the Assumption of the Blessed Virgin Mary dating principally to 1724-36, the baroque fountain to 1686 (Bishop Liechtenstein was again responsible). The area to the north of Riegrovo náměstí was the site of the Jewish ghetto and several parts of the original ghetto wall (1680) survive. The most interesting building is the former Jewish Town Hall (1687, restored 1974-80) at number 259 Moravcova which today serves as a local cultural centre. Jewish town halls basically used to serve as community houses with rooms available for meetings, a records office, a classroom, a winter prayer room and sometimes also the rabbi's living quarters. The synagogue used to be on Komenského náměstí; it was demolished by the Nazis in 1942.

Ten minutes walk west of the old town centre are the highly photogenic Květná Gardens (entrance along gen. Svobody) which were originally laid out at the instigation of Bishop Liechtenstein in the late 1660s over an episcopal vegetable garden. The gardens feature a highly photogenic 764ft (233m) long Colonnade (1665-71) designed by G.P. Tencalla which boasts forty-six columns, each topped by a statue from ancient history or mythology. According to drawings made at the time the appearance of the garden has not actually substantially changed since its inception and the Lion and Triton fountains are original though the Rotunda in the middle was reconstructed in 1904. On gen. Svobody, between here and the old town centre, is the former Bishop's Granary (1714).

Four miles (7km) north of Kroměříž lies the château of **Chropyně**, a former hunting lodge of the Bishops of Olomouc. It has a quite delightful setting along the banks of the Chropyně lake and in the midst of newly restored parkland. Inside there is an exhibition dealing with the history of the town which incorporates two historic halls, the Ječmínek Hall and the Knight's Hall which houses a large collection of (mostly seventeenth century) weapons. There is also a small exhibition of paintings by local

The Květná Zahrada gardens at Kroměříž

avant-garde artist Emil Filla (1882-1953) on the second floor. Meanwhile about 4 miles (6km) to the south of Kroměříž, near the village of Velké Těšany, stands a completely reconstructed and visitable windmill.

Kroměříž to Zlín

Four miles (6km) east of Kroměříž at **Hulín** there is a church with an attractive Romanesque portico dating from 1224. The church itself was reconstructed in the 1740s and occupies the site of a former manorial seat.

About 6 miles (9km) beyond Hulín stands **Holešov** which is dominated by a baroque château erected in 1650 by Filiberto Lucchese, inside which there is a small exhibition of furniture and behind which is a very tidily kept French garden whose layout dates from the mid-eighteenth centuy. On the town's main square is a parish church next to which is the so-called Black Chapel dating from the mid-eighteenth century and containing the tomb of František Antonín Rottal whose family once owned the château — the chapel contains some beautiful sculptured decorations, the work of Gottfried Fritsch. The Jewish ghetto used to be in the north-western part of the town and many of the rural type one-storey houses there have survived from the eighteenth century. At the centre of the former ghetto is the synagogue, built in 1560 and extended in the seventeenth century, which contains a museum dedicated to the history of the Jews in Moravia. If the synagogue looks quite plain then this is due to a series of laws enacted from the Middle Ages until the mid-nineteenth century (when Jews were finally made equal before the law) which restricted synagogue builders in terms of dimensions, seating capacity, exterior decorations and the like so that their buildings could not compete with the size and beauty of Christian churches. Until the first half of the nineteenth century the seating inside synagogues used to run along the walls of the prayer room facing inwards to the bimah (or alemar, a raised platform from where the Torah scrolls are read) and this original interior design has survived in the Holešov synagogue; in most synagogues the seats are now arranged in parallel rows (as in a Christian church) facing the eastern wall.

At least sixty synagogues were destroyed by the Nazis during World War II in the area of the present day Czech Republic and after the end of the war nearly 300 synagogues fell into disuse. About 100 of them were demolished either because of their poor condition or to make way for the Communist urban renewal programmes leaving some 200 synagogues presently left. Of these only three still serve as their original function (two in Prague and one in Brno), the rest have been variously converted into Christian churches, museums, concert halls, libraries and storehouses. Across from the synagogue, on Zámecká, is an unkempt Jewish cemetery. The oldest legible tombstone dates to 1647 (the last burial was in 1975) and the tomb under glass belongs to Rabbi Shabtai ben Meir ha Kohen, the author of *Sifse Kohen* (1662). The Jelíneks of Vizovice (of the famous, and kosher, plum brandy *slivovice*) are also buried here. There is also a memorial tablet for the town's 250 Jewish victims of Nazism during World War II.

Two miles (3km) north-west of Holešov is the small, rural village of **Rymice**, incorporated into which are a number of cottages dotted through the village which comprise a *skansen*. Exhibitions are housed in number 6, 14 and 116 though many more are being set up; each house will reconstruct the particular interior of what would have been a local tradesman's dwelling eg a saddler or a smith. Most of the relevant houses are loosely identifiable by being freshly whitewashed and thatched.

About 9 miles (15km) south-east of Holešov, near the town of Frystak, stands the **Lešná** château and game park complex which covers a monumental 178 acres (72 hectares). The château is a relatively modern construction dating from between 1887 to 1894 and housing a permanent exhibition of that period. The extensive English park surrounding was laid out at the same time and contains some 240 species of animals including zebras, hyenas, gibbons and tapirs. There are excellent parking facilities and ample eating opportunities as well as a special children's corner. Just to the north-east of Lešná at **Štípa** one may like to pay a visit to the pilgrim baroque Church of the Birth of the Virgin Mary (1759), the village also boasts a Dutch-type windmill with complete internal furnishing (1850). Slightly to the north of Štípa lies the village of **Lukov** above which lie the ruins of a Gothic castle dating from the first half of the thirteenth century which was abandoned in 1780.

It would be something of an understatement to say that there was a shoe factory in **Zlín**. The existence of the town is first mentioned in 1322 but the most important date in the town's history is undoubtedly 1894 when two brothers Antonín and Thomáš Bat'a and their sister Anna first established shoe production here. At the time the population of Zlín was under 3,000; today it is over 85,000 and the dramatic increase is almost wholly as a result of the Bata factory. Following his brother's death in 1908 Tomáš became the sole proprietor of the firm and he immediately began to implement entrepreneurial skills picked up during a visit to the United States in 1904. The initial Bata fortune was made during World War I when the company supplied the Austro-Hungarian army with its footwear and during the inter-war years the company expanded dramatically and began exporting. It eventually became the largest manufacturer of shoes in the world with an amazing 50 million pairs produced annually.

In 1923 Tomáš Bat'a became mayor of Zlín and set about designing, with the aid of the famous French architect Le Corbusier and locally-born Cubist architect František Gahura, a new type of town based around the factory built of concrete, bricks and glass; entirely functional yet also providing for the cultural and recreational needs of its population. It is somewhat ironic that such a devout capitalist as Baťa (he even banned Comunists from the workplace during the 1920s) should be seen to have spawned what many would regard as a quintessentially 'Communist' looking town. Certainly the basic principles of Zlín architecture were repeated after the war throughout the country (and within Zlín itself), but with much less imagination and with a generally depressing effect.

In 1932 Tomáš Baťa died in a plane crash near Otrokovice. His son, Thomáš Junior, took over the running of the company until 1938 when the family was forced to leave the country. Upon the end of World War II (during which the factory sustained severe bomb damage) the company was nationalized and renamed Svit while Zlín itself was renamed Gottwaldov after the country's first Communist president, Klement Gottwald, who was born nearby (it was changed back to Zlín in 1990). Thomáš Junior settled in Canada where he built another town on similar principles near Ottawa called Bataville while his brother Antonín continued to run the foreign branches of the business from Brazil. After the Velvet Revolution in 1990 Thomáš Junior was invited back to Zlín and he received a rapturous reception. Negotiations with the government saw the return of much property to the family (including a store on Wenceslas Square in Prague) but not the factory.

The town is still dominated by the huge red-brick shoe factory (next to which are the main bus and train stations) designed by Vladimír Karfík who was one of Gahura's assistants. Baťa himself used to work in a moveable glass office situated in an elevator so that he could see what was happening on every floor and also be accountable himself. In the basement of the factory is a unique Shoe Museum which used to open at the same times as the rest of the factory (7am to 1pm). The museum was originally founded in 1931 at Tomáš Baťa's initiative within the Zlín château and today houses some 3,000 shoes documenting the changing styles of footwear across the centuries and around the globe. It also of course focuses upon the production of footwear in Zlín and is almost as worthwhile visiting for the display of old photographs of the town and factory.

Just over the river to the north of the town centre along Gahurova one finds Baťa's own villa which he had designed by the leading Czech architect of the time, Jan Kotěra, in 1911 though it is remarkable mainly for its understatement. Walking back over the river along Gahurova you will pass on your left the town's sixteenth-century château (rebuilt in 1870) which houses the museum of south-east Moravia as well as temporary art exhibitions and a unique collection of the history of orienteering. The town's main square, náměstí Míru (the Peace Square), is beyond the château. Walk back to Gahurova and follow the road up the hill where it changes its name to náměstí T.G. Masaryka. What you see here is in effect a large, sloping, leafy square, flanked by a succession of simple cube-shaped buildings, the most obvious remains of the original town plan. At the top of the hill is the House of Art, built in 1932 to the designs of Gahura as a memorial to Baťa and originally containing the remains of the plane in which he died; it presently serves as a concert hall (performances are usually held on Thursday evenings) and a contemporary art gallery. Walking back down the other side of the square, to your left is the enormous eleven storey Hotel Moskva, erected in 1933, in front of which one finds the Grand Cinema (also erected in 1933) which seats 2,000.

To the south of the city is another of Gahura's municipal monuments, the Woods Cemetery, built in the 1930s and conceived on a grid rectangular layout as the town's main cemetery.

Tomáš Baťa was one of the first people to be buried here. Finally, in the very western part of Zlín in the part of the town known as Malenovice stands a very well-preserved castle dating from the second half of the fourteenth century. Damaged during the Hussite wars, it today contains a museum devoted to the prehistory of south-east Moravia. Both the cemetery and the castle are accessible by municipal transport.

Local tourist literature seems blissfully unaware of it, but Zlín is actually the birthplace of British playwright and screenwriter Tom Stoppard whose father was a Czech doctor by the name of Eugene Straussler. When Stoppard was 2 years old the family emigrated to Singapore where his father died; his mother later married a major in the British army (called Stoppard) and settled in England. Stoppard has produced definitive English translations of many of Václav Havel's plays, and some of his writing, such as the plays *Dog's Hamlet* and *Cahoot's Macbeth*, focus on Czech themes, particularly the repression of artistic freedom during Communist days. Another famous person to be born in Zlín is Ivana Trump (as Ivana Zelníčková) who first rose to fame as a member of the 1972 Czechoslovak Olympic skiing team, a fame sustained during her career as a model in Canada. After her marriage to Donald Trump she became even more famous (as well as disturbingly rich).

From Zlín to Uherské Hradiště via Slavičín and the White Carpathians

Ten miles (16km) east of Zlín, in the northernmost part of the Bilé Karpaty mountains, stands the town of **Vizovice** which was first documented in 1261. Today most people come here to visit the late eighteenth-century château bujilt for the Brno nobleman F.A. Grimm inside which there is a collection of old masters paintings (including works by Brueghel and

Teniers) along with exhibitions of Louis XVI furniture, china and home-made tools from the Podřevnicko region. Behind the château is a quiet English park with a lake. Very near to the château entrance stands the late baroque Church of St Lawrence (1792) while in the centre of town is a Marian Column (1690), by now a familiar sight. Vizovice is probably most famous for the delicious plum brandy (*slivovice*) it has been producing at the Jelínek Distillery in the western part of town since 1712 and every year in early September there is a festival called the Trnkobraní to mark the plum harvest which features, amongst other things, very much plum brandy tasting. Four miles (6km) north-east of Vizovice in **Jasenná** one may visit the attractive wooden *fojtství* (house of the bailiff) and pay respects to the late seventeenth-century parish Church of Mary Magdalene before continuing on the final 5 miles (8km) up to Vsetín.

The first historical record of **Vsetín** dates back to 1309. In the seventeenth century it became a major centre of resistance to the Habsburg policy of Catholicisation and it was also a centre for resistance during World War II due to the activities of the Jan Žižka brigade in the surrounding forest. The Renaissance château on the main square (remodelled in the eighteenth century) contains a museum dedicated to the history of the town and the folklore of the surrounding area. Also on the square is the former Town Hall which dates from 1721 and the Mastaliska, a baroque building with battlements dating from 1710, which originally functioned as stables. From Vsetín one may like to venture eastwards along the narrow valley of the Vsetinská Bečvapay and pay a visit to one of a number of villages which feature attractive Wallachian timber-framed houses. Alternatively one may care to use Vsetín as a base for exploring the surrounding Beskydy mountains (discussed more fully in chapter 8 on north-east Moravia).

From Vsetín it is 17 miles (27km) south to the small settlement of **Valašské Klobouky**, first mentioned in 1241 in connection with a military defence camp to defend against the Tartars. Today the town is a relatively popular holiday resort with two well-known tourist centres close to the town, Jelenovská and Královec, both in the White Carpathians (Bílé Karpaty) — Jelenovská is primarily a ski resort but does offer some good hiking possibilities. One place to head for is the clearing known as Ploština where a partisan community was established during World War II and twenty-four people died when the Nazis burned their homes and today a National Monument commemorates the events. The Královec ridgeway in the White Carpathians probably offers better views but it is more popular as a consequence. As for the actual town of Valašské Klobouky itself, a fire in 1896 unfortunately destroyed all but a handful of buildings, but on the U-shaped main square, Masarykovo náměstí, stands the wooden-roofed City Hall which houses a museum of the primeval history of the area. Around the corner of the square at the bus stop is a Marian Column dating from 1762 near to which is the baroque Church of the Holy Cross (rebuilt 1761-5) which boasts a fourteenth-century Gothic spire. Leaving town on the road to Broumov along Soukenická ulice are some old houses built of wooden logs, some are up to 200 years old.

Slavičín is similarly well placed for a summer walk in the country along one of the dense network of cross country skiing tracks that begins near Haluzice and goes along the mountain ridge via Bojkovice to Luhačovice. In the centre of the town itself is a baroque-classicist château built in the first half of the eighteenth century. Today it functions as a mini shopping centre which includes a restaurant. In the cemetery at **Šanov**, about 2 miles (3km) south-east of Slavičín, there is a memorial to twenty-eight Anglo-American airmen who lost their lives during an air battle with the Germans on 29 August 1944. Originally buried in a common grave in Slavičín cemetery, their remains today lie in France where they were taken at the end of the war.

Six miles (10km) west of Slavičín is situated the utterly pleasant spa town of **Luhačovice**. Even though the springs were known about as far back as the twelfth century the town's history essentially dates back to 1920 when it was first developed as a spa resort by František Veselý who founded the Luhačovice company and created a therapeutical and cultural centre. The spotlessly clean and neat and tidy town centre is best remembered for the odd and colourful half-timbered villas dotted around, the largest of which is the Jurkovičův dům at the centre of the spa gardens next to the curved concrete colonnade (the nearby Lípova villa houses an ethnographic museum). All these are the work of architect Dušan Jurkovič and plainly show the influence of local folk architecture (Jurkovič was also responsible for the tourist complex at Radhošt in the Beskydy). A short walk 1 mile (2km) north-east of the centre there is a large lake (or more properly reservoir) used for swimming and boating where there is a caravan site and restaurant. Luhačovice's bus and train stations are at the south-western end of the spa.

One final stop 10 miles (16km) before Uherské Hradiště could also be made at **Uherský Brod** which was founded as a royal town in 1272. In the late seventeenth-century stables of the town's castle there is a small museum devoted to the life of the scholar Jan Comenius (1592-1670) who is thought to have been born here. The castle itself is a sixteenth-century Renaissance structure that was remodelled during the seventeenth century. The baroque Town Hall originally dates from the fifteenth century and the town also has some remains of its medieval walls. The Jewish community in Uherský Brod was one of the largest in Moravia and during the eighteenth and nineteenth centuries many Jews left the overcrowded ghetto to found communities in Slovakia — the well-known Jewish surname Brod has in all probability been derived from the town. During the mid-nineteenth century about 900 Jews resided in Uherský Brod making up just over a third of the town's total population. All that is left today of the Jewish quarter (in the south-eastern part of the walled town) are a few houses next to the city wall and a school at number 823 Jirchářská. The synagogue was destroyed in 1941 by Czech fascists; the remains of the old Jewish cemetery are by the southern part of the city walls — it was devastated during the German occupation and the more valuable tombstones have been transferred to the new cemetery on the eastern edge of the town.

Anyone still left with a bit of time and energy on their hands might like to pay a visit to the nearby communities of Vlčnov, Veletiny and Hluk to the south and west of Uherský Brod which feature many attractive and characterful folk buildings.

Further Information
— South-Eastern Moravia —

Places to Visit

Buchlov Castle
☎ 0632 95161
Open: May to August 8am-5pm, September 9am-4pm, closed Mondays. April and October 9am-4pm, weekends only.

Buchlovice
Château
☎ 0632 95110
Open: May and June 8am-5pm, July and August 8am-6pm, September 9am-4pm, closed Mondays. April and October 9am-4pm weekends only.

Kroměříž
Galerie Švabinský
Velké náměstí 38
Open: 8am-12noon and 1-5pm, closed Mondays.

Archbishop's Palace
Sněmovní náměstí
☎ 0634 21360
Open: May to September 9am-5pm, closed Mondays. April and October 9am-5pm, weekends only.

Zámecká zahrada
Behind Archbishop's Palace
Open: 7am-6.30pm daily.

Květná zahrada
Entrance along gen. Svobody
Open: 7am-7pm daily.

Lešná
Château
☎ 067 918331
Open: May to September 8am-5pm, closed Mondays. April and October 8am-4pm, weekends and holidays only.

Malenovice Castle
☎ 61379
Open: May to October Tuesdays, Thursdays and Sundays 10am-12noon and 1-5pm.

Rymice
Folk buildings
Open: Saturdays and Sundays 9am-12noon and 1-4pm.

A lake in the Bohemian paradise

The colourful fruit and vegetable market in Brno (Chapter 5)

A park in Olomouc, famous for its flower exhibitions (Chapter 7)

The main square at Fulnek, featuring buildings from baroque and Renaissance times (Chapter 8)

Uherské Hradiště
Slovácké Museum
Smetanovy sady
Open: April to October 8am-12noon
and 1-4pm, closed Mondays.

Ruins of Staré Město
Open: April to October 8am-12noon
and 1-4pm, closed Mondays. Ruins at
Sady and Modra accessible at all
times.

Uherský Brod
Château
☎ 0633 2288
Open: 9am-5pm, closed Mondays.

Valašské Klobouky
Town Museum
Town Hall
Masarykovo náměstí
Open: 9am-12noon and 1-3.30pm,
closed Mondays.

Velehrad
Church Museum
Open: 9am-12noon and 1-5pm, closed
Mondays.

Vizovice Château
☎ 067 952762
Open: May to August 8am-5pm,
September 9am-4pm, closed Mondays
and Saturday mornings. April and
October 9am-4pm weekends only.

Zlín
Shoe Museum
Shoe Factory Basement
☎ 511 ext 2203
Open: Monday to Friday 8am-4pm, Sat-
urday 8am-2pm.

Regional Museum
Zlín Château
Soudní 1
☎ 23145
Open: Tuesday to Friday 9am-5pm,
Saturdays and Sundays 10am-6pm.

Dům Umění
State Art Gallery
☎ 231 50
Open: 9am-5pm, closed Mondays.

Useful Information: Zlín

Banks
Agrobank, Zarámí 88 ☎ 333 41
Investment Bank, Kvitková 4323
(Hotel Ondráš) ☎ 328 11
Commercial Bank, T. Bati 152,
☎ 220 85

Car Rental
Brnocar ☎ 318 60

Car Repairs (Garages)
Autoservis, Na výsluní 318 ☎ 240 26
Autodílna, Gahurova 226 ☎ 613 46
Autonova, Burešov 3215
Pneuservis, Nerudova 158 ☎ 331 11

Chemist (24-hour)
Dlouhá street 4215, ☎ 255 72

Cinemas
Velké Kino, náměstí Práce ☎ 329 36
Kino Družba, T. Bati ☎ 225 91

Dentistry
During working hours an emergency
service is provided at the
Stomatological Polyclinic, T. Bati.
Out of office hours try the hospital at
Havlíčkovo nábřeží 600.

Exchange Offices
Apart from Čedok and the aforementioned banks the following hotels offer
exchange facilities:
Hotel Sole, T. Bati 3692
☎ 25191 (24-hour).
Interhotel Moskva, náměstí Práce
2512 ☎ 514 (6am-9.30pm daily).

Fire Brigade
☎ 150 (emergency)

Hospital
Havlíčkovo nábřeží 600
☎ 155 (emergency)

Left-Luggage Offices
Bus station, Monday to Friday
7am-7pm, Saturday 7am-12noon,
closed Sundays. Railway station open
24 hours.

Lost Property
Vestibule of the Town Hall, Míru
náměstí.

Police
☎ 158 (emergency)
Town Police ☎ 333 03

Main Post Office
Míru náměstí ☎ 52 52 11

Pubs
Hanácká pivince, náměstí Míru 18
☎ 261 32
Januštice, Zálešná ☎ 277 02
Pivince se Samoobsluhou, náměstí
Práce 1099 ☎ 315 51
U Máců, Tyršovo nábřeží 486
☎ 261 83

Taxis
Taxi stand in the car park by the RYO
snack bar ☎ 311 11 or 241 92

Theatres
City Theatre, T. Bati 4091/32
☎ 250 11
Tickets may be purchased in advance
at the theatre box office Monday to
Friday 10am-12noon and 1-6pm and
one hour before each performance
(☎ 241 06). This is also the main
ticket counter for all cultural performances in Zlín.

House of Culture (Dům Umění)
☎ 231 50
Performances of the philharmonic
orchestra of Bohuslav Martinů are
usually held here on Thursdays.

Tourist Information Offices
Čedok
Kvitková 80
☎ 270 18

CKM
Inside the bus station building
☎ 278 95

Travel Information
ČSAD (buses) station ☎ 264 51
ČSD (trains) station ☎ 245 29
Municipal Transport ☎ 233 52
Czech Airlines, Dlouhá ☎ 243 91

Wine Bars
P-Club, arch. Lorence 9 ☎ 258 93
Rey Club, Rašínova street ☎ 337 94
Zámecká Vináma (Château) Soudní 1
☎ 222 67

Tourist Information Offices

Kroměříž
Čedok
Komenského náměstí

Luhačovice
Čedok
Masarykova 137
☎ 93 22 45

Luhatour
Masarykova
☎ 93 23 89

7 • Olomouc and Central Moravia

Olomouc

Olomouc is the largest city in Central Moravia and lies at the confluence of the Morava and Bystřice rivers. It is the second most important architectural unit in the country after Prague and the historical core is surrounded by a number of beautiful parks — flower exhibitions have been a feature of the city since 1958. Equally famous are the city's many fountains which are dotted all around the centre; most date from the eighteenth-century rebuilding programme. Buy a bar of native chocolate in the Czech Republic and chances are it will have the name Zora-Olomouc on it. The Zora chocolate factory is situated near the bus and train stations and, on a warm day with the wind in the right direction, the whole area becomes suffused with the aroma of gently steaming cocoa. The bus and train terminals are 1 mile (1½km) east of the old town, so take a tram. For information concerning hotels and private rooms head for Čedok on the main square.

There is evidence of a settlement here dating back to the seventh century though it is not believed to have been one of the major centres of the Great Moravian Empire. In the early tenth century a fortress was constructed here by Bretislav I and in 1063 the town that grew up was made into an episcopal see. Under its fifth bishop, Jindřich Zdík (1126-50), the unfinished Basilica of St Wenceslas was consecrated and a Bishop's palace, which still survives today in a fragmentary state, was built. From 1187 to 1641 Olomouc was the capital of Moravia and it was here in 1469 that King Matthias of Hungary proclaimed himself to be king of the Czechs. Situated on an important trade road to Krakow the town continued to prosper economically and during the Hussite wars of the early fifteenth century Olomouc became a staunchly (indeed fervently) Catholic town which led in 1454 to the expulsion of the Jewish population (they were not allowed back until 1848). In 1566 a Jesuit college was founded here which in 1573 was raised to the status of a university, only the country's second. During the Thirty Years War however the town was occupied, and largely destroyed, by Swedish troops and replaced as the capital of Moravia by Brno — both the bishopric and university subsequently moved there. An extensive, and very necessary, rebuilding campaign was curtailed in the late eighteenth century by the construction of city fortifications built on the orders of Empress Maria

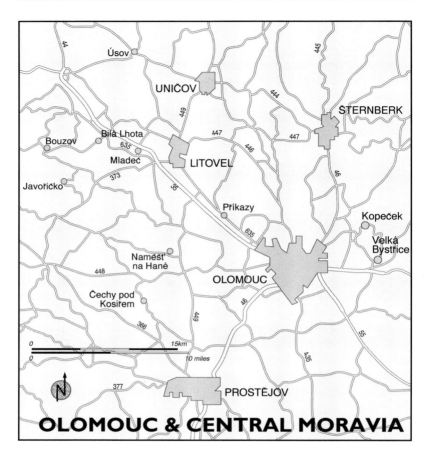

OLOMOUC & CENTRAL MORAVIA

Theresa, fearful of a Prussian military advance. This led to a great restriction on the town's commercial development which lasted until 1888 when the fortifications were finally pulled down. Since then industry has been quick to expand here and after World War II Olomouc once again became a university town. During the Communist era the town was the grudgingly accepting host to one of the largest concentration of Soviet troops on Czech soil.

The town centre is based around two large squares. The upper one, **Horní náměstí**, has at its centre an amalgamation of buildings that make up the Town Hall (Radnice). The nucleus of the building belongs to a Gothic market hall, the tower dates from 1378 and was given its spire in 1443. The complex is probably most famous for its astronomical clock (1420-2) which was destroyed during World War II and given its modern mosaic of workers, peasants and intellectuals in 1955 (the town's coat of arms used to be there); there is a form of procession every hour, and the whole thing is an interesting

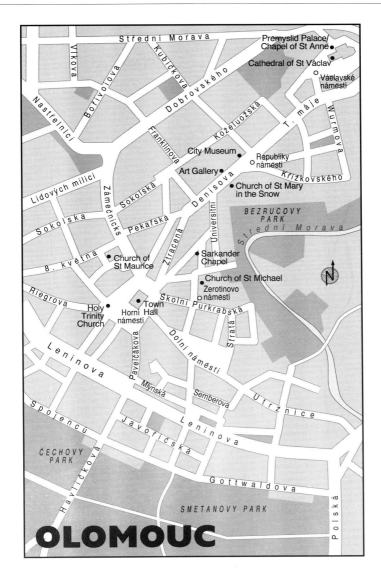

'Stalinist' version of the one on the Old Town Hall in Prague. On the southern side of the **Town Hall** projects the apse of a fifteenth-century chapel while on its eastern side is a Renaissance loggia rising above a flight of steps dating from 1564. Next to the Town Hall is the monumental baroque **Holy Trinity Column** dating from the first half of the eighteenth century and at 118ft (36m) high the largest plague column in either Republic. The base contains a tiny chapel and at the top there are some eighteen figures depicting the

Holy Trinity. Plague columns are a frequent feature of Catholic towns, being an expression of gratitude for being left untouched by an epidemic with the hope that it might have some sway when the next one came around. As well as this they are very much entwined with the attempted re-Catholicisation of the country during the seventeenth and eighteenth centuries. The widespread devastation caused by the Thirty Years War led to a vast rebuilding campaign and a vital role in this programme of urban renewal was played by the Jesuits who were anxious to embody the mystery and splendour of the Catholic religion in town architecture. Baroque architecture in general is an expression of beautification and of mystery, it was designed to inspire an emotional response (preferably awe) in the onlooker in direct opposition to the Protestant creed whose main raison d'être was to de-mystify and to simplify, to explain in the vernacular rather than to frighten and suppress people (as they saw it) with theatre, superstition and a language (Latin) they could not understand. Plague columns later became regarded by Czech nationalists as symbols of Austrian imperialism and many were dismantled following the foundation of the Czechoslovak Republic in 1918 (including the one that used to stand in Prague's Old Town Square).

Among the more interesting buildings around the square are the early eighteenth-century Salm's Palace at number 1, the Renaissance-style Edelmann's Palace at number 5 and at number 10 the Provincial Chemists house rebuilt in the Empire style in 1900 upon Gothic foundations. On the western side of the square is the Oldřicha Stibora Theatre built in 1830 where a young Gustav Mahler spent an unhappy 3 months as Kapellmeister in 1883. Today the theatre puts on a good selection of opera and the city's philharmonic orchestra also regularly performs here. During May Olomouc holds its own spring music festival (Hudební jaro) when concerts take place all over the city — ask at Čedok for details.

Horní náměstí also boasts two of Olomouc's famous fountains, one of Hercules (1687) and one of Julius Caesar (the supposed founder of the city) astride a horse (1724). Two more fountains can be found in the lower square (Dolní náměstí) depicting Jupiter (1707) and Neptune (1695) and in the centre of the lower square is another Plague Column (1720). One other thing to note in this square, apart from the rather plain church of the Capuchins (1665), is the single Renaissance oriel of the Haunschild House on the corner of Lafayettova. From Dolní náměstí take a short walk along Kateřinská to St Catherine's Church which features a rare Gothic portal dating back to 1400 and a wonderfully carved wooden entrance door.

Back just to the north of Horní náměstí is the largest Gothic church in Moravia, the fifteenth-century **Church of St Maurice** which actually looks more like a castle when viewed from the west. The largest organ to be found in either republic is also on show within the church (2,311 pipes), it dates

The modern astronomical clock on the wall of the Old Town Hall in Olomouc

from 1740 to 1745 and is the work of Michael Engler of Breslau. Every September an international organ festival is held here. Just in front of the nearby Prior department store there is another fountain; this one features a representation of Mercury (1730).

Exiting Horní náměstí at its south-eastern corner along either Školní or Michalská leads one up to **Žerotinovo náměstí** which is dominated by the former Dominican **Church of St Michael**, originally founded in 1230 though what you see today dates mostly from the reconstruction of 1676-1701 (it has a quite wonderfully baroque interior). Nearby, on the corner of Na hradě and Mahlerova, is the neo-baroque **Sarkander Chapel** built on the site of the town prison in 1721 in memory of the Holešov vicar Jan Sarkander who was tortured to death there in 1620 during the Czech uprising against the Habsburgs when Protestants briefly gained control of the town council and the Jesuits were expelled from Olomouc (in the nineteenth century Sarkander was made a saint). The chapel was enlarged (1909-10) in Pseudo-baroque style; in the basement there are various instruments of torture and descriptions of seventeenth-century torture procedures.

Carry on your walk along Mahlerova and then Universitni to Denisova. To your right is the early eighteenth-century Jesuit **Church of St Mary in the Snow**, notable only for the fact that one tower is higher than the other, opposite which is the city's **Art Gallery** which houses various temporary exhibitions of a very modern nature. Next to this is the **City Museum** which is housed in a former Clarissine convent dating from 1773. Exhibitions of varying degrees of fascination cover Egyptology, ethnography, mineralogy, zoology and botany.

From here walk across **Republiky náměstí** with its delightful Triton fountain (1709) and then along Mariánská to **Biskupské náměstí** upon which is situated the very clean Archbishop's Palace which was financed by the Liechtenstein clan during the 1660s. Around here are the main university buildings which are housed in attractive seventeenth-century dwellings.

Walk down Wurmova then cross the main street and head up Dómska which will lead you to Václavské náměstí and the **Cathedral of St Václav**. It was originally a twelfth-century Romanesque basilica but owes its present day appearance to the nineteenth-century neo-Gothic restoration when the 328ft (100m) high east tower was added. Inside the crypt is a rich display of religious treasures. Next door to the cathedral is the **Přemyslid Palace** which contains the remains of the twelfth-century Bishop's Palace, only revealed at the end of the nineteenth century, probably the most historically valuable monument in Olomouc. On the ground floor is a late fourteenth-century Gothic cloister decorated with early sixteenth-century murals, while upstairs is the magnificent original Romanesque arcade. Next door to the palace is the baroque **Chapel of St Anne** (1593), where new bishops were elected, and the Cathedral Deanery where at the age of 11 Mozart lay close to death for 6 weeks with smallpox in 1767. A plaque on the Deanery also remembers the murder here of the 16-year-old Wenceslas III which took place on 4 August 1306 (responsibility for the deed is still a matter of conjecture). Today the building houses the Historical Institute of the Palacký University (named after the famous Czech historian considered to be the 'Father of the Nation').

Back on the main road (at this stretch known as 1. máje), walk eastwards to the first canal of the Morava river and then beyond to the river itself. From the bridge look northwards to the bulky baroque former-Premonstratensian monastery of Hradisko built between 1661 and 1750 but originally founded in 1078. Since the late nineteenth century the building has served as a hospital (for a closer inspection take either bus number 14 or 25).

One may like to walk in one of the parks that practically encircle the town; traces of the original town walls may be seen in the Bezručovy sady though the nicest gardens are in the Smetanovy sady. At the beginning of May there is an annual flower festival in the Flora Exhibition Grounds. The town fortifications to the west of the town centre once stretched along the wide avenue called Svobody; at the bottom of this street you will find the only remaining town gate.

Excursions from Olomouc

Velká Bystřice lies some 5 miles (8km) east of Olomouc on the traditional borderline between the German and Czech-speaking areas. First mentioned in historical records in 1276 it was raised to the status of a town in 1460; the local church of the Beheading of St John the Baptist was first mentioned in the thirteenth century. The town today is principally worth visiting during the annual Haná folklore festivals known as the Lidový rok. Ask at Čedok in Olomouc for details.

Much more worthy of attention, 6 miles (10km) from the centre of Olomouc and accessible by municipal bus number 11 from outside the railway station, is the baroque pilgrimage church at **Kopeček** built between 1669 and 1679 by the monks from the Hradisko monastery. It is a truly spectacular sight perched some 656ft (200m) above the plain and positively throbs with activity on Sundays. A 5-minute walk behind the church is the Olomouc Zoo, founded in 1956, where there are some tigers, zebras, lions, llamas and kangeroos. The surrounding hills are laid out as a recreation wood-park and are ideal for a picnic or strolling.

For the last seven centuries the town of **Šternberk** has been dominated by its Gothic castle, founded in the 1240s by Zdislav of Šternberk and last owned (privately) by the Liechtensteins who kept the castle from 1700 to 1945. Between 1536 and 1538 the castle underwent a Renaissance reconstruction but it was rebuilt in neo-Gothic style in 1886. Regarding the interior, its most unusual aspect is a weird and wonderful clock museum largely here because of the presence of the old state watch manufacturers Prim in the town below. The museum contains more than 200 exhibits including metal clocks from the fifteenth century, sixteenth-century wooden clocks, a Renaissance astronomical clock from 1580, a collection of baroque clocks and a miniature watch made from pure gold dating from the second half of the eighteenth century. Nearby is the huge baroque Church of the Annunciation of the Virgin Mary (1775-83) attached to which is an Augustinian monastery. Be slightly warned that Šternberk's bus and train stations are about 1 mile (2km) from the centre of town. A tourist trail heading east from Šternberk leads you through some very pleasant scenery via the villages of Lipina, Stachov and Těšíkov to the Těšíkovská kyselka mineral spring.

Eight miles (13km) north-west of Šternberk, **Uničov** was founded in 1213 by the Moravian margrave Vladislav Jindřich and the municipal documents are the oldest extant in the republic. A former mining town, at

The Gothic castle at Šternberk, near Olomouc

one time Uničov was the second biggest settlement (after Olomouc) in northern Moravia. The town was largely destroyed by fire in 1643 when occupied by the Swedish army during the Thirty Years War and over the next century the ethnic make up of the town changed dramatically due to the influx of a large number of German immigrants who founded a great many German schools. In 1918 the German population declared Uničov to be a province of the Sudetenland and refused to accept the new Czechoslovak Republic; on 9 October 1938 the Czech population of the town was expelled for the duration of the war. Unfortunately, due to a number of serious fires over the years relatively few buildings have been preserved in Uničov. The Gothic three-nave parish church originally dates from 1330 to 1341 and was rebuilt in 1889. Of the four original town gates only two survive today; the Medelská and Vodní brána gates. The two fountains and the statue of the Virgin on the main square all date from the eighteenth century, the town prison dating from the fifteenth century has also been preserved. An amateur film festival, the Mladá kamera Uničov, is held in the town every year.

Four miles (7km) to the west of Uničov is **Úsov** where there is a château containing a museum of forestry which incorporates hunting trophies from the House of Liechtenstein among its insects and timber species (also included is an exhibition devoted to the history of the château). The origins of the château date back to the thirteenth century when a Gothic castle was built here. During the Swedish invasion it suffered much damage and so had to be reconstructed at the end of the seventeenth century (according to the designs of the Italian architect D. Martinelli) by Jan Adam of Liechtenstein whose family had acquired the castle by marriage. A complex of folk buildings is in the process of being prepared in **Příkazy** 5 miles (8km) north-west of Olomouc. The first building to be opened here is Kameníček's farmhouse (at number 54) which has a permanent display on the history of the Haná village. At the northern and southern end of the village are baroque crosses dating from 1772 while in the middle of the village is a baroque statue of the ubiquitous St John of Nepomuk (1345-1393) dating from 1716. John of Nepomuk is basically famous for having the severe misfortune of being the vicar general for the Archbishop of Prague at the time when his master fell out with King Wenceslas IV over the excommunication of one of his favourites. Arrested as the Archbishop's chief agent and personally tortured by Wenceslas before being gagged, shoved into a goatskin and thrown into the Vltava from the Charles Bridge in Prague his story was largely forgotten but then revived during the seventeenth century by the Catholic church in a conscious attempt to create a new national mythology to back up their re-Catholicisation programme. Numerous myths and legends began to circulate about him such as how he refused to betray Queen Sophia's secrets revealed at confessional (officially declared false only in 1961) and of how a constellation of stars could be seen hovering above his dead body floating in the river. In 1693 he was finally canonised as St John of Nepomuk, becoming the patron saint of the Czechs and thus inspiring numerous new religious statuary and the consecration of many new churches. The icing on the cake came in 1719 when his tongue was discovered in a completely undecayed state, the Jesuits having had his body dug up just in case any miracles had happened meantime (it was in fact a piece of his brain).

Due to the presence of six streams flowing through the town (one of them running under the main square) **Litovel** is sometimes referred to, perhaps a touch misleadingly, as the 'Venice of Hana' though the town is probably best known for its beer which has been brewed here since 1892 and which is exported to some thirty-eight countries. Litovel was founded in the early thirteenth century and granted town privileges in 1281 but the town's modern day expansion is principally due to the arrival of the railway in 1848. Regular buses from Olomouc take about 45 minutes to get to Litovel. The centre of Litovel is the large main square náměstí Přemysla Otakara which is dominated by the Town Hall built in 1572 and boasts a beautiful Renaissance stucco ceiling in its main hall. Leaving the square along Kostelní ulice one comes to náměstí Svobody which is dominated by the parish Church of St Mark which was rebuilt between 1529 and 1532 upon an originally Gothic structure. At the corner of Komenského ul. and náměstí

Litovel, a typical medieval Moravian town, with a castle rising above the roofs of the houses

Svobody is the chapel of St George, built in 1444 by the nobleman Karel z Vlašimi for the local Protestant community. Across and beyond the other side of the main square is a large park, the Smetanovy sady, which features a musical pavilion and a large pond. Arguably the most beautiful building of the town, the Opletalovo gymnasium built in neo-Renaissance style in 1904, is also set in the park. It is named after Jan Opletal, a former student of the school, who was the first person to be killed during the October 1939

The náměstí Přemysla
Otakara square in the
centre of Litovel

anti-Nazi student demonstrations in Prague (he is buried nearby in the village of Náklo). On 17 November 1989 on the fiftieth anniversary of Opletal's funeral a crowd of 50,000 gathered in Prague; their attempted March to Wenceslas square and the resulting confrontation with the police (dubbed a 'massacre' though nobody was actually killed) was the trigger for the events that led up to the Communist downfall.

There are a cluster of interesting sights that are visitable from Litovel, which may be visited either via an infrequent bus service that runs from

Litovel to Mladeč to Bilá Lhota to Bouzov (total journey time about 40 minutes) or under one's own steam.

It is a pleasant 4 mile (6km) stroll (much of it along the Morava river) from Litovel to **Mladeč**, famous for its system of limestone caves (Mladečská jeskyně). Archaelogical evidence suggests that the caves were known to Stone Age man and the caves now accessible to the general public are only a small part of an extremely complex labyrinth of crevice corridors and larger ruined domes reserved exclusively for speleologists. The guided tour lasts about 40 minutes. From Mladeč to **Bilá Lhota** is a 3 miles (5km) walk along a slight incline. On the far side of the village of Bilá Lhota is a very pretty arboretum based in an old castle park. The site takes up 6 acres (2¹/₂ hectares) and represents almost 300 species of trees and bushes, interspersed among which are both classical and modern sculptures.

It is a further 5 miles (7¹/₂km) walk from Bilá Lhota to **Javořičko**, scene of one of the many atrocities of the last war when on 5 May 1945 the SS destroyed the village and murdered thirty-eight men aged between 15 and 80 in revenge for the help given by the villagers to the partisans; a monument commemorates the event. The village is also the home of a complex of limestone caves, domes, corridors and abysses that rank among the most impressive in the country. The karst system (the Javořičské jeskyně) is easily as good as that near Brno but comes without the crowds. It is 3 miles (5km) from Javořičko to **Bouzov** which is dominated by a fourteenth-century castle, substantially rebuilt at the turn of the century, which was owned from 1690 until 1939 by the Grand Order of German Knights and occupied during World War II by the Nazi SS. The interior features an unspectacular display of paintings, furniture and weapons (some of the more valuable treasures were appropriated by the Nazis). The most interesting section is the Pseudo-Gothic chapel which houses a fifteenth-century statue of St George, transferred from a house of the Order in Venice. The town below has no discernible point of interest, though one hotel should you need it.

The château at **Náměšť na Hané** (about 6 miles/10km due west of Olomouc) was constructed in the 1760s by Ferdinand Bonaventura Count Harrach (his previous residence being a castle situated in the town below). It was held in aristocratic hands until 1916 when it was bought by an Olomouc wholesale merchant by the name of František Ottahal (in 1945 the château was forfeited to the state). The hourly guided tour is most enjoyable for the excellent collection of Meissen porcelain on display and for the collection of baroque coaches in the coach house outside that belonged to various Moravian bishops and archbishops. The largest and oldest dates from 1745 and was owned by bishop Ferdinand Julius Troyer of Olomouc. The town itself, first mentioned in 1141, is a little isolated, connected by bus

Bouzov Castle, north-west of Olomouc

or train to Olomouc but not much else. The surrounding countryside is recommended only for those seeking complete solitude.

There is another château at **Čechy pod Kosiřem** just to the south of Náměšť na Hané. Between 1708 and 1716 a four-winged baroque château was built here which was then reconstructed in Empire style by the Syla Tarrouca family between 1834 and 1846. Since 1945 the building has been publicly owned. Inside there is a memorial hall dedicated to the painter Josef Mánes who often stayed here as a guest; in the surrounding park you can still see his summer studio. His stays here are also noted by a memorial tablet over the main entrance.

Further Information
— Olomouc and Central Moravia —

Places to Visit

Bilá Lhota
Arboretum
Open: 8am-6pm, closed Mondays.

Bouzov
Castle
☎ 0644 93202
Open: May to September 8am-5pm,
closed Mondays. April and October
9am-4pm weekends and holidays
only.

Čechy pod Kosířem
Château
☎ 0508 92717
Open: April to October 9am-5pm,
closed Mondays.

Kopeček
Olomouc Zoo
☎ 91521
Open: 8am-6pm daily.

Javořičko
Javořičské Jeskyně (Limestone Caves)
Open: 9am-4pm, closed Mondays.

Mladeč
Mladečká Jeskyně (Limestone Caves)
Open: 9am-4pm, closed Mondays.

Náměšť na Hané
Château
☎ 068 733
Open: May to August 8am-5pm,
September 9am-4pm, closed Mondays. April and October 9am-4pm,
weekends only.

Olomouc
City Museum
Náměstí Republiky 5
☎ 22741
Open: 9am-5pm, closed Mondays.

Art Gallery
Denisova 47
☎ 284 70
Open: 9am-5pm, closed Mondays.

Přemyslid Palace
Václavské náměstí
☎ 068 22741
Open: 9am-5pm, closed Mondays.

Příkazy
Kameníček's Farmhouse (No 54)
Open: 9am-5pm, closed Mondays.

Šternberk
Castle
☎ 7643 2714
Open: May to September 8am-5pm,
closed Mondays. April and October
9am-4pm weekends only.

Úsov
Castle
☎ 0648 41287
Open: May to August 8am-5pm,
September 8am-4pm, closed Mondays. April and October 9am-4pm
weekends and holidays only.

Useful Information: Olomouc

Banks
Agrobanka, 1 Blanická ☎ 245 21
Investiční banka, 1 Kollárovo náměstí
☎ 237 91
Komercni banka, 14 Třída Svobody
☎ 232 51

The Holy Trinity statues in the main square at Olomouc (Chapter 7)

A solitary cross at Paludza, near Liptovský Mikuláš, in the Low Tatras (Chapter 9)

The Low Tatras in winter. A chairlift to Chopok (Chapter 9)

Books

Antikvariat at 2 Opletalova has foreign-language books.

Car Parks

Rooseveltova ulice
Jeremenkova ulice
Náměstí Republiky
Legionářská ulice
Hodolanská
Třída 17 listopadu
J.V. Pavelky (indoor) ☎ 31062

Car Rentals

Autofachs, 73 Chválkovická ☎ 31036
Brnocar, Pavlovická ul. ☎ 32722
Mototechna, Domovina 1 ☎ 24276
Otisek, 2 Polská ☎ 239 74

Car Repairs — Garages

CSAO, Holická ul. 16 ☎ 26713
CSAO, Smetanova ul. ☎ 25171
Mototechna, Holická ul. ☎ 24468
Kovodřevo, Lazecká ul. 70a ☎ 26174
Barum, Holická ul. ☎ 25126 (tyre replacement)
Autotourist, Neředín ☎ 26215 (towing service)

Casinos

Admirál Club, Ostružnická
Admirál Club, Fontána Restaurant, 630 Smetanovy sady
Admirál Club, Palác hotel, 27 Tr. 1 máje
Národni dům hotel, 21 8. května
Herna-bar, 2 Opletalova

Chemist

24-hour service at Dolní náměstí 51, ☎ 243 89

Cinemas

Central, 47 Denisova ☎ 235 97 (good selection of subtitled 'arthouse')
Kinokavárna Jas, 26 Kinopasaz ☎ 233 16 (old-style café-cinema)

Lípa, tř. Svornosti ☎ 4137 81
Metropol, 25 Sokolská ☎ 224 66

Exchange Offices

Try Čedok or at one of the banks listed, the following hotels have exchange offices:
IH Flora, 34 Krapkova ulice ☎ 232 41
Národní dům, 21 tr. 8 května ☎ 24806
Palác, 27 tr. 1 máje ☎ 240 96
Sigma, 36 Jeremenkova ☎ 269 41
ČSAD Motel, 37 Sladkovského ulice ☎ 337 28

Filling Stations

Brněnská (unleaded)
Ferona (unleaded) — 24-hour service
Lipenská
Pražská (unleaded)
Krapkova (Monday to Saturday only)
Tabulový vrch (Monday to Saturday only)

Fire

☎ 150 (emergency)

Hospital

I.P. Pavlova 6
☎ 155 (emergency)

Police

☎ 158 (emergency)
Žižkovo náměstí 4 ☎ 23333

Post Offices

PO No. 1 at Náměstí Republiky 2 ☎ 29220
PO No. 2 at Jeremenkova 60 (by the railway station) 24-hour service ☎ 22241

Sport

Olomouc Sigma ZTS football stadium, 12 Legionářská ☎ 270 49
Ice hockey stadium (zimna stadión), 9a Hynaisova ☎ 287 65
Swimming pool, 11 Legionářská ☎ 413 181

Tennis courts, TJ Milo, Na střelnici,
☎ 235 15 and TJ Lokomotiva, 1 Tr.
17. listopadu ☎ 227 24
Golf, TJ Lokomotiva, 1 Tr. 17.
listopadu (from 1 April).

Taxi
5 Horní náměstí ☎ 27181
V. Poljakov, 30 I.P. Pavlova
☎ 414401
Janík, 40 Bukovany ☎ 954 87

Theatres
Moravské divadlo (Moravian Philharmonic Orchestra), 23 Horní náměstí
☎ 235 31
Hudební divadlo, Hodolany,
1 Ostravská ☎ 337 27
Divadlo hudby, 47 Denisova
☎ 235 65

Tourist Information Offices
Olomouc
Čedok
Horní náměstí 2
☎ 28831

Tourist Centrum
Rooseveltova ulice
☎ 27191

Olomouc Information Service
Town Hall
Horní náměstí
☎ 24547

CKM
Denisova ul. 4
☎ 29009

Travel Information
ČSAD (buses) Bus Station,
Sladkovského ulice ☎ 33291
ČSD (trains) Railway Station,
Jeremenkova 60 ☎ 476 2175

Wine Bars
F1, 8 Janského
'S Klub, 17 Listopadu

Tourist Information Office
Šternberk
Janatour
Radnicka 3
☎ 7643 3490

8 • Silesia and the Beskydy Mountains

This region provides an undeniable contrast, from the Silesian industrial heartland down to the pretty little towns and villages perched on the edge of the Beskydy mountains. The Beskydy hills are the main destination in this region, where wooden houses and churches are dotted around the countryside and a whole range of folk buildings have been gathered in the republic's largest open-air museum in Rožnov pod Radhoštěm. In addition to the folk culture and walking there are a cluster of interesting museums in the nearby villages; a car museum in Kopřivnice, a hat museum in Nový Jičín and memorials to Sigmund Freud in Příbor and to Leoš Janáček in Hukvaldy, their respective birthplaces. The largest town in the region is Ostrava which is usually given short shrift by guide books; admittedly its attractions are few but it is as good a base as any from which to see much of this region.

Ostrava

Ostrava is the regional capital of North Moravia and the Czech Republic's third largest city with a population of 330,000, a large proportion of whom are Polish. There is not a great deal of sightseeing to be done in the city but the plethora of hotels and restaurants together with the obviously good communications with the surrounding region may persuade you to use it as a base. Guide books paint a universally grim picture of this part of the Czech Republic and nothing can disguise the fact that Ostrava is a very large mining town (in fact the biggest industrial centre in the country) founded on coal and steel, but even so it comes as quite a surprise to discover the amount of green there is right up to the city's limits (even if it is just wasteland) and once in the centre it really is not that bad — giving the impression of a reasonably lively, provincial city. Having said that the huge Hlubina works at the south of the town, clearly visible from the bus station and unmissable when approaching by road from the south, is straight out of some surrealist film or work of art; viewed at night, when it is partially illuminated as it bellows noxious white fumes into the cold, still air, it resembles some strange other-worldly beast that just happens to be living on the edge of town and it is undeniably one of the few truly breathtaking sights in the whole of

163

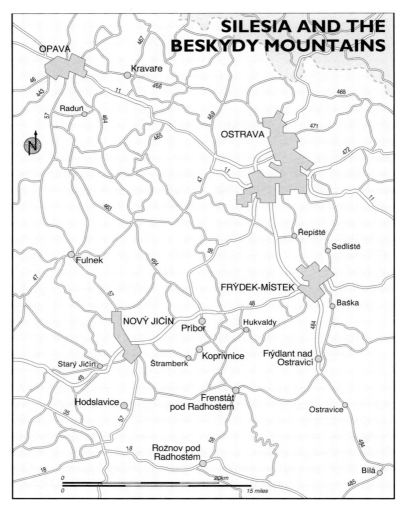

Moravia. The main railway station is to the north of the city centre (tram number 2, 8 or 12) while the main bus terminal is just to the west of the centre over the large bridge.

Ostrava was founded in 1267 by Bruno von Schaumburg, Bishop of Olomouc, as a Moravian border fortress. It soon gained a reputation as a clothmaking centre but remained a small and insignificant town until the late eighteenth century when the local bituminous coal deposits were first discovered. Soon afterwards the local aristocracy began to have the coal extracted and in 1828 the Vítkovice Ironworks were opened. The construction of a railway to Vienna in 1847 consolidated the town's growth and by 1880 only one of the 97 weaving mills operating in 1834 was still in existence, so fully had everything been turned over to coal and steel. Between 1980 and 1981 playwright and future president Václav Havel spent the worst months of a thoroughly miserable 4-year prison term at a camp near Ostrava.

For simplicity's sake Ostrava can essentially be divided up into three districts; to the east Slezská Ostrava, where the first coal deposits were found back in 1767, to the south Vítkovice, where Moravia's first iron foundry was set up, and in the middle of it all Moravská Ostrava (district 1) where most of the town's 'sights' are. The centre of the city is the large former marketplace and main square **Masarykovo náměstí** in Moravská Ostrava, upon which is situated the sixteenth-century Town Hall (rebuilt in 1859) which houses the **City Museum** featuring well-meaning natural history, archaeological and historical collections.

Just to the east of Masarykovo náměstí on Kostelní náměstí is **St Wenceslas Church**, a valuable late Gothic construction built at the end of the fourteenth century on Romanesque foundations. Its present baroque appearance dates back to a reconstruction of 1805. Next to the church there is a baroque statue of St John of Nepomuk dating from the eighteenth century. To the south-west of Masarykovo náměstí on **Smetanovo náměstí** is the Antonín Dvořák Theatre Hall which was built between 1906 and 1907 according to the design of Viennese architect A. Graf. Today it is the home of Ostrava's philharmonic orchestra and opera, ballet and theatre are also performed here. Walk north of Smetanovo náměstí along Nádražní, the Union bank building at number 10, which was constructed in the 1920s, formerly housed a museum dedicated to the working class movement but now has reverted to its original function (the Investiční bank now own the building).

Just off Nádražní along Jurečkova is the city's **Art Gallery** with a collection of works by twentieth-century Czech artists including Slavíček, Preisler, Kubin and Filla. It is not a large collection but there is some good work on display here. Walk back up along Nádražní and then turn right down Čs. Legií where opposite the huge 4,000 capacity basilica (designed by H. Meretta in 1889) is a late nineteenth-century Theatre Hall owned by Jiří Myron which in 1918 was used by the District Revolutionary National Committee. A short walk north of here is Prokešovo náměstí upon which is situated the **New City Hall** built between 1924 and 1930 and standing 282ft (86m) tall. The four sculptures outside symbolize the activities of the town — coal mining, metallurgy, science and commerce. A lift in the main hall takes you to the top of the building (pay at the top) from where there is an impressive view of the city and the factories that encircle it.

To the east of the town centre over the Ostravice river in the district of Slezská Ostrava are located the ruins of **Slezskostravsky Castle** (found along the street Hradní). The castle stands at the confluence of the rivers Ostravice and Lučina and guarded the border between Poland and Bohemia until 1327; in 1548 it was converted into a château by Jan Sedlnický. At the time of writing it is being renovated but it is due to reopen in the near future; there is a stylish wine bar here to occupy your time meanwhile. On your way to the castle ruins you may like to make the small detour along Těšínská to the **Church of St Josef**, a late baroque one-aisled building dating from 1780 to 1783 — the main altar features a painting of the Madonna dating from about 1410. As a result of mining in the vicinity the church actually sank 26ft (8m) during the years 1913 to 1928 and it has subsequently had to be strengthened with reinforced concrete.

Also to be found in that part of town known as Slezská Ostrava is the stadium belonging to FC Baník Ostrava, one of the Czech Republic's foremost footballing sides and incidentally the first European team to play an English side (Aston Villa) following their re-introduction to European competition in 1990. If you fancy attending a game most matches take place on a Saturday or Sunday afternoon and are usually advertised on flyposters around the town. Matches attract a good mix of age and sex but tend to be a little short of atmosphere (and indeed crowd) for all but the most important fixtures. The actual play is technically very good though English supporters will inevitably miss the pace and aggression of their domestic game. It is a good idea to bring along something to sit on (most fans do) as the seats are very dirty — it may be worth buying a programme for this purpose. Souvenir hats and scarves are hard to come by so you will just have to make do with a metal badge and a packet of nibbles. Ostrava's other main football team is FC Vítkovice who are situated on Závodní ul. in the suburb of Vítkovice — both sides have enjoyed long runs in the Czech (and formerly Czechoslovak) first division. Anyone feeling more adventurous may like to pay a visit to one of the many ice-hockey games which usually take place on Tuesdays or Fridays and begin at around 6pm; again look around the town's flyposters for details. Ice hockey is the country's second favourite sport and it is not unusual to see children playing a version of the game in the streets or on frozen ponds in winter. The season starts at the end of September.

Opava to Fulnek

Despite heavy damage sustained during the Thirty Years War and in the last days of World War II some interesting buildings have managed to survive in **Opava**. A settlement first developed here in the tenth century under the protection of a Slavic moated castle. In the late twelfth century a large number of German merchants from Lower Saxony were attracted here and in 1224 Opava was raised to the status of a town, prospering under the protection of the Teutonic Order. In 1318 Opava became the capital of the duchy of Troppau which under Duke Nicholas II separated from Moravia and became part of Silesia; Silesian diets (parliaments) were occasionally held here. In the mid-eighteenth century Silesia broke up, with the greater part (now in Poland) falling to Prussia, though the duchy of Troppau remained within the Habsburg empire as 'Austrian Silesia'. After the Great War this became 'Czech Silesia' which in 1938 was made part of the 'Reichsgau Sudetenland'. At the end of World War II, when the town's large German population was expelled, this became known as plain old 'North Moravia'. The bus station is just less than ¹/₂ mile (1km) south-east of the old town square.

The centre of town is Horní náměstí which is dominated by the 236ft (72m) high Municipal Tower (given its present form in 1618) on top of the Town Hall. Directly opposite this is the neo-baroque Bezruč Theatre (1882), behind which is the red-brick Church of the Assumption built between 1360

The Town Hall
at Opava

and 1370 in North German Gothic style (the interior was given a baroque revamp in the eighteenth century). Slightly to the north-east of Horní náměstí beyond the Town Hall on Dolní náměstí stands the late seventeenth-century baroque Jesuit Church of St Adalbert next to which is an eighteenth-century Jesuit college where the Silesian Diet used to meet. A short walk south of here along Masarykovo třída is the Gothic Minorite Church of the Holy Ghost, the burial place of the Silesian Přemyslids and (later) of the Dukes of Troppau. In the eighteenth century the church underwent a baroque remodelling. A short walk from the town centre along Komenského (on the way to the bus station) is the grand nineteenth-century Silesian Museum set in a very pretty park area. Its collections cover archaeology, the applied arts and natural history.

Four miles (7km) east of Opava at **Kravaře** there is a baroque château housing a museum dedicated to the so-called Ostrava Operation, one of the most important manoeuvres of World War II. Along the main road between Ostrava and Opava around the town of Štítina the roadside is strewn with military equipment used during the fighting. At Hrabyně (7 miles/12km south-east of Opava) there is a memorial and a symbolic cemetery.

Five miles (8km) due south of Opava above the village of **Hradec nad Moravicí** (accessible from Opava by bus or train) stands a large château in the middle of a beautiful English-style park. There was a Slavic fortification standing here in the tenth century and during the thirteenth century this developed into a Gothic castle which in 1600 was transformed into a château. It was rebuilt in Empire style in 1796 and then further altered in neo-Gothic style in 1880. During the early nineteenth century a number of leading musicians stayed here including Beethoven (in 1806 and 1811), Liszt (1846 and 1848). Because of a very serious fire the château is presently undergoing a slow restoration programme and will not be open to the public until at least 1997. Some of the furniture and exhibits have been moved to the Empire château (built on the site of a former keep) in the nearby village of Raduň — 4 miles (6km) south-east of Opava and accessible by bus.

Fulnek (about 14 miles/22km south of Hradec nad Moravicí), though quite severely damaged by bombing during World War II, has been very well restored and is a surprising treat. First records of the town date back to 1293 and it was formerly the residence of the Lords of Kravaře and Žerotín. The charming main square is surrounded on three sides by original Renaissance houses with baroque façades and on its fourth side by a beautiful early eighteenth-century baroque church, steps behind which lead up a wooded hill to a baroque castle (built on an original thirteenth-century Gothic structure) which unfortunately does not bear up to close scrutiny. Next to the church on the square is the rebuilt school of Lutheran Brethren where the great scholar and Czech nationalist Jan Komenský (1592-1672) taught between 1618 and 1621. During his time here Komenský wrote numerous treaties covering subjects ranging from the beauty of the Czech language to social criticism and he was later to describe his years in Fulnek as the happiest of his life. In the middle of the square is a Trinity Column dating to 1718.

Nový Jičín to Frýdek-Místek

Nový Jičín was founded in the latter half of the thirteenth century by Czech and German settlers and remained, along with most of the region, bilingual until World War II. The town is probably most famous for its hat factory — in the second half of the nineteenth century the firm of Hückel (called Tonak after nationalization) located in the town was the biggest manufacturer of hats in the Austro-Hungarian Empire with over 2,000 employees. The central Masaryk's square is of medieval origin, the arcade was built after a fire of 1503 though the façades changed after fires in 1768 and 1773. The boxy Town Hall (whose tower looks as if it belongs to another building) was established in 1501 and rebuilt in 1661 and again in 1930. Directly opposite this is the gleamingly white Old Post Office built in 1563 by an unknown Italian architect. The baroque Plague Column dates to 1710 and the delightful Peasants Fountain by Franz Barwig is also eighteenth century. Just beyond the main square past the Town Hall along Lidická is the Renaissance Žerotín château, converted from a medieval fortress between 1538 and 1541. The château today houses a museum dedicated to the history of the town, a display of millinery fashions and a memorial to the local artist Adolf Zábranský. The Praha Hotel opposite dates from the late nineteenth century. The building that now houses Čedok at the end of 28 října used to house the regional court; it dates from the 1830s. Back on the main square, the church standing tall above the eastern corner is the baroque Parochial Cathedral of the Virgin Mary of Redemption built between 1729 to 1732 on the site of an old Gothic cathedral. The church tower dates back to the late sixteenth century, the dome to 1854. A little way out from the centre along Knemocnici is the Spanish Chapel built on the site of a mass grave of 500 Spanish soldiers killed during the battle of Nový Jičín in 1621. The stone church dates from 1721 though a side chapel was added in the mid-eighteenth century. There are two small train stations on either side of the town centre, the bus station is right in the heart of the town.

About 3 miles (5km) to the south-west of Nový Jičín is **Starý Jičín** above which tower the ruins of a thirteenth-century castle. This was converted into a Renaissance palace during the sixteenth century though it has been deserted since the latter half of the eighteenth century.

Five miles (8km) south of Nový Jičín in **Hodslavice** is the tiny wooden Church of St Andrew (1551) and the house where the famous Czech historian, poet and politician František Palacký (1798-1876) was born. The house today contains an exhibition about his life and work. Palacký was a key figure in a remarkable group of intellectuals who had a common purpose of reviving Czech culture. Palacký's production of the dauntingly enormous tome *The History of the Czech Nation* (first volume published in 1836) has led to him being called the 'Father of the Nation'.

Five miles (8km) east of Nový Jičín is **Štramberk**, accessible by an occasional bus or a two hour walk. This is a real gem, a picturesque town founded in 1359 and crowned by a ruined medieval castle with a renovated lookout tower (called 'Trúba') that houses an exhibition of the history of the castle, below which is a excellently renovated baroque main square upon which is situated a Jesuit church and the town museum (which displays findings from the nearby Šipka cave where in 1880 remains of Neanderthal Man were discovered). On the narrow winding streets beyond the main square are some unique eighteenth- and nineteenth-century traditional Wallachian folk houses, mostly semi-timbered and featuring some beautiful carving. The Wallachs, or Vlachs, first came to this region from present day Romania during the fifteenth century. The name Vlach is simply a generic term for a sheep farmer and initially at least it seems that their existence was semi-nomadic. Today these distinctive timbered dwellings dotted around the region are just about the only tangible remains of the Wallachian culture — their folk costumes survive only in museums.

Literally around the corner from Štramberk (about a half hour walk) is the town of **Kopřivnice**, an ugly, sprawling place famous for its Tatra Car Plant and Museum. The present day Tatra engineering works was originally founded in 1850 to produce horse-drawn carriages. After the coming of the railways in 1882 it began to produce freight wagons, but its first blockbusting success came in 1897 with the production of the so-called 'President', the first automobile of the Austro-Hungarian Empire. From then on car production became the main speciality of the plant though today the factory specializes only in sturdy lorries and distinctive heavily built limousines which were once used to carry Communist party dignitaries. The museum is situated in a large glass and steel building beside the railway station and is filled to the brim with old cars (including the 1897 'President' model). There is also another museum in the town on Záhumenní which contains some of the factory's original horse-drawn carriages and a memorial to Emil Zátopek, long distance runner and Olympic champion in the 1950s, who was born in Kopřivnice.

A short 3 miles (5km) bus or train ride north of Kopřivnice stands **Příbor**, the oldest town in the region and the birthplace of Sigmund Freud (1856-1939). Even though his family left for Vienna when he was only four the town museum, situated in a baroque former Piarist College (1694-6) on

Lidická, still manages to find some space for the man in its exhibition devoted to the history of the town. The modest house of Freud's birth is at number 117 Zámecnická. The familiarly arcaded baroque main square is named after him and there is also a bust of Freud on a plinth by the large supermarket between the museum and the square. Freud attached great importance to his early life here and wrote later: 'Deep within me, although overlaid, there continues to live the happy child from Příbor, the first-born child of a young mother who received from this air, from this soil, the first indelible impressions'. At the age of 17 Freud returned to Příbor for a summer holiday and fell in love for the first time with a girl whose cot he had shared during his first 3 years.

Four miles (6km) east of Příbor is the homely village of **Hukvaldy**, sheltered under the woods of a large and impressive ruined castle which was founded by Arnold von Huckeswagen in 1240 and burned down and abandoned in 1782. Hukvaldy is the birthplace of a contemporary of Freud, composer Leoš Janáček (1853-1928) who was born in what is still the village school (his father was a teacher). The ninth of fourteen children, at the age of 11 Janáček was sent to Brno to be a chorister and it was there that he subsequently made his home though when he was in his seventies Janáček returned to Hukvaldy and it was here that he wrote some of his greatest works including his opera of the countryside *The Cunning Little Vixen*. Janáček was very much interested in the folk songs of the surrounding region (which he collected with František Bartoš) and he made use of their melodic characteristics in both his operas and his purely instrumental works — he also used to model his writing for voices on the inflections of his native language and so consequently has been credited for developing a distinctly Czech style. Janáček used to stay in a cottage called Podobora near to the school where he would entertain his muse Kamila Strösslová (not to be confused with his wife) and it was while looking for her son in the surrounding woods that he caught a fatal cold. Inside the cottage there is a small and charming museum dedicated to his memory.

Charm is perhaps one thing (among many others) that the town of **Frýdek-Místek** rather lacks. Frýdek-Místek is actually two towns; Místek, where the bus station is, was founded in the thirteenth century on the Moravian left bank of the Ostravice river while Frýdek, where the train station is, was founded in the fourteenth century on the Silesian right bank. Both towns have an old town square; the one in Místek (náměstí Svobody) is quite unremarkable, though it may be good for an ice-cream, and so it is best to head from here along the main road Hlavní třída over the river and then left up the hill to the main square in Frýdek (Zámecke náměstí) which is presently being restored. The seventeenth-century château on the square (adapted from a Gothic castle) once belonged to the lords of Těšín and now houses a small folk museum and tributes to composer Janáček and the Silesian poet Petr Bezruč (1867-1958) who spent many years here bemoaning the fate of local poverty-stricken miners. There are plans also to establish a memorial room to the local poet Óndra Łysohorsky who derived his name from a combination of the local Robin Hood figure Ondráš (who was imprisoned in Frýdek castle in the seventeenth century) and the Lysa hora, the highest peak in the Beskydy. Łysohorsky chose to write his verses in Lachian, a local dialect somewhere between Czech and Polish which survives in some of the border towns and which was spoken by an estimated one million people (mostly miners) between the wars. This made him none too popular with the Communist authorities who accused him of stirring up Polish nationalism and promptly banned his work. Łysohorsky died in 1989 in Bratislava but his vast archives are deposited in the château. Also on the main square is a fountain with a statue of St Florian, the patron saint of firemen. With a couple of hotels here (one by the railway station and one just south of the main square in Frýdek) the town could possibly be considered a suitable starting point for walks in the Beskydy region though there really are better places.

Two miles (4km) north of Frýdek-Místek in **Sedliště** there is a seventeenth-century wooden church while 4 miles (6km) north-west of Frýdek-Místek in **Řepiště** there is a wooden church dating from the sixteenth century.

Walking in the Beskydy Hills

Three miles (5km) south of Frýdek-Místek is the small village of **Baška** which with its camping site may be seen as a more convenient base to explore the neighbouring countryside. There is a large artificial lake here that is used for watersports and also a nudist camp. Three miles (5km) south of this is **Frýdlant nad Ostravicí**, a larger settlement with two hotels, a motel, a tourist hostel and an autocamping site as well as numerous restaurants and a couple of beerhouses. First written mention of the place came in 1275 but it was not until 1948 that it was raised to the status of a town. In the centre of the town is an early baroque church dedicated to St Bartholomew, a museum dedicated to the painter and graphic artist Ferdiš Duša (who lived here) and a Marian Column dating from 1713. Attractive hiking paths lead from the town to Łysa hora (4,339ft/1,323m) the highest peak in the region which is topped with a TV transmitter and, in the other direction, the massif of Ondřejník.

The real heart of the walking area however lies a little to the south of here and is based around the settlements of Ostravice, Staré Hamry and Bílá which feature a number of hotels and a plentiful supply of private accommodation. The sixteenth-century settlement of **Ostravice** is by far the

Preserved buildings in the Beskydy Mountains

largest of these but anyone passing through **Bílá** should take the time to visit its small Scandinavian-type wooden church dating from 1875. With its high mountains, deep valleys, mountain streams, barrier lake and beautiful views this is very good hiking territory with the most obvious focal points for walks being the forested peak of Smrk (4,185ft/1,276m), the aforementioned Łysa hora and the recreational resort on the ridge Bílý Kříž. There is also another attractive small wooden church at Gruň, if you are in the vicinity.

South-west of Frýdlant nad Ostravicí is **Frenštát pod Radhoštěm**, another major resort. The town, which was owned by the Olomouc bishops in the Middle Ages, has an attractive main square (surrounded by a number of hotels) in the centre of which is a Marian Column dating to 1686. The late nineteenth-century neo-Renaissance Town Hall on the square houses a museum with a display concerning the local linen and cloth industry and an exhibition of the work of the painter Břetislav Bartoš. From here the most popular peak to aim for is Radhošť; from Frenštát there is a frequent bus service to the rest house Ráztoka (just beyond the village of Trojanovice) from where you can either walk or take the chair lift which operates every hour up to the top of the hill where there are a number of attractive nineteenth-century timber-slat buildings and a small belfry. A mile (2km) along the path from here to Radhošť is a totem featuring the mountain's legendary pagan god Radegast (perhaps better known as a brand of local beer). It is another mile (2km) to the peak at Radhošť, marked by the presence of a wooden chapel and observation tower. The views are very good and from here it is an easy 2 mile (4km) walk back down the hill to the rest house Ráztoka.

Radhošť could actually just as well be accessed by a 7 miles (12km) hike from **Rožnov pod Radhoštěm** which is home to the biggest *skansen* of folk architecture in either republic. It is found in the former spa park and consists of about ninety buildings. The museum is divided into three parts and has three separate opening times. The first part of the museum is the Dřevené městečko, the inspiration of local artist Bohumír Jaromek upon returning from a visit to the original folk museum in Stockholm (from where the word *skansen* is derived). In 1925 Rožnov's eighteenth-century wooden Town Hall was moved from the town's main square to its present site in the museum, this was followed by a number of other timber buildings from Rožnov and the surrounding villages including a seventeenth-century wooden church from Větřkovice u Príbora. The second part of the museum is the Valaška dědina, built in the 1970s, which recreates a typical highland sheep farming settlement (complete with live sheep!). The final section, the Mlynska dolina, is yet to be fully completed but is centred around an old water mill.

Further Information
— Silesia and the Beskydy Mountains —

Places to Visit

Frenštát pod Radhoštěm
Town Museum
Old Town Square
Open: Tuesday to Friday 9am-12noon and 1-4pm, Sunday 9am-12noon.

Frýdek-Místek
Château
Zámecké náměstí
Open: Tuesday to Friday 8am-12noon and 12.30-4pm. Sunday 1-5pm.

Hukvaldy
Janáček Museum
Open: May to September 9am-12noon and 1-4pm, closed Mondays. April and October weekends only.

Hukvaldy Castle
☎ 0658 97323
Open: May to August 9am-6pm, September 9am-5pm closed Mondays. April and October 9am-4pm weekends and holidays only.

Opava
Silesian Museum
Open: Tuesday to Saturday 9am-12noon and 1-4pm. Sunday 9am-12noon and 2-4pm.

Ostrava
City Museum
Old Town Hall
Ostrava 1
Masarykovo náměstí 1
☎ 23 37 60
Open: Monday to Friday 9am-5pm. Saturday 8am-12noon.

Art Gallery
Dům Umění
Ostrava 1
Jurečkova 9
Open: Tuesday to Friday 10am-
12noon and 12.30-6pm. Saturdays and
Sundays 10am-3pm.

Nový Jičín
Hat Museum
Zerotin Château
Lidická
Open: Tuesday to Friday 8am-12noon
and 1-4pm. Saturdays and Sundays
9am-12noon.

Raduň
Château
☎ 0653 211706
Open: May to September 9am-4.30pm,
closed Mondays. April and October
9am-3pm weekends and holidays only.

Rožnov pod Radhoštěm
Skansen
Wooden Town
Dřevené městečko
Open: July and August 8am-7pm
daily. May, June and September 8am-
6pm daily. October to 15 November
8.30am-5pm daily. 15 December to
March Monday to Wednesday
8.30am-3.30pm, Saturday 8.30am-
1pm, Sunday 12noon-4pm.

Wallachian Village
Valašká dědina
Open: daily, 16-31 May 8am-6pm,
June to August 8am-6pm, September
9am-5.30pm.

Mill Valley
Mlynska dolina
Open: daily, 16 May to August 8am-
6.30pm, April to 15 May and September to 15 October 8.30am-5pm.

Štramberk
Town Museum
Old Town Square
Open: April to October only 10am-
5pm, closed Mondays.

Trúba Tower
Open: April to October only 8.30am-
4.30pm, closed Mondays.

Town Museum
Lidická
Open: Tuesdays and Thursdays 8am-
12noon and 1-4pm, Sundays 9am-
12noon.

Useful Information: Ostrava

Banks
Investiční banka, Ostrava 1, Nádražní 10
Komerční banka, Ostrava 1, Nádražní 12
Obchodní banka, Ostrava 1, Nádražní 4

Car Rental
SNAP, Ostrava-Vítkovice
Štramberská 21

Car Repair
Autoservis, Ostrava 1, Cihelní 49
☎ 23 39 66

Chemists
24-hour service at:
Ostrava 1, Nádražní 26 ☎ 23 56 61
Ostrava-Hrabůvka, Dr. Martínka 7
☎ 34 42 22
Ostrava-Zábřeh, Pavlovova 65
☎ 37 06 72
Ostrava-Poruba, Opavská 959
☎ 44 11 81

Cinemas
Vesmír, Ostrava 1
Zahradní 17
☎ 23 43 25

Náročného diváka, Ostrava 1
28. října 124
☎ 26 13 21

Vítek, Ostrava-Hrabůvka, Hasičská ul.
☎ 595/164 59

Luna, Ostrava-Zábřeh
Výškovická 113
☎ 37 08 58

Dukla, Ostrava-Poruba
Hlavní třída 706
☎ 44 11 01

Máj, Ostrava-Přívoz, Jirská ul.
☎ 23 56 11
In summer there is an open-air cinema
at Černá louka in Ostrava 1.

Exchange
As well as Čedok and the aforementioned banks the following hotels offer exchange facilities:
Imperial Hotel, Ostrava 1, Tyršova 6
Palace Hotel, Ostrava 1, 28 října 59
Hotel Atom, Ostrava-Zábřeh, Závodní

Filling Stations
24-hour service at:
Ostrava 1, Novinářská
Ostrava-Zábřeh, Rudná

Fire Brigade
☎ 150 (emergency)

Hospital
☎ 155 (emergency)

Market
Ostrava 1, Kostelní náměstí

Opticians
Oční Optika; Ostrava 1, Nádražní 153
and Ostrava 1, Poštovní 5
Servis Optika, Ostrava 1, Tyršova 31

Police
☎ 158 (emergency)
Police stations at:
Ostrava 1, Poděbradova 12
☎ 23 50 66

Ostrava 1, Milličova 20 (passports and visas)
☎ 21 44 49
Ostrava 1, Českobratrská 13 (foreign department)
☎ 21 48 03

Post Offices
Ostrava 1, Poštovní 20
Ostrava-Přívoz, by the main railway station (hlavní nádraží)

Sport
FC Baník Ostrava, Bazaly stadium, Ostrava-Slezská Čedičová ul.
FC Vítkovice, Ostrava-Vítkovice, Závodní ul.
Gymnastics Hall, Ostrava 1, Cingrova 10
Ice-hockey stadiums; Ostrava 1, U kluziště 2 and Ostrava-Poruba, Čkalovova ul.

Swimming Baths
Ostrava 1, Sokolská tř.
Ostrava-Hulváky, ul. U koupaliště
Ostrava-Bartovice, Těšínská ul.
Ostrava-Vítkovice, Závodní ul.
Ostrava-Vítkovice, Zengrova 14
Ostrava-Stará Bělá, Junácká ul.
Ostrava-Poruba, gen. Sochora

Taxi
Ostrava 1, corner of Tyršovy and Zámecké ul.
☎ 23 51 41

Theatres
Divadlo Antonína Dvořáka, Ostrava 1, Smetanovo náměstí ☎ 23 40 21
Divadlo Jiřího Myrona, Ostrava 1, tř. Čs. legií 12-4 ☎ 23 17 48
Divadlo Petra Bezruče, Ostrava 1, tř. 28. října 124 ☎ 514 22
Divadlo Loutek (puppet theatre), Ostrava 1, Masarykovo náměstí 33
☎ 23 43 22
Divadlo Hudby Ostrava (musical theatre), Ostrava 1, 28 října 23
☎ 23 54 00

Tickets are available at the venues one hour before performance or from Čedok or Sport Tourist in the town centre. Every year in May there is an international music festival — look out for concerts at venues all over the city.

Tourist Information Offices

Ostrava
Čedok
Nádražní 9
☎ 23 14 24

Sport Tourist
Nádražní 43
☎ 23 61 08

CKM
28. října c. 102
☎ 23 45 61

Autotourist
Husova 9
☎ 23 62 23

Travel Information
ČSAD (bus) station, Ostrava 1, Vítkovická, 511 00
ČSD (trains) station, Ostrava-Přívoz ☎ 23 60 49
Ostrava Airport Mošnov ☎ 5 82 16, regular flights to Prague. Tickets

available from Trans-Tour at 28. října 119, Ostrava 1 ☎ 577 31. Buses depart to the airport from Nádražní 7, Ostrava 1.

Wine Bars
Elektra, Ostrava 1, Nádražní tř.
Pavilón, Ostrava 1, Černá louka
Alexandria,Ostrava-Zábřeh, Výškovická tř.
Burgas, Ostrava 1, Nádražní 59
Rotunda, Ostrava-Slezská, Hradní 10
Srbská, Ostrava 1, Nádražní 21

Tourist Information Offices

Frýdek-Místek
Information Centre
Hlavní 112
☎ 42 658187

Kopřivnice
Town Information Office
Čs. armády

Nový Jičín
Cedok
Ulica 28. října
☎ 222 31

WES
19 Riegrova
☎ 228 36

Part Three
SLOVAKIA

Introduction

The Slovak Republic — which has been in existence as a separate state only since 1993 — is by turns one of the most beautiful, and ugliest, countries in Europe. Its capital, the city of Bratislava, built on the banks of the River Danube, boasts some of the most depressingly neglected high-rise estates anywhere in the former Communist world, often located adjacent to the factories in which their residents worked. These factories now either lie idle, rendered redundant by the demands of the new market-led economy, or they still belch out pollutants into the air or pump them into the Danube, contributing further to the massive environmental problems that parts of Slovakia face. Yet it is also a country of starkly beautiful and contrasting landscapes — the flat, monotonous plains around the Danube, baked dry by the sun in summer, give way in the north to some of the highest and most spectacular mountains in Europe. Modern development from Communist days, when cheap and wholly functional architecture was the order of the day and the look of towns almost completely ignored, still blights the look of many places, but there are also many remote hill villages, seemingly untouched by the twentieth century, where traditional ways of life still survive. In rural Slovakia, in particular, the overriding impression is one of poverty: people farm from timber-built shacks, using horses and carts to ferry produce to markets, and often the whole family is employed on the land: a common sight is one of women and girls in the fields, picking fruit or tending crops, while men and boys load the crop onto carts or walk with the horses along the roads. The land is often steep and stony and farming is very hard. That the farmer's young son, walking behind or riding on the cart pulled by the family horse, is wearing a T-shirt with the logo of a western rock band, is an indication that the older ways are not as all-pervasive as they might initially seem; that on Sunday morning, the whole family, children included, will dress up in their nicest clothes and, with other villagers, pack the local stone-built or wooden village church to the brim, is an indication that Catholicism is still as powerful a force in Slovakia as it always has been and that many traditions still thrive.

Slovaks are a proud race and nationalism has always been important here. For centuries the country was a neglected Imperial outpost: in 906, with the defeat of the Great Moravian Empire, Slovakia came under Hungarian control. From 1526 it was part of the Austro-Hungarian empire, ruled (without much interest) from Vienna and then, from 1867, from Budapest; the Hungarian rulers made no effort to improve the appalling social and economic conditions in the country (with the result that many Slovaks emigrated, particularly to the United States), but they did make every effort to stamp hard on any show of support for Slovak nationalism or cultural identity — whether voiced by dissidents and campaigners or portrayed in art, music or writing. The Slovak language (different to Czech, though similar enough for both peoples to be able to understand each other) was suppressed (unsuccessfully) and those who tried to propagate its use were imprisoned. Nationalist heroes emerged, such as Juro Jánošík, who, in the early eighteenth century, robbed rich Hungarians and gave the money to poor Slovaks; more than two centuries later, a colonel called Jan Golian organized an uprising in 1944 against the Nazi occupation of Slovakia, setting up an illegal national government in Banská Bystrica and organizing partisan groups in the mountains to try to oust the Germans. The coup failed and Nazi reprisals resulted in the deaths of over 30,000 Slovaks, many of them innocent villagers whom the Germans thought nothing of exterminating as bloody revenge for Slovak defiance of their rule.

Before and after World War II, Slovaks were ruled from Prague, and thought that the Prague government actively neglected them in favour of the Czech lands to the west; industrialization and economic growth was very apparent in Bohemia and Moravia, while Slovaks thought that their country was being allowed to remain an impoverished agricultural backwater. After 1948 the Stalinist leaders of Czechoslovakia saw centralization as the key to control, and hopes for any sort of Slovak self-government were dashed for 20 years; then in 1968 Czechoslovakia became a federal state and Slovakia was allowed its own government, located in Bratislava, which controlled a lot of its internal affairs. Slovak grumblings and demands for greater independence became even more vocal after democracy was introduced in 1989, and hard-line nationalists began to claim that the government in Prague was ignoring the very real problems of poverty and industrial decline that Slovakia was facing in the new market economy of Czechoslovakia. They maintained that Slovakia's problems could only be tackled by a fully independent Slovak government and that the two parts of Czechoslovakia needed to develop economically and politically in different ways. After the government in Prague had spent over 2 years trying to hold the country together, they relented and Slovakia became an independent state on 1 January 1993. It soon began to mint its own coinage and took

Typical rural landscape of Slovakia is captured below

control of a Slovak army, although the two Republics are still linked by various trading and economic agreements and arrangements.

Since gaining independence, Slovakia has seemed a country unsure of which path to take towards development. The full impact of a market-led economy has needed to be softened here, to prevent mass unemployment occurring as inefficient industries are shut down, and the reformed Communists were elected into power in Bratislava in the belief that they would keep the old industries running for the benefit of those employed in the old factories. Meanwhile, extremist right-wingers have also become prominent, stressing Slovak nationalism and speaking out against Slovakia's sizeable ethnic minorities, particularly Hungarian speakers (who live in the south-east of the country) and the gypsies, who live predominantly in the east, particularly around the city of Košice. These right-wing sentiments also mix in anti-Semitism and other nasty elements and have worried many observers; similar movements have grown up in other areas of Eastern Europe which, like Slovakia, have been freed from doctrinaire Communism but now face a very uncertain political and economic future.

The geography of Slovakia divides the country into three distinct regions: in the south-west of the country are the Danube Plains — an extension of the plains of Northern Hungary — where there are many industrial towns and cities, such as Bratislava and Nitra. This area has very strong historical links with Hungary; Bratislava was a Hungarian city until the early part of the twentieth century. Only a short distance from Vienna, and conveniently approached from that city by hydrofoil, bus, train or car, Bratislava is in many ways a gateway to Slovakia without being a destination in its own right — and is not covered in this book. The northern part of Slovakia is occupied by the Carpathian Mountains; the highest range is the High Tatras, the most popular destination for visitors to Slovakia. Many of the lower ranges are much less visited — such as the Low or West Tatras, or Malá Fatra and Veľká Fatra; all are described in depth in this book, as is the area to the south of the high mountains, around Banská Bystrica (Central Slovakia). Finally, the eastern part of Slovakia — going under the awkward name of Carpatho-Ruthenia — is the poorest and most remote region of the Czech and Slovak Republics, with rolling hills covered with beech forests which lead up to the Ukrainian and Polish borders, the countryside dotted with tiny timber-built villages complete with wooden churches; a real back-of-beyond where few visitors venture — and which is all the more rewarding a destination for that reason.

9 • The Slovak Mountains

For those who have entered Slovakia through Bratislava, that city — despite being the capital of the Republic — really provides travellers with a very false window into this land. Although Bratislava may have a modern, youthful appearance, urbanization and industrialization have come to this region relatively recently. Slovakia is a mountainous country, and Slovaks are, by tradition at any rate, a mountain people, more at home in wood-timbered villages than amidst the industrial throng of a place like Bratislava. It is no accident that the two largest towns in Slovakia (Bratislava and Košice) both have strong cultural links with Hungary, rather than being purely Slovak creations. Whereas Czech culture is traditionally centred on Prague and the Vltava, Slovaks do not hold their capital or the Danube in such high esteem. The title of their National Anthem, *Lightning is flashing above the Tatras*, admirably highlights the fact that Slovaks look to the mountains, rather than urban centres, as the true heartland of their country.

The Carpathian Mountains are the principal geographical feature of Slovakia. Stretching in a broad arc through half a dozen countries, from Vienna to Bucharest, they form one of the highest mountain ranges in Europe away from the Alps. All the ranges described in this chapter — Malá Fatra, Veľká Fatra, and the West, Low and High Tatras — are all part of the Carpathians. The High Tatras themselves, the primary destination for most visitors to Slovakia, include the highest mountains in the Carpathians as a whole, with a few peaks in the range soaring to over 8,200ft (2,500m) in height.

The mountains in Western Slovakia — the White Carpathians — are not covered in this chapter; but all the mountain ranges in the northern part of Slovakia, between the towns of Žilina in the west, and Poprad in the east, are described in detail. The broad itinerary around which the chapter is structured is a very obvious one, running along the Váh valley from Žilina to the High Tatras, where the Váh rises. The Váh is obvious on any map, as its valley forms the major communications corridor of northern Slovakia, with principal roads and railways running through it, linking the towns that have grown up on the banks of the river. Thus, the suggested itinerary presented

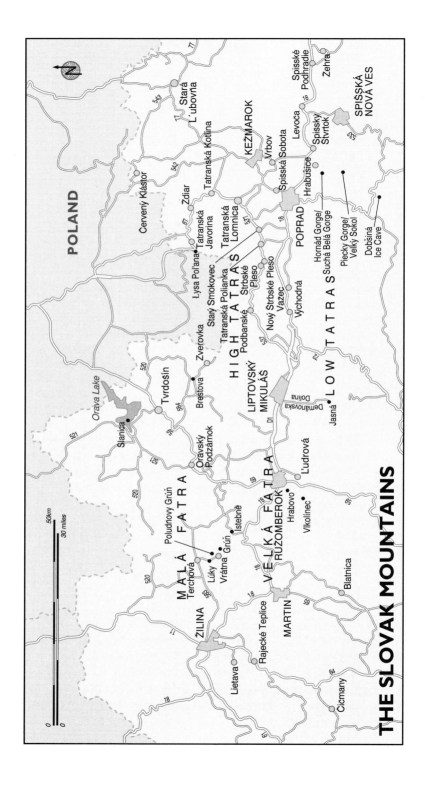

THE SLOVAK MOUNTAINS

here can be followed by both road or rail travellers. Virtually all the important towns in northern Slovakia — Žilina, Ružomberok, Martin and Liptovský Mikuláš — are situated in the Váh valley. Often visitors will find accommodation in these towns before heading out into the surrounding mountains on day excursions.

Malá Fatra

Malá Fatra is the first of the high mountain ranges which stretch in a west-east direction along the northern border region of Slovakia. The most important centre in the mountains is Žilina, a pleasant though rather dull town in the Váh valley, with fast road and rail connections to Bratislava, Prague and many other Czech and Slovak cities. Žilina is the easiest place from which to visit the highest part of the range, between Terchová and Šutovo, to the east of the town. Veľký Kriváň, at 5,606ft (1,709m) the highest peak in the range, is accessible from both these places, as are other high mountains, such as the rocky peaks Stoh and Veľký Rozsutec. This northern part of the range is the best walking countryside and is also very popular, with many paths busy in summer; southern and eastern parts of the range allow for gentler walking in less busy surroundings. The road running south from Žilina to Rajec gives access to the south-western part of the range, while Martin, further along the Váh valley to the east, is the centre for exploring both the south-eastern parts of Malá Fatra, and also parts of the neighbouring range, Veľká Fatra, which lies to the east. Malá Fatra covers a wide and popular area and many maps are available to walkers: the best, covering most places described below, is probably map number 110 in the series published by VKU (Harmanec), entitled *Malá Fatra-Vrátna*. Number 120 in the same series, *Malá Fatra-Martinske Hole*, describes the southern part of the range.

Žilina and the Northern Malá Fatra

Žilina itself is a largely unexciting town in the Váh valley; but many visitors to the Malá Fatra will choose to stay here, as it is an important road junction, and is well served by public transport, including trains to Poprad, Bratislava and Prague, and buses to many parts of Malá Fatra and beyond.

Žilina's origins are medieval. Earlier in the twentieth century, the oldest known manuscript written in Slovak, was discovered here. Known as the *Slovak book*, dating from 1370, it details the rights of the town's citizens. However, the real growth in the importance of the town came in the last decades of the nineteenth century, when the railway along the Váh valley was built. Now one of the most important railway junctions in Slovakia, the town has important forestry, chemical and engineering industries. Over

1,700 Russian soldiers who died fighting for the towns liberation during World War II are buried on a hillside outside the town. There are two main squares in the centre of Žilina. Námestie SNP, the lower of the two squares, is a modern, large ugly open space. A ramp and stairway lead up from this square past the pink-covered Gothic Church of the Most Holy Trinity, with its distinctive free-standing belfry, dating from the fifteenth century. Continuing along a narrow alley from the church (Pučikova Street) brings one out into Námestie Dukla, a more pleasant square surrounded by baroque and Renaissance houses with arcades. Here one can find the big yellow frontage of the Jesuit church (1743, with monastery next door), and the Považská Galeria, with temporary exhibitions and displays of the work of a local sculptor, Rudolf Pribiš. In the western suburb of Budatín is Budatín Château, founded in the thirteenth century to guard an ancient ford across the River Váh, which houses a museum of the Váh valley and work by craftsmen of the area, such as figurines made from tin and wire, once sold as far away as Australia. In another suburb, Zavodie, is Žilina's most noteworthy building, St Stephen's Church (Kostol sv. Štefana) which was founded in the thirteenth century and whose interior is decorated with medieval wall paintings, traces of which survive. The church is also surrounded by a medieval wall.

The mountains in the immediate vicinity of Žilina are neither very high, nor very interesting. One must travel about 15 miles (24km) to the east to reach the most popular part of the Malá Fatra, the Vrátna Dolina area which is centred on the three villages of Terchová, Vrátna and Štefanová, with the village of Šutovo, just off the main road along the Váh valley to the east of Martin, a gateway to approaching this small area from the south.

The village of **Terchová** is 14 miles (22km) east of Žilina. It must be reached by crossing the road bridge over the River Váh at Žilina, and then following the roads which run along the north side of the Váh. There is a hotel here and a supermarket (the latter just after the turning to Vrátna). Terchová is the birthplace of Juraj Jánošík (1688-1713), a Slovak folk hero who, Robin Hood style, robbed from the rich to give to the poor. Jánošík was supposed to have joined the anti-Habsburg alliance under the Hungarian rebel leader, Ferenc Rákóczi, when a young boy of 14; the rebels were eventually defeated (at Trenčín, in 1711), and Jánošík, after 2 years' training for the priesthood at Kežmarok, became an outlaw and took to the hills, engaging in periodic bouts of wealth distribution in favour of the local peasantry. His move into banditry was partly done as revenge for the death of his father, who had been killed by his employers for taking time off work to attend his wife's funeral and build her a coffin. In 1713 Jánošík was captured and executed in the main square at Liptovský Mikuláš, where he was hung by a hook attached to the rib cage and took over a day to die.

Jánošík subsequently became the most important Slovak folk hero; his exploits have been described by countless poets, novelists and songwriters. More recently, he has been seen as a hero by those fighting for Slovak nationalism and self-rule, such as those rebels who fought in the Slovak National Uprising in 1944. In Terchová there is, predictably, a small museum about him (on the other side of the river from the main road through the village) exhibits include his brass-studded belt and items of folk art.

The road leading south from Terchová takes one past a modern aluminium statue of Jánošík (on the left hand side of the road), and then through the spectacular Tiesňavy Pass, which is at the entrance to the Vrátna Dolina valley. The road winds up past craggy ridges which come right down to the banks of the fast-flowing River Vrátnanka, which rises just beyond Vrátna. After a mile or so of fine scenery, one reaches **Lúky**, a popular winter and summer resort set amidst a fine backdrop of hills, where is a road off to the left to the village of Štefanová (see below). The main road continues along the valley, past popular skiing areas on both sides, to terminate at **Vrátna**, 2,460ft (750m). From here, a very popular chairlift (arrive early in the morning to avoid the worst of the queues) takes one up Snilovské Sedlo (1,500m, 4,920ft). There are good views from the top over the peaks of Malá Fatra. There are more skiing grounds around Snilovské Sedlo. From the top station of the chairlift it is a five minute walk along the green-marked track to Snilovské Sedlo itself (4,986ft/1,520m), a high pass on the mountain ridge of Malá Fatra. From here, it is an easy walk to the summit of Chleb (5,402ft/1,647m) or, in the other direction, the summit of Veľký Kriváň, at 5,606ft (1,709m) the highest mountain in Malá Fatra (both are about half an hour's walk from Snilovské Sedlo, on the red-marked track). Another option from Snilovské Sedlo is to follow the blue markers down to the buffet pod Chlebom (refreshments) and then on down into the forest and the Šútovské Vodopádý waterfalls, which are spectacular; the blue-marked path goes on to the village of Šutovo, which is just off the main Žilina-Ružomberok road in the Váh valley. There are a few buses here, but more buses from the bus stop on the main road, next to the railway station from where there is the option of taking the train back to Žilina. This is a lengthy walk, probably an all day affair taking into account transport from Žilina to Vrátna and from Šutovo back to Žilina. The walk from Snilovské Sedlo to Šutovo takes about 3 hours.

The turning off the main Vrátna Dolina valley, mentioned above, takes one through the Nová Dolina valley. On the right, almost immediately after the road junction, is the bottom station of a chairlift up to Grúň (3,280ft/1,000m). There is pleasant scenery at the top, dominated by the solid-looking peak **Poludňovy Grúň** (4,789ft/1,460m). Visible from the top station of the chairlift, to the left, and a short walk away, is the mountain

The Tiesňavy Pass in Malá Fatra

hut Chata na Grúñi, which should sell refreshments in season. Poludňovy Grúň rises ominously above the wooden chalet, and one can ascend the peak from here. It takes 1 1/2 hours on the yellow-marked track, up a fairly steep path.

The road along Nová Dolina from the chairlift continues to **Štefanová**, (2,050ft/625m), a pretty mountain village with shops and a good restaurant. The road terminates in the village, which is a very popular starting point for walks. Among the wide variety of walks from Štefanová are ascents of two Malá Fatra peaks, Stoh and Veľký Rozsutec. A green-marked track runs up from Štefanová to (Sedlo) Medzieholie, a pass on the main ridge of the Malá Fatra (1 to 1 1/2 hours). From Medzieholie, walking in either direction along the red-marked track takes one up fairly steep paths either to the right, up Stoh (5,274ft/1,608m), or in the other direction, to the left, up the distinctive rocky peak of the summit of Veľký Rozsutec (5,281ft/1,610m); both walks take 1 to 1 1/2 hours from Medzieholie. Also in this part of the mountains is the valley Horné Diery, a ravine which must be walked along by using chains and ladders fixed into the rock. This is just one of the paths accessible from Štefanová the high density of walking tracks means that they are not as busy as those starting from Vrátna.

Čičmany and the Southern Malá Fatra

Heading south along the road from Žilina towards Rajec and Prievidza, the first place one comes to is Lietavská Lúčka, whose cement works belches out off-white dust into the otherwise pristine mountain air. A little further on, a turning left brings one to a tiny, pleasant village called **Lietava** with a ruined castle rising above it on a steep bluff, its towers peeking up over the tops of the trees and its walls appearing to crumble into the forest. The castle was built in the fifteenth century and was abandoned in the eighteenth century. There is a path up to it (blue markers), which runs through fields and then round the back of the hill on which it is situated; a nice, desolate spot, with good views. The castle could just as easily be approached from Lietavská Svinná, a hamlet in the next valley south (green markers).

Further on along the road, **Rajecké Teplice** is a spa, with hotels, camp sites and swimming pools. A number of marked paths start from here which take one up into the low, fairly undramatic but empty southern part of the Malá Fatra. Heading east, via the hamlet of Kunerad (where the early twentieth-century château is closed to the public), brings one up to Veľká Lúka (4,821ft/1,476m), following the blue markers; an alternative route back is following the yellow markers along the Svitacova dolina. This is a whole day affair. Veľká Lúka is much more easily approached from Martin using the chairlift from Podstráne. From Rajecké Teplice westwards there are fewer possibilities, but possible destinations include the castle at Lietava or the 'Rock City' called Súľovské skaly, with the ruined castle of Súľov at its centre; a 3-hour walk from Rajecké Teplice, following the yellow markers, but much more easily approached from the village of Súľov to the south of the castle (to drive to Súľov from Žilina, head west towards Trenčín and then turn off to the left just after Hrabové).

Čičmany, an isolated village situated in a broad valley right on the southern fringes of Malá Fatra, is also one of the most visited villages in Slovakia. The wooden houses are strewn haphazardly along the side of the road, as is the case of many Slovak villages, but where Čičmany is different is in its preserved folk architecture — abstract, simple decorations adorn many of the houses in a style unique to this remote mountain region. Most of the designs are abstract patterns, with birds and other animals also featured. The designs are meant to be based on the intricate patterns of lacework; folk costumes and other items of folk arts and crafts can be bought and seen in the village, with white the predominant colour. Brightly coloured footwear called *válenky*, made from felt and cloth, is manufactured in the village. Čičmany is at quite a high altitude (3,191ft/973m) making it cold in winter and often cool in summer. Though fascinating, Čičmany receives fewer visitors than it might because of its inaccessibility: bus links, from Žilina in particular, are poor. There is a hotel in the village but there is actually little to do here, except look. The village is on the road between Fačkov, south of Rajecké Teplice, and Ilava, in the Váh valley well to the south-west of Žilina. A number of walks can be made from both Fačkov and the high pass on the road to the south, Fačkovské Sedlo; the summit of Kľak (4,431ft/1,351m) is the most obvious destination.

Žilina to Martin and the Eastern Malá Fatra

The main road and railway line along the Váh valley continue east from Žilina to Martin, a town at the confluence of the Váh and Turiec rivers which also marks the boundary between the Malá and Veľká Fatra ranges. Seven miles (11km) from Žilina, the flattish land of the Váh valley is suddenly interrupted by the main massif of Malá Fatra, which road and railway pass through by means of the steep-sided Strečno Gorge, which has been cut through the mountains by the River Váh. Both the main road and railway run along the complete length of the gorge, competing with the river for space on the narrow valley floor (the railway goes through a tunnel for a short distance). The entrance to the gorge, at the village of Strečno (which the road bypasses), is overlooked by the ruins of Strečno Castle, situated on a sharp, precipitous rock right above the road; the best view of the castle is actually from the railway, which is on the other side of the river at this point. The castle was founded in 1321 and guarded the trade routes that passed along the valley. It was destroyed on purpose in 1678, to prevent anti-royalists from using it as a base from which to attack the forces of the Austrian emperor. When it re-opens, after a lengthy period of restoration, access to the castle will be from the minor track that leads behind the rock on which it is situated.

Another, less noted ruined castle overlooking the Váh valley is accessible from here. The village of Strečno is situated immediately below the castle, by-passed by the main road. A metal foot bridge in the village (or an ancient car ferry) takes one over to the north bank of the river. From here it is a 45-minute walk along the red-marked track to the castle, Starý hrad, founded a century before Strečno Castle to protect an ancient crossing place over the Váh. The castle can be reached by walking along the road which runs alongside the north bank of the river, and then scrambling up through the trees an awkward ascent for not much of a view from the top (which is mostly shrouded in trees).

The main road and railway continue through the gorge from Strečno. A mile further on, Starý Hrad can be seen from the road, on steep cliffs on the opposite bank of the river. It cannot be reached from here as there is no way of crossing the river. The gorge soon widens out and the road runs through the northern part of the town of **Martin**, bypassing the centre. Martin is at the head of the Turiec valley, along which road and railway run south to

Turčianske Teplice and Banská Bystrica (see next chapter). This ostensibly unremarkable town is surprisingly rather proud of itself, and its present industrial facilities (until recently, it was an important centre for Warsaw Pact tank production) belie a political history that has given the town a prominent place in Slovak history. In the 1860s the first, muted demands for Slovak independence from Hungary came from this town. These demands were ignored by the Imperial Parliament in Vienna, and in 1863 an organization called Matica Slovenská, which is still in existence, was founded in Martin to preserve and promote Slovak language and culture — which was actively suppressed by the Hungarians after 1867 when the Austro-Hungarian Empire was divided and Slovakia came under the rule of Budapest. Martin was even once considered by nationalists as a viable capital of an independent Slovakia in preference to 'Hungarian' Bratislava. In 1918, the Martin declaration proposed that Slovakia should join with Bohemia and Moravia to form a united Czechoslovakia. Martin was a major centre of the Slovak National Uprising and its brewery produces the strongest beer in Slovakia (12 per cent proof). Matica Slovenská still survives, in a pompous neo-baroque building in the town, and the museums in Martin give an idea as to the importance which Martin holds for Slovaks. Along Muzeálna is the Slovak National Museum, with the largest number of folk costumes and artefacts from all over Slovakiá 1 mile (2km) south of the town, along the road to Žiar, is the largest *skansen* in Slovakia, with buildings uplifted from villages all over the country and rebuilt here. North of the town, around the railway station, are two art galleries and another museum. The main reason for which walkers come to Martin is to take the chairlift up through the forest to Martinské Hole. The bottom station is in the western part of the town, and drivers will find themselves crossing the railway and the River Turiec by a modern road bridge to reach it. There are skiing grounds at the top. From the top station, carry on along the road to the red-marked track which runs along the mountain ridge, and take this track to the left to ascend Mount Veľká Lúka (4,841ft/1,476m). The valley to the south of Martin gives access to the western parts of Veľká Fatra.

Beyond Martin, the main Žilina-Poprad road and railway continue east along the Váh valley through another steep-sided gorge formed by the River Váh. From Šutovo, a sleepy village off the road, a road runs into the mountains towards the Šutovo Waterfalls (the road only goes part of the way; those with a car must walk the last 45 minutes. For those without a car, the falls are 1¹/₂ hours from Rieka, immediately east of Šutovo; it takes about half an hour to walk from Šutovo station and bus stop, in the Váh valley, to Šutovo itself). The falls are fabulous, with water cascading down many gulleys in a verdant, almost tropically wet woody valley. Beyond the falls the blue-marked track gets much steeper and goes up into the hills to the bufet pod Chlebom (another 2 hours) and then up to Snilovské Sedlo (another $^1/_2$ hour, on green markers) on the main ridge of Malá Fatra, from where many walks are possible (see under 'Northern Malá Fatra'). There is a green-marked path from Šutovo to Snilovské Sedlo, which is slightly shorter (just over 3 hours to cover the whole distance) but which does not go via the falls.

Beyond Šutovo, Kraľovany is notable only as a road and rail junction, from where one can head to Dolný Kubín and the Orava Region and Western Tatras, or on along the Váh valley to Ružomberok, the main starting point for Veľka Fatra.

Veľká Fatra

Beyond Kraʾlovany, the main road and railway along the Váh valley enter the Veľká Fatra range; lower but wilder than Malá Fatra, the range is bounded by the towns of Martin, Ružomberok and the Váh valley to the north, and to the west and east by the Turiec and Revúca valleys, respectively. The highest peak is Ostredok (5,222ft/1,592m), in the southern part of the range.

Martin lies in the Turiec valley and is the best place from which to explore western parts of Veľká Fatra. South of the town is a village called **Blatnica**, where there are nice wood-timbered houses and, in the local manor house, a museum dedicated to the work of Karol Plicka, one of the most famous photographers of the Slovak countryside. From the village, one can gain access by marked walking track to the valleys Blatnická dolina (green markers) and Gaderská dolina (yellow markers), both of which are craggy limestone valleys, walking along which gives one access to the central part of the range and the ridge of highest mountains. Use one of the maps published by VKU (Harmanec) to plan walks — Number 100 in their series includes the southern fringe of the mountains, but most of the range is shown on map 121, *Veľká Fatra*. The network of paths is dense, with a red-marked track running along the main ridge and going over the main peaks, and there are other tracks which lead up valleys to it; other villages in the Turiec valley (for example, Necpaly, Belá-Dulice, Sklabiňa Podzámok), give access to the main peaks, as do villages in the Revúca valley on the western side of the mountains — for example, the best way to approach Ostredok is from paths which lead off the road south of the village of Liptovský Revúce.

The town of **Ružomberok** is usually considered to be the best starting-point for exploring Veľká Fatra — and other areas beyond. An important road junction, roads lead off from Ružomberok south to Banská Bystrica (see next chapter) and north to the Orava region (see next section). It is an excellent base from which to visit Malá Fatra, the Western and Low Tatras and the Orava region, as well as Veľká Fatra itself. Turčianske Teplice,

Harmanec and Banská Bystrica, all on the southern fringe of the mountains, are described in Chapter 10, Central Slovakia. Ružomberok is a fairly uninteresting industrial town: the factory beside the main road, impossible to miss, manufactures synthetic fabrics, of which the town smells. On Májekova Street is a gallery devoted to L'udovít Fulla, and the parish church is worth a quick look. It is known as being the church of one Andrej Hlinka (1864-1938), a fervent Slovak nationalist who was imprisoned in 1906 by the ruling Hungarians who were suspicious that his nationalism spilt over to active campaigning against them. While in prison he was seen to be the organizer of protests against the ordination of a pro-Hungarian priest at Černova — his home village. The crowds that turned up to protest against the ordination on 27 October 1907, were fired on by police, and fifteen were killed, making it one of the most famous and bloody instances of Slovak demands to be rulers of their own land. Hlinka's reputation as a martyr, however, has been tarnished by his later tendencies towards fascism; the Slovak People's Party that he later founded openly voiced opposition to Jews, Poles, Gypsies and other minorities living in Slovakia. Had he lived to see World War II there is no doubt that he would have fitted in to the pro-Nazi government that ruled Slovakia after 1939. Current efforts of many to rehabilitate his reputation have been seen as evidence of the powerful forces of the nationalistic neo-fascism which has risen alarmingly in Slovakia since democracy — and with it, freedom of speech — came in 1989.

Just before entering the town, a sign on the main road from Žilina points the way to **Hrabovo**, a small village just south of the main valley, where there is an outdoor swimming pool and a hotel. A cable car runs up from here to Malina, a low ridge set above a dry valley. The slopes on the other side of the valley are used for downhill skiing. A number of walks are possible from the Hotel Malina, to the left and down a little from the top station. One can walk back down to Ružomberok (just over an hour; blue markers) or along the red-marked track to the summit of Sidorovo (3,605ft/1,099m), then, following the same track, on down into Ružomberok (3 hours in total from the Hotel Malina). These walks bring one down into the centre of Ružomberok.

A number of villages south of Ružomberok have nice wooden folk architecture; these include **Vlkolínec** (where some of the buildings were badly damaged by the Nazis in 1944, in retaliation for the Slovak National Uprising), **L'udrová** (where the Gothic church is a museum of Gothic art), and the neighbouring villages of Nižný Sliač, Stredný Sliač and Vyšný Sliač.

The Western Tatras and the Orava Region

The Western Tatras (Západné Tatry) are the westward extension of the High Tatras; not as high, but wilder and more deserted than the neighbouring range. Where the Western Tatras become the High Tatras is open to question, but a rough indication of their area is that they stretch from Dolný Kubín in the west to the first High Tatran resort, Podbanské, in the east. The main gateways to the range are Liptovský Mikuláš, in the south (also the main gateway to the Low Tatras, and the village of Zuberec, to the north). Zuberec is reached via the Oravica valley, which runs north from Ružomberok to the Polish border; the Orava Hills rise to the west of this valley, while the attractions in the valley itself are Orava Castle and, at its northern end on the Polish border, the artificial Orava Lake.

The lake is approached along a wide valley (of the River Orava) from either Ružomberok or Kral'ovany, in the Váh valley. Once famed for its poverty — when the Lithuanian army marauded its way through here in 1683, they burnt most of the villages, disgusted at there being no provisions to pillage — and emigration to the USA from here was endemic (as it was from other remote parts of Slovakia). The towns themselves are not very interesting and there is some ugly industrialization, introduced to the region after 1945 to stop the outward movement of people. Outrageously slow branch-line trains trundle up the valley from Kral'ovany (a junction on the main line) to Trstená, on the Polish border; there are also buses on the main road along the valley, which crosses into Poland just beyond Trstená.

Just after the first major bend to the right that the road out of Kral'ovany takes, there is a bridge over the river and a yellow-marked track which leads to a deserted village in the hills, called Podšip. Some of the houses are now being rebuilt, in original styles. The track continues beyond the village up to the summit of Šip (3,749ft/1,143m) — a nice walk. Back on the road, the first place one passes through beyond Kral'ovany is **Istebné**, where there is a huge metal foundry and its attendant quarry, still scarring the landscape but no longer belching out so much smoke that the sky became darkened during the day, and the inhabitants of the town threatened to move to somewhere else (as they did in the mid-1980s). The old village, above the new one, boasts some old wooden buildings, including a wooden Lutheran church (1686). Dolný Kubín is the regional capital but has nothing to make it worth stopping for; further on up the valley, however, everyone seems to stop off at **Oravský Podzámok**, where Orava Castle dramatically stands guard over the village, perched at various levels on a rock which rises to over 328ft (100m) above the valley floor. Founded in 1264, the lords of the castle once taxed the merchants who came this way, on their way to Poland. It has changed hands very frequently — two of the owners were the Hungarian magnates Ferenc Thurzo and his son György, who rebuilt the castle in

Renaissance style in the seventeenth century; György's tomb can be seen in the chapel of the castle. The current appearance of the castle dates mainly from the early nineteenth century, when it was extensively renovated. Inside the castle are displays of medieval torture gear and some dull furnished rooms (you must go round on a guided tour). The castle is more impressive from the outside than the inside. There is also a small museum in the village.

Further on still up the valley, Podbiel is the gateway to the Roháčska Dolina valley and the main walking centres of the Western Tatras. At **Tvrdošín**, the fifteenth-century church, tucked along a back street in the northern part of the town and surrounded by a walled cemetery, contains some altar paintings which date from the time the church was built. From the town, a road heads north to the Orava Lake, created in 1954 when a dam was built for hydro-electric purposes. People swim, sunbathe and go boating from a number of spots along the shore: just pick any one — there is not much to choose between the places. Creating the lake meant that five villages became completely submerged, but the baroque church of one of them, **Slanica**, was high enough to remain above the water. It now stands on a wooded island in the lake and can be reached by boat from the campsites along the southern shore, or from Námestovo, the New Town at the western end of the lake. The village was the birthplace of a Catholic priest named Anton Bernolák (1762-1813), who made great efforts to preserve the Slovak language. The church now contains memorials to Bernolák, as well as folk art and ceramics.

The most popular place to walk in the Western Tatras is from the **Roháčska Dolina** valley. There is a good network of paths here. A road leads along to the valley from the village of Podbiel in the west, in the Orava valley. This road then passes through Zuberec (the last village in the valley) and then through **Brestova**, where a *skansen* (open-air folk museum) has been constructed next to the road. This is the Orava Village Museum, where traditional buildings from surrounding villages have been rebuilt; the most important building here is a wooden church from Zábrež, with nice folk panel painting inside. It is not possible to drive beyond Chata Zverovka, where there is a small car park. From here, one must walk along the road for about 2 miles (3km) to the head of the valley. Then there are several options: a blue-marked track runs up from Adamculov to some mountain tarns (the largest is Renáčske Plesá). From the lakes, take the green-marked track down to the Smutna Dolina and then the Tatliakova Chata, before walking along the road to the place where you started. Alternatively, from Adamculov there is a steep path up to Baníkov (the lakes are a short diversion off this path; the last bit up to the summit (7,144ft/2,178m) is along a very steep red-marked track and a tough climb.

Right at the head of the Roháčska Dolina valley is **Tatliakova Chata**, where the road ends and a steep blue-marked path begins. The ascent of the pass over the main ridge of the Western Tatras, called **Smutne Sedlo**, is tough going, even though the summit of the rocky pass is visible to walkers long before you get there. At the top, one could take the red markers along the ridge, westwards to **Baníkov** (less than an hour) and a second peak beyond it, Brestova. Following the red markers eastwards takes one to **Ostrý Roháč** (6,845ft/2,087m), also less than an hour, and to peaks on the Polish border. The better option, however, is to drop down from the pass following the blue markers to the **Žiarska Dolina** valley; this path is rocky for a while but then gets a lot easier. The **Žiarska Chata**, in the valley, should sell refreshments. This is a satisfying climb which goes over the central part of the range: allow 4 to 5 hours at least, from Zverovka to Žiar. There are a few buses to Zverovka (from Dolný Kubín and Podbiel); those without transport at Žiarska Chata will have to walk down the road (or keep following the blue markers through the forest) for an hour or so to Žiar, a small village to the north of Liptovský Mikuláš, and linked to that town by fairly frequent buses. The walks described here are shown on the map *Západné Tatry: Roháče*, number 112 in the series published by VKU (Harmanec). The key to the map is in English.

The Western Tatras cover a wide area and there are many other walking possibilities: just study the map and head out. The further one gets away from the head of the Roháčska Dolina valley, the less crowded paths become. From **Oravice**, for example, a remote village to the north of Zverovka where there is a campsite (accessible by road from a turning off the Roháčska Dolina at Habovka), there is a red-marked path up a limestone gorge, Juraňova Dolina, and then to peaks strung out along the Polish border.

The Low Tatras

The Low Tatras form the second highest mountain range in Slovakia. They also form the largest range by area, stretching from Banská Bystrica and Ružomberok in the west to Poprad and Švermovo in the east, and bounded to the north and south by the broad valleys of the Váh and Hron respectively, along which run main roads and railway lines. Although there has been development in some areas of the mountains — Jasná, for example, is one of the top ski resorts in the country — much of the Low Tatras is unpopulated, and it is much easier for walkers to get away from the crowds in the Low Tatras than in the other ranges in Slovakia. The country's greatest numbers of bears, lynx and wolves live in the thick pine forests that cover the lower slopes of the mountains.

Like Malá Fatra, the peaks of the Low Tatras are typically rounded, rather than jagged or sharp. The Low Tatras are primarily granite mountains,

Enjoying the spectacular scenery of the Low Tatras

although the number of caves in the area also points to limestone being an important component in their geology. There is a certain amount of evidence that the area was glaciated during the last Ice Age. The main ridge of the mountains runs in an east-west direction and includes the highest peaks, Ďumbier (6,701ft/2,043m) and Chopok (6,639ft/2,024m) — both easily accessible by walkers who make use of the Jasná chairlift. The only road to cross the Low Tatras from the Váh to the Hron valley does so at the lowest point of the ridge, the Čertovica pass (4,061ft/1,238m). No railways cross the main ridge. Many streams rise in the vicinity of the ridge, and flow perpendicular to it — north to the River Váh, or south to the Hron — and the steep valleys they have eroded are often very picturesque. The most developed part of the Low Tatras is along two of these valleys, Demänovská Dolina in the north and Bystrá Dolina in the south. The main ski resorts are Jasná, on the northern slopes of Chopok, and Bystrianska Dolina on the southern slopes, above Hotel Srdiečko. There is also the much smaller resort of Čertovica at the summit of the Čertovica Pass, which is more popular with less advanced skiers. Jasná is also an important centre for cross-country skiing. In the summer, all these resorts, and others, provide accommodation for those who want to walk or tour by car in the mountains.

Liptovský Mikuláš, further on from Ružomberok in the Váh valley, is the gateway to the Low Tatras. It lies on the eastern shore of an uninspiring artificial lake, Liptov Mara, which does at least provide some cool swimming when the surrounding plain, squeezed between high mountain ranges, becomes too hot as with Orava Lake, to the north, a number of villages were destroyed when the lake was created, and now lie beneath its surface. Like so many of the settlements in the Váh valley, the town is a place to stay in rather than to look round. Its points of interest are two museums in the centre: one dedicated to the pastor, writer and nationalist Michal Hodža, who played a part in the 1848 uprising against the Habsburgs by helping to publish the *Demands for the Slovak Nation* and then fled to avoid execution the second, on poet Janko Král, situated on the town's main square, is possibly the more interesting of the two, dedicated to Slovakia's most famous nineteenth-century poet, who was born here. Both museums make little sense unless one can read Slovak or knows about the individuals concerned. This said, most people arrive in Liptovský Mikuláš with the sole intention of coming out again and getting into the mountains; road travellers at least can safely avoid the town since it is bypassed by a short motorway. It is, however, the centre for public transport in the region, with trains on the main Žilina-Poprad line stopping here and with many buses from here along the Demänovská Dolina valley to Jasná (where the road ends), following the route described. The bus station is opposite the railway station in the town. Accommodation in the area can be found in many centres, including

Touring by car through the Demänovská Dolina valley in the Low Tatras

Liptovský Mikuláš and Jasná, but many people come here on day excursions from the High Tatras or from Malá Fatra.

The following is a step-by-step guide to the attractions in the **Demänovská Dolina** valley and in the Bystrá Dolina area, the most visited valley on the other side of the Low Tatras. The two valleys are linked by chairlift (from Jasná and Hotel Srdiečko) but not by road. Although this section is laid out as a continuous itinerary, those who want to see all the attractions here will need to set aside more than a day to cover it. Those intending to do some serious walking or skiing at Chopok or other centres could easily spend 2 or 3 days exploring this relatively small area.

The main road through the Demänovská Dolina valley to Jasná, runs south from Liptovský Mikuláš, and the junction on the motorway bypass, through the village of Demänová and then into the Low Tatras National Park. The lower part of Demänovská Dolina is a beautiful limestone valley cut by the River Demänová, with steep sides and many steep bluffs which tower above the road. Clumps of trees also grow on the sides of the valley that are not sheer rock faces. Water has also been at work inside the cliffs themselves, and the total length of the nine storeys of interconnected caves here is 12 miles (19km). Two of the caves in the valley, which are part of this system, have been opened to the public (be warned: both caves are extremely cold to visit — even in summer).

Soon after entering the National Park, 5 miles (8km) south of Liptovský Mikuláš, a car park on the left hand side of the road is for the **Demänovská**

L'adová Jaskyňa (Demänová Ice Cave), reached by a short walk up the hillside. This cave, cut by the River Demänová on four levels, boasts many bizarre ice patterns and flows, as well as stalactites and other limestone formations on its upper storeys. Spring is the best time to visit the cave, when the melting ice means that the formations are at their best. The existence of the cave has been known since medieval times. A circuit 2,230ft (680m) in length has been open to the public since 1952.

A little further on along the valley is a second cave, the **Demänovská Jaskyňa Slobody** (Demänová Cave of Liberty), so named because partisans hid weapons here during the Slovak National Uprising against the Nazis in 1944. It can be reached by walking up the hillside from the car park on the road, but there is also a short chairlift which runs up to the entrance. The cave, also formed as the result of the actions of the River Demänová, was discovered in 1921, and it boasts many limestone formations and beautiful subterranean lakes.

Beyond the latter cave, the gradient of the road increases, and from Chatá Záhradky, on the left hand side of the road, as it curves around, there is a chairlift up to Mount Chopok. Just beyond here, the road terminates at **Jasná**, at the top end of the Demänovská Dolina, which in winter becomes one of the most important skiing resorts in the country, with fine downhill skiing on the slopes of Mount Chopok, where there are many skilifts and tows. From Jasná there is a two-stage chairlift up to the summit of Mount Chopok (6,639ft/2,024m), and like many other lifts in the mountains, a ride up it often entails waiting in a long queue. Another chairlift from Jasná goes up to Luková which really only gives access to more skiing grounds, rather than a specific summit. Jasná has hosted many international skiing championships and many of the downhill runs, particularly those further up towards the summit of Chopok, are used by very advanced skiers.

There are excellent views from Mount Chopok, partly because it is on the main ridge of the Low Tatras, so that one can look one way over the Demänovská Dolina, and the other way over the valley on the other side, the Bystrá Dolina. A red-marked track runs all the way along this ridge, and one can walk along this in either direction, over more peaks and past mountain chalets. One popular option is to walk for about 2 hours from Chopok along the main ridge of the Low Tatras to the summit of Ďumbier (6,701ft/2,043m), the highest peak in the Low Tatras. From Ďumbier, another track brings one, after 5 hours, to the campsite at the bottom of the Demänovská Dolina valley, very close to Liptovský Mikuláš. One can also walk from the top station of the chairlift back down to Jasná (blue markers). Heading from the top of the chairlift in the other direction along the red-marked track brings one after 5 hours to Magurka, an isolated hamlet with skilift and a *chata* — which in theory will provide food and even accommodation; and, after

The main ridge of the Low Tatras provides good skiing in winter

another 5 hours, to Donovaly, the pass on the road from Banská Bystrica to Ružomberok in the westernmost part of the range.

A chairlift also runs down from Chopok to Hotel Srdiečko, in the Bystrá Dolina valley, on the opposite side of the ridge to Jasná. One can also ski on these slopes, although they are south-facing, compared to the north-facing slopes on the Jasná side of Chopok, and conditions and facilities here are not as good as those at Jasná. By now it must be assumed that those who have driven to Jasná will be without their cars, since there is no road link between Jasná and Hotel Srdiečko (unless you drive back to Liptovský Mikuláš and then over the Čertovica pass — a distance of over 50 miles/80km). So, those who want to continue beyond Hotel Srdiečko must make use of the regular bus service that runs along the valley. Bystrá Dolina is a similar valley to Demänovská Dolina, although not as attractive. Four miles (6km) from Hotel Srdiečko, the valley broadens out at Tále, another important winter and summer resort, with hotels and campsites; this is the start of a yellow-marked track up to Dereše (6,570ft/2,003m) on the main ridge of the Low Tatras. A short distance south of Tále, the minor road in the Bystrá Dolina valley meets the more important Road 66 at the village of Bystrá. In the village, just along the road towards Banská Bystrica, is the **Bystrianska Cave** (Bystrianska jaskyňa), the third of the limestone caves in the area.

This itinerary could easily be followed, in reverse, by those approaching from the direction of Banská Bystrica (for which, see next chapter). One could drive to Hotel Srdiečko, via the Bystrianska Cave, then go up Mount Chopok by chairlift and down the other side into Jasná, from where one can catch a bus along the Demänovská Dolina valley to the two caves. The area just described is a highly developed part of an otherwise largely deserted mountain region. Villages away from the central valleys are often little more than isolated mountain hamlets, with wooden houses occasionally adorned with fine examples of Slovak folk art. Roads are poor and public transport is often non-existent. The valley of the River Hron, east of the industrial town of Brezno, has many possibilities for walkers who really want to get away from the crowds: Heľpa, Pohorelá and Šumiac are all traditional mountain villages, as is Liptovská Teplička on the other side of the mountains. The railway and road along the Hron valley east of Brezno provide some great scenery. The map *Nízke Tatry — Kráľova hoľa* (number 123 in the series published by VKU of Harmanec) will show the walking possibilities in the remote eastern part of the range, where accommodation is limited, food-stops few and where bears roam in the dense forests, through which paths head up to the peaks. Some suggestions: from Heľpa station, one can reach the summit of Veľká Vápenica (5,546ft/1,691m) in 2 to 3 hours (yellow or blue markers); or Kráľova hoľa (6,389ft/1,948m), the highest peak in the eastern part of the range, can be reached on a blue-marked track from Šumiac. At Telgárt, at the very eastern end of the Hron valley, the railway runs through a spiral in the mountainside and reaches an altitude of 3,277ft (999m) shortly before Vernár station, on the main road through the Slovak paradise. The railway continues on to the station for the Dobšiná Ice Cave before continuing to Košice (see chapter 11).

Other options for walking or driving excursions on the northern side of the mountain include the Janská Dolina valley, to the east of Demänovská Dolina. A blue-marked track runs up along here from Liptovský Jan. It takes 5 hours to reach the summit of Ďumbier (red markers at Pred Bystrou, then yellow from sedlo Javorie, finally getting onto the red markers for the final leg to the summit itself). From the track junction at Pred Bystrou, one could head in the other direction, following the green markers, to the nature reserve Ohnište (limestone rock formations and a good view) and then onto the peaks Slema and Smrekovica and, if necessary, back down to Liptovský Jan. A good walk through dramatic scenery in an uncrowded part of the mountains which can be reached from Liptovský Mikuláš.

It is 22 miles (35km) from Liptovský Mikuláš to the road up to the High Tatran resorts at Tatranská Štrba. From Liptovský Mikuláš, road and railway continue eastwards, passing through the village of **Východná**, where the largest folk festival in Slovakia is held, usually at the end of July. Since there is no accommodation in the village, visitors usually camp out in haylofts belonging to local farmers, which are specifically let out for this purpose. The next village beyond Východná is **Važec**. The main road bypasses the village (there is also a railway station) but, on the opposite side of the village to the road and station is the entrance to **Važec Caves** (Važecká Jaskyňa). The caves were formed by the actions of one of the tributaries of the River Váh, and they boast many stalagmites and stalactites. The caves were discovered only in 1922, and the length of the circuit open to the public is comparatively short. There is a good view of the High Tatras from the entrance to the caves. Važec used to be one of the most beautiful villages in the Tatras until 1931, when most of the buildings were damaged in a fire, but a small folk museum in the town shows how things used to be. The next place beyond Važec is Tatranská Štrba, from where road and rack railway run up to Štrbské Pleso, the westernmost High Tatran resort.

The view down a gulley from the summit of Ďumbier, the highest of the
Low Tatras mountains

The High Tatras

The highest mountains in Slovakia also rank amongst the highest in Europe the Alps and the Pyrénées may be higher, but the High Tatras are rarely anything less than spectacular, offering some of the best high-mountain scenery anywhere in Europe and presenting walkers and climbers with challenging territory. These are serious mountains for serious mountain-lovers. The only truly 'Alpine' part of the Carpathians, they occupy a comparatively small area of Northern Slovakia (a smaller, and lower, part of the range lies in Poland). The highest peak, Mount Gerlachovský Štít (8,708ft/2,655m) is the highest mountain in north-eastern Europe. In summer, the mountains are excellent walking country; in winter, skiers come here from all over Europe.

Geologically, the Tatras were formed about 35 million years ago, at the same time as the Alps and the Pyrénées. This makes them (in geological terms, at least) very young mountains — the Scottish Highlands and the Appalachians are both about ten times older than the Tatras. There are no glaciers here today, but much of the present day appearance of the landscape is a result of glacial erosion of the granite rocks during the last Ice Age, which has resulted in many sharp, pyramidal peaks appearing, high, jagged ridges and dozens of tiny tarn lakes which are situated high up in the mountains. The lower slopes of the mountains are very thickly forested; bears and deer live here. Higher up, there are chamois and marmot, and there are also many beautiful Alpine flowers, which visitors are not allowed to pick. Other animals which live in the Tatras include rock eagles, wolves, lynx and wild cats. Above an altitude of 7,544ft (2,300m), there is no vegetation or animal life, just bare, steep, rocky slopes.

Tourism began in the High Tatras in the late eighteenth century, but until World War II it was mainly rich Hungarians who were able to afford to travel to, and stay in, the three fashionable resorts of Štrbské Pleso, Tatranská Lomnica and Starý Smokovec. Many lifts were built in the 1940s, including the cable car up to the summit of Lomnický Štít, the second highest peak in the range. The greater accessibility that resulted from the opening of the railway to Poprad, and of the Tatran Electric Railway which links the resorts themselves, meant that the Tatras grew in popularity as a holiday destina-tion. In the 1960s and 1970s, more hotels, and many skiing facilities (especially at Štrbské Pleso) were built. The Tatras have long proved popular with East European tourists, but they receive relatively fewer visitors from Western Europe.

At first sight, this area is hardly off the beaten track. Covering a small area (the main ridge of the mountains is only 16 miles/26km in length, and in theory can be walked in under a day), and receiving many visitors, the area is crowded for much of the year. The three resorts — Štrbské Pleso, Starý

Smokovec and Tatranská Lomnica — each have dozens of hotels and other places to stay, and their bars, restaurants and clubs give a varied, if unsophisticated (and inexpensive) version of the *après-ski* life of Alpine resorts. Some of the most popular peaks to climb (such as Rysy) become smothered in bodies, sporting rucksacks and water bottles and maps, during weekends in high summer. The conversation everywhere seems polyglot — Czechs and Slovaks come here, of course, but so do plenty of Germans, Poles, Hungarians and Russians — and smaller numbers of English speakers, too. Yet there is a pronounced contrast. Away from the resorts and the most popular walks, it is possible to get away from the crowds into the remote wilderness of forests and mountains. By visiting at the right time of year, by using a map to plan adventurous walks carefully, it becomes easy to step from places that heave with the sheer weight of visitors, to areas where the only sounds come from circling eagles or from mountain wildlife, living, unseen, in the rocky valleys.

Practical Advice For Those Visiting The High Tatras

It is pointless trying to see the mountains by any means other than on foot. Roads run up to the resorts but not into the mountains proper. The aim of this chapter is very firmly to get people out of cars and trains, and then into the mountains by chairlift, funicular or cable car, and from there to take to walking as the principal way to enjoy these mountains. Because of the popularity of this location, it is advisable to book accommodation in the High Tatras well in advance, at any time of year. Hotels exist in the resorts, and Poprad, the main town in the region (from where there are excellent public transport connections up into the mountains) also has hotels and private rooms on offer. The main Čedok office in the High Tatras is at Starý Smokovec, just up from the station and on the main road through the resort. They can advise travellers who turn up without having booked a room on which hotels have space left. They are also the main source of tourist information for the region.

The weather in the High Tatras is variable and unpredictable, as it is in any other mountain area. The first snow arrives in November and does not melt completely until May or June. Significant pockets of snow remain on north-facing slopes all year round. The main season for skiing is from January to March. In winter, days will often start grey and misty, but as the sun gets higher in the sky, it will evaporate the mist away, resulting in fine, bright and often very cold afternoons. Spring may not start until April or May. In summer, it can get very hot in the High Tatras, and there will often be very short, sharp thunderstorms in the late afternoon, which then clear very quickly to give fine evenings. In summer, walkers should always try to get underway early, to avoid the heat of the day and the ensuing storms.

Walking in the High Tatras

August, September and early October are more settled months. Late October and November are damp and rainy, and are the slackest season in the High Tatras, so far as tourists are concerned.

Since they cover such a small area, and are so popular, the High Tatras often get very crowded. It may even be advisable not to visit the area in July and August, when it may seem that much of Eastern Europe is taking its holiday here. The same goes for January and February, which are the main skiing months. September or May are probably the best months for walkers to visit the High Tatras, when they can avoid the worst excesses of the heat and the crowds.

Access to, and transport in, the High Tatras, is easy and convenient. Poprad is the main town in the region; it is not in the mountains, but the peaks are visible from it, on the near horizon. Poprad is an industrial town, and can safely be avoided by those with their own transport (a suburb of Poprad, Spišská Sobota has a few minor points of interest. See under The Spiš Region, for more details). Poprad is the main centre in the region, the focus of all the public transport routes in and to the High Tatras. In fact, those who are using public transport will find it almost impossible not to pass through Poprad at one time or another. The main airport for the High Tatras, Poprad-Tatry, is near the town; there are flights to there from Prague, via Bratislava, and fares are comparatively cheap. Poprad is on many internal and international rail routes, and the station here (also called Poprad-Tatry) is one of the most important railheads in Slovakia. There are many trains to Prague (about 9 hours) and Bratislava (about 6 hours), both of which run via Žilina (see the start of this chapter). The journey from Prague is best and most conveniently done overnight, in couchette (sleeping berth) or sleeper trains.

Poprad is also the centre for public transport within the High Tatras. There are many buses up to the resorts, which leave from the bus station next to the railway station. More entertaining, if slower, is the Tatran Electric Railway, a metre-gauge railway which winds its way along the northern slopes of the mountains, linking the three resorts with each other and also with Poprad. The narrow gauge tracks upstairs in the modern, glassed-in part of Poprad station, mark the lower terminus of the line. Another part of the line is a rack section, from Tatranská Štrba up to Štrbské Pleso, one of the main resorts. Many trains on the Poprad-Žilina line stop at Tatranská Štrba (the station here is just called Štrba).

Poprad is an important road junction as well, but motorists approaching from the west will branch off the main Váh valley road before reaching Poprad, probably at Tatranská Štrba, to take the road up to the three resorts. Poprad is about 335 miles (540km) from Prague. Motorists making the journey might want to arrange a route which passes through some of the places described in the section in this book on Moravia. Between Žilina and

The alpine peaks of the High Tatras

the High Tatras, road travellers will follow the itinerary presented in this chapter — through the Strečno Gorge, and through Martin and Ružomberok. The roads in the mountains are good, and are cleared in winter.

The area of the High Tatras was designated as a National Park in 1949. National Park rules must be followed when walking in the area: do not pick flowers, do not disturb the wildlife and do not stray off the marked paths. Route-finding in the High Tatras is, in fact, very easy, since all the paths are obvious, well-signposted and marked, and well trodden-on (but some paths well above the tree line, are very difficult to ascend and are only recommended for the nimble footed — and fearless! Some of these harder walks, or scrambles, are described further on in the chapter). There are other basic rules which should be followed. Do not walk too far from the settlements, or too far up, if the weather is bad. If the weather changes (and it can change very quickly), turn back immediately. Try to find out the weather forecast before setting out on a long walk. Take the following things: warm clothing — even on a hot day in summer, it may be cold at high altitudes, or it may become colder later in the day or if the weather changes; protection from the sun — sun hat, sun glasses, sun cream; some food and drink; basic first aid; wear good shoes, particularly for walking on paths above the tree line, which are often rocky; and take a whistle, which can be used in an emergency to attract attention (the normal 'distress call' is to blow six times every minute). It is usually possible to buy food in one of the huts in the mountains, but check if they are open before setting off. One last indispensable piece of equipment is a walking map of the High Tatras of which several are available, such as the *Turistická Mapa: Vysoké Tatry*, published by Slovenska Kartografia (Number 21 in their series), or the Edícia Turistickych Máp No.113: *Vysoké Tatry,* published by VKU (Harmanec), which is slightly clearer. These maps show all the colour-coded walking tracks described in this section, as well as dozens of others, which walkers can obviously use to plan their own trips. In addition to the three main resorts, and all the walking tracks and lifts that start from them, most maps on sale also show the other places mentioned in this section — Východná, Važec, Poprad and Ždiar. The maps are sold at news stands, hotel reception desks, bookshops and tourist offices in the main resorts. Note that most of the high-altitude paths are closed in winter, and some of the best paths are only open from 1 July to 30 October, and are closed during the rest of the year for environmental reasons (mainly to prevent walkers disturbing animals during the breeding season). The Belianske Tatry, to the immediate north of the High Tatras, are closed completely to walkers and skiers for the same reasons. Some paths in the Tatras are 'one way' (to ease passage over rocky bits) and are indicated as such on maps; during summer a minimal fee may be charged by the National Park authorities for visitors to use certain popular paths. Some difficult sections over steep, rocky parts of the mountains need to be tackled by walkers making use of chains and ladders fixed into the rocks. To ascend these safely you must have both hands free — always carry food, spare clothes etc in a backpack, rather than hand-held carrier bags.

More ambitious walkers might want to spend the night in one of the many mountain huts (called *chata*) in the Tatras. Unfortunately, these are often booked up, and it is definitely advisable to reserve a bed in a chalet in advance, before setting off. The place to do this is Slovakoturist, who have an office in Nový Smokovec, a short distance east of the station in Starý Smokovec. A couple of the chalets are sizeable hotels, with private rooms, but others such as Pod Rysmi and Téryho, both situated above 6,560ft (2,000m), are ancient stone-built huts way up in the mountains, which only sleep a dozen or so people in very basic dormitories. Most chalets will sell food, but walkers should not rely on them doing so, and should always take an adequate supply of food and drink with them. Because the Tatras cover a small area, a full programme of walking can be arranged without having to make use of these huts — it is possible to get up and down any of the peaks in a day; nevertheless, the sight of a Tatran sunrise or sunset is a memorable experience for anyone who gets a bed in a *chata*. Many of the highest peaks in the Tatras do not have marked trails leading up to their summits. Nevertheless, these can be ascended by climbers and walkers who hire a mountain guide. Guides can be hired from Horska Služba, the mountain rescue service, who have an office in Starý Smokovec next door to Čedok, just up from the railway station. In fact, anyone considering doing a lot of high-altitude walking, with or without a guide, should seek information from this office on planning trips, to find out, for example, the weather forecast, whether any paths have been closed, which mountain huts are open etc.

Climbing and skiing both require specialist equipment and (in the case of climbing) knowledge, experience and perhaps the use of guides. People who are not members of a recognized climbing club in their home country, must make use of a guide (again, Horska Služba is the place to go for information). Ice-climbing is popular in winter. Skiing gear can be borrowed from some sports shops in the area, and from the largest hotels in each of the resorts but it is best to have your own with you. The best time for skiing is from Christmas until the end of March. Štrbské Pleso is the most important downhill skiing centre, with two ski jumps. The gentler slopes around Ždiar, on the northern side of the mountains, are popular with beginners and families. Podbanské, in the western part of the range, is the centre for cross-country skiing. Specialist winter maps of the area are available, showing ski-runs (graded in terms of difficulty) and cross-country skiing tracks.

Resorts and Villages in the High Tatras

This section describes the Tatran resorts, and other settlements in the mountains, as one travels by road (or, for much of the way, railway) from Podbanské, in the south-western part of the range, round to Łysa Pol'ana, on the Polish border. Suggestions for walking from the settlements are given in a separate section, below. The places described here — but for the odd museum and limestone cave — are really places to stay or eat in, rather than places to visit in their own right. They fall neatly into two categories: the resort towns, which are geared towards the needs of skiers and walkers; and the smaller villages, which, although tainted by tourism to some degree, still retain to a large extent the air of traditional country villages.

Podbanské is the western-most town in the High Tatras, and is on the (undefined) boundary between the Western Tatras and the High Tatras. It is a small village with a few hotels, and is surrounded by forests which are dotted with small holiday homes that were, in Communist days, established by Trades Unions for the benefit of their members working in industry. The village is in a quiet location, the surrounding countryside lower and less dramatic than the area immediately to the east.

Štrbské Pleso, a short distance east of Podbanské, is the premier ski resort in Slovakia. Accessible by road and rack railway from Tatranská Štrba, on the main Váh valley road (NB the station there, where the rack railway meets the main Žilina-Poprad line, is just called 'Štrba'), this is a fairly featureless sort of place, which gives access to some of the best walking and skiing areas in the country. Hotels here are mostly modern, concrete box affairs; the other two resorts to the east have more character about them, and Štrbské Pleso is an unashamedly functional place, giving its (mostly foreign) visitors a place to sleep, eat and party. At 4,444ft (1,355m) it is the highest resort in the mountains, in a spectacular location and overlooked by two dominant ridges, with a glacial valley running between them. The town was actually founded as a spa; bronchial and respiratory diseases are treated here, not by spring waters but by the fresh mountain air. In 1970 the resort hosted the World Alpine Ski championships and much of the modern development is associated with that and other skiing events that are held here. The town covers a sizeable area, with parks and wide, mostly traffic-free streets. Above the railway station, and slightly to the left, is a big glacial lake, also called Štrbské Pleso, where boating and bathing are forbidden (but, in winter, when the lake freezes over, it is used for skating). Many of the town's hotels are built on its shores, including the triangular-shaped Patria Hotel, which has one of the town's best panoramas. Beyond the lake, near the Hotel Fis, there are two ski jumps. The larger one, whose ugly triangular silhouette is a blot on the Tatran landscape for miles around, was built in 1970 for the World Ski Jumping Championships. It is still used for international competitions. In winter it is often possible to see people using the smaller jump next to it. Beyond the hotel are the main skiing grounds. Near the jumps is the bottom station of a chairlift up to Solisko, a ridge above the town which is the starting point for many walks (beware of long queues forming in summer to use the lift). A mountain hut at the top provides a view with your refreshments.

Nový Štrbské Pleso is situated just below the railway station. It is a southward extension of the town, founded by an architect from Banská Bystrica who drained the swamps and created a small artificial lake and built cheap hostel accommodation around it, to cater for those who could not afford the hotels around the resort proper.

The main road, and the Tatran Electric Railway, run eastwards along the side of the main massif of the High Tatras, towards Starý Smokovec. **Vyšné Hagy** is a large health complex, most of which is secluded in the thick forest; it was once a private health farm owned by a Prussian count, but since 1948 it has been in the care of the state. Respiratory diseases are treated here, using the twin benefits of pure mountain air and modern state-of-the-art medical technology. **Nová Polianka**, further on, is another, less famous, health resort, and **Tatranská Polianka** is a rather neglected former winter sports centre. **Tatranské Zruby** is a military training camp, where the old Czechoslovak army was trained in the techniques of mountain warfare; the army built many of the paths that lead from here into the moutains.

Nový Smokovec, **Dolný Smokovec**, **Horný Smokovec** form a whole

Téryho Chata, one of the many stone-built walking and climbing centres in the High Tatras

with **Starý Smokovec**, the next important resort along the road. There is more character to this resort: only a few of its buildings are modern, and many of its hotels still retain the elegant grandeur of the nineteenth century, when the place was a favourite holiday resort of wealthy Hungarians. Starý Smokovec was established in 1793 and, along with the spa of Horný Smokovec nearby, soon became very fashionable as a spa and holiday resort. Some buildings from the village that used to stand here still remain: for example, opposite the Grand Hotel, just above the station, there is a nice wooden church, typical of many in the Carpathians. The Grand Hotel itself, right in the middle of town, is a half-timbered building, dating from 1905 — one of the most expensive and popular places to stay in the High Tatras. Next to the church is the bottom station of a funicular railway up to Hrebienok, skiing grounds above the town and a starting place for walks. The funicular is not very long, and one can also reach Hrebienok by a $^1/_2$ hour stroll along the green-marked track that runs up through the forest beside it. Starý Smokovec is a road and rail junction, with branches of the Tatran Electric Railway running from here to Poprad and to Tatranská Lomnica. There are also good bus connections and it is arguably the best place in the mountains for walkers to base themselves, with many possibilities for walks beginning at Hrebienok, and with easy public transport connections to other Tatran centres. Just above the railway station are the offices of the Mountain Rescue Service, which can give information to walkers, and, next door, the main Čedok office in the region, through which accommodation can be obtained. Horný Smokovec and Dolný Smokovec both have important spa sanatoria for children. The latter resort, which stretches along the road down to Poprad, has a nice park and a 100-year-old wooden chapel, built in the local style. The Tatracamp campsite, further on along the Poprad road, is one of the largest campsites in Europe — not recommended as a place to stay. The main road through the mountains continues north-east to **Tatranská Lomnica**, the third of the resorts. There are bus and rail connections from here to Poprad (both the Tatran Electric Railway, via Starý Smokovec, and a branchline off the main railway). Like Starý Smokovec, the place has an air of faded grandeur about it, many of the hotels being over 100 years old. The landmark of the resort is the Grandhotel Praha, which dates from 1905. There are a number of parks, and the resort is overlooked by the pointed peak Lomnický Štít. The excellent Tatra National Park Museum, housed in a grey building below the Grandhotel Praha, has exhibits on the plant and animal life of the Tatras, and on the people who first lived in and explored the mountains.

Tatranská Lomnica is not such a good base for walkers and skiers, but it is from here that the greatest number of lifts in the Tatras operate. Next to the Grandhotel Praha is the bottom station of a cable car up to Skalnaté Pleso (5,743ft/1,751m), a tiny lake situated below Lomnický Štít. From here, a single-cabin cable car takes fifteen people at a time up to the summit of Lomnický Štít, at 8,633ft (2,632m) the second highest mountain in Slovakia, and first climbed, in 1615, by a 15-year-old boy from Kežmarok called David Fröhlich. The lift was installed in 1941, and dismantled, modernized and rebuilt during the 1980s; now many of the cars operating on it are Swiss-built. There are often very long queues to ride up on this cable car, as it is the most popular tourist draw in the High Tatras, and a time-booking system is often in operation. If the weather is fine, and the queues are bearable, the view from the top is, of course, fantastic. There is an observatory and a meteorological office at the top, in addition to the usual place selling food. One can walk around outside at the top, though not very far. One must remain at the top for 35 minutes, until the next car comes up.

There is another cable car from Tatranská Lomnica to Skalnaté Pleso, which runs from the other end of town, from near the Hotel Horec. The top stations at Skalnaté Pleso are, however, next to one another. It is normally possible to approach Lomnický Štít by using this second cable car — one has to change at Skalnaté Pleso, in any case — but check first. In addition to the Lomnický Štít cable car, there is another lift from Skalnaté Pleso, a chairlift up to Lomnický Sedlo (7,183ft/2,190m), a rocky, wind-swept mountain ridge. There are possibilities for walking from both Tatranská Lomnica and

Skalnaté Pleso, but not from Lomnický Sedlo or Lomnický Štít.

The main road in the High Tatras continues east from Tatranská Lomnica, through another spa, Tatranské Matliary, where Kafka stayed for 6 months in 1921, suffering from tuberculosis. After 6 miles (9km) it meets road 67. Turning left here, towards Zakopane (Poland), one reaches the village of **Tatranská Kotlina**. At the far end of the village there is a path up to the entrance to the Belianská Jaskyňa caves, where running water has created many stalagmites and stalactite features in the rocks here. It was discovered in 1881, and in 1896 the cave was opened to the public and was lit with electric lighting, only 12 years after the invention of the electric light bulb. The caves are very substantial and the circuit visitors are led around is fairly long. Fewer people hike from Tatranská Kotlina, so those who want to get away from the crowds could use the map to plan some walking in this area.

A short distance on along the road that leads past the caves, one passes a turning on the right which leads to the bottom station of a chairlift up to Spišská Magura (3,720ft/ 1,134m) — there are excellent views from the top. However, the main road continues on into the village of **Ždiar**, which is well-known for its many wooden houses, similar to those built in Alpine areas. One of the buildings is a folk museum, open every day. The local people here (the Gorals, who are half-Polish, half-Slovak) are still very much mountain dwellers, living in traditional wooden houses decorated with folk designs — half a world away from the brash Tatra resorts. The main street in the village, unsurfaced, runs parallel with the main road, and is lined with the best examples of traditional architecture. Often whole families are out in the fields around the village, tending animals or small-holdings of crops; animals are used to draw ploughs and to transport farm equipment or produce around. Unfortunately some disfiguring modern buildings have sprung up, but many parts of the village can still lay a genuine claim to be a traditional mountain community.

The valley around Ždiar is very scenic and provides road travellers with some good views: the ridge on the left is the Belianske Tatry, an area of the Tatras that has been closed to all walkers, climbers and skiers as a nature conservation measure. The Belianske Tatry are limestone rocks (hence the caves at Tatranská Kotlina), rather than granite, which is the rock that forms the High Tatras. Just beyond Ždiar, on the left hand side of the road, is a small skiing ground which is very popular with families and less advanced skiers. From here, the road meanders down through the quiet village of **Tatranská Javorina**, a former centre of iron-ore mining, where there is a nineteenth-century wooden church, typical of many remote parts of Slovakia. The next place along the road is **Łysa Poľana**, a dusty collection of buildings grouped around a car park and disused customs house on the Polish border. Passports are checked on the other side of the road bridge across the Biela Voda

(Slovak) or Biatka (Polish) River. Both these places are starting and finishing points for walks in the quieter part of the northern High Tatras. Frequent buses run from Łysa Pol'ana to Tatranská Lomnica and Starý Smokovec, via all the places mentioned above.

Walking in the High Tatras

The High Tatras allow for some of the most challenging and exciting mountain walking anywhere in Europe; though the main routes get very busy during weekends in high summer, it *should* be possible, even at these times of the year, to choose walking paths which are less popular; in general, paths on the northern side of the mountains are much less busy than those which start from the main resorts on the southern slopes. The walks described below are graded according to difficulty and length; possibilities have been given in turn from each of the resorts and settlements mentioned in the previous section. For recommended walking maps see page 209.

From Podbanské

1. The Kamienista Dolina valley is a peaceful, forested valley; after 2 hours the blue-marked path along the valley gets suddenly much steeper and harder as it ascends the pass, Pysne sedlo, on the Polish border; from here, a red-marked path runs westwards along the ridge which marks the border, to the peaks Blyst and then on to Klin and peaks in the West Tatras. From Blyst there is a blue-marked track to the summit of Bystrá (7,373ft/2,248m), the highest peak in this part of the mountains. Possibility of returning from Bystrá, via the yellow-marked path along the Bystrá Dolina Valley, to the road at Pri Bystrej, and a bus back to Podbanské. This circular walk easily takes a day and is hard once you get outside the main valleys. Check that the red-marked path along the Polish border can be used by foreigners (in the recent past only Slovaks and Poles have been allowed to use it).

2. Heading up the Ticha Dolina valley, on the yellow-marked path (most of which is along a track), is not as interesting; a whole day's excursion might involve heading up this long, quiet valley to the point where the road forks, and then heading up one of two passes on the Polish border by the red-marked track — Tomanovo sedlo or the much steeper Suche sedlo (red, then yellow markers); paths get much steeper after the fork in the road and the red markers start.

3. A short distance east along the road from Podbanské is a collection of buildings at Tri studničky (bus stop); from here a steep, demanding green-marked path runs up to the summit of Kriváň (8,180ft/2,494m). This is a 3-hour ascent (allow 2 hours for the descent). Tri Študničky is also linked to Podbanské by an easy red-marked path.

From Štrbské Pleso

The biggest walking centre in the Tatras; paths from here run deep into the mountains, are demanding and can get crowded. Rysy and Kriváň, the highest peaks in the Tatras accessible to walkers who do not use mountain guides, can be reached from here. Tracks are signposted from the marker board in the square just above the railway station.

Easy Walks

1. Red markers to the lake, Jamské Plesó just over an hour, along the level. A nice walk.

2. Yellow markers to the Skok Waterfalls (Vodopády); 1 hour 20 minutes. The track runs along the bottom of the Mlynska Dolina valley, which is bare and rocky. Above the waterfalls is another tiny lake, Pleso nad Skokom.

3. To Popradské Pleso, a much larger glacial lake, picturesquely set in the bowl of the mountains, which can be reached after an hour on the red-marked track. There is a mountain chalet on its shores, called Chata Morávku, where one can stay in dormitories or private rooms. A very popular walk; the lakeside is often busy in summer. The red-marked path continues on, very steeply, from the *chata* and snakes up the mountain side to the pass sedlo pod Ostrvou, from where there is a magnificent view of the lake. Close to the lake is the 'symbolic cemetery' (*symbolický cintorín*), wooden crosses and a chapel built in the 1930s to commemorate those who have died in the Tatras. The motto reads, 'For the dead in memory, for the living as a warning.' Find it along the yellow-marked track.

4. From Solisko, at the top of the chairlift, to the glacial lakes at Nišné Wahlenbergovó blue, then yellow markers — 1¹/₂ hours. This walk is a bit harder. The lakes are beautifully situated, in the valley Furkotská Dolina.

Harder Walks

5. From Solisko, at the top of the chairlift, to the peak above it, Predné Solisko (6,865ft/2,093m), is a short but very steep climb up the red-marked track; reckon on taking just over half an hour to ascend.

6. The ascent of Mount Kriváň (8,180ft/2,494m) is fairly tough — a 7-hour return trip from Štrbské Pleso. The first part of the trip is along the red markers to Jamské Pleso; from the lake, take the blue-marked track for another 2¹/₂ hours to the summit of Kriváň. Kriváň is a distinctive pyramidal peak, which often features in Slovak poetry and folklore.

A welcome rest after walking in the High Tatras

7. The ascent of Mount Rysy (8,197ft/2,499m) is possibly the most demanding walk in the Tatras; a 9-hour return trip from Štrbské Pleso. Get an early start to avoid the crowds — on fine afternoons in summer the summit of the mountain can often be obscured by sheer numbers of walkers sitting on it! Rysy is on the Polish border (it is actually the highest mountain in Poland) and many people walk up it from a track on the Polish side. Lenin walked up Rysy in 1914, and from 1957 to 1989, in true Communist style, the 'International Ascent of Youth' up the mountain was organized every year, to commemorate the event.

From Štrbské Pleso, take the red-marked path to the lake, Popradské Pleso; after the lake, follow the blue markers along the valley, then branch off on the steep red-marked path to the right, which snakes up past tiny, ice-cold pools and which requires walkers to use chains and ladder-rungs fixed into the rock to ascend the steepest bits. The highest mountain hut in Slovakia, Chata pod Rysmi, is a short distance below the summit. It is built of stone and has dormitory accommodation for about a dozen people — and hopefully will sell refreshments. There are usually pockets of snow around the *chata*, even in high summer. The view from the summit itself is extraordinary; note that it is not possible to cross the border here and go down into Poland.

8. From Solisko, walk along the blue, then yellow-marked track to Nišné Wahlenbergovo; from here, the yellow-marked path gets much steeper, as it ascends the pass Bystré Sedlo (7,590ft/2,314m). One reaches the top of the pass, from the lakes, after just over an hour. The path over the pass is indistinct; one just has to pick one's own way over the rocks, and then down the other side (although it is impossible to get lost). From the top of the pass, the path takes one down into the next valley, Mlynická Dolina. The walk back to Štrbské Pleso from here, still following the yellow markers, goes past the Skok waterfall. The walk described, from Solisko to Štrbské Pleso over the pass, takes 5 to 6 hours. This is a good walk, as it is circular and does not require the walker to use the same track twice.

From Tatranská Polianka
A whole day's walk is from the railway station here, right over the High Tatras to Łysa Pol'ana, on the Polish border; green markers along the Velicka Dolina valley, to the Sliezsky Dom hotel, then along the blue-marked track over Polsky hreben (7,216ft/2,200m) and then along the long Bielovodsk dolina valley to Łysa Pol'ana, from where there are frequent buses to Tatranská Lomnica for the train or bus back to Tatranská Polianka. Allow at least 9 hours.

From Starý Smokovec

1. Starý Smokovec is overlooked by a bulky-looking mountain called Slavkovský Štít (8,043ft/2,452m), which can be ascended from the town along a blue-marked track. This is a 9-hour return trip from the resort.

2. From the top of the funicular at Hrebienok, walk for 20 minutes past Bilíkova Chata and then down to the waterfalls, Studenovodské Vodopády. From here, follow the blue-marked track for 5 minutes to the track junction in a forest clearing. Then, take the red-marked track from here for 15 minutes to the waterfalls, Obrovsky Vodopády. Carry on along the red-marked path for another 20 minutes, as it climbs the side of a hill; a track junction in the forest clearing points the way to the Nalepkova Chata, a minute's walk away along the green-marked track. This chalet is a picturesque wooden building, set in trees and overlooked by a sharp, high ridge.

From here, the green-marked track quickly climbs out of the forest and into more open, rocky terrain. Téryho Chata is 2 hours along this track — the second part of the walk, up to the ledge on which the *chata* sits, is steep. Téryho Chata is a stone-built mountain hut situated at 6,609ft (2,015m) near a number of small glacial lakes which are perfect for swimming in.

From Téryho Chata, one can of course return to Hrebienok the way one came. A much more adventurous, and hair-raising, alternative is to cross over the Priečne sedlo pass (7,715ft/2,352m) to Zbojnicka Chata. It takes 2 hours along the yellow-marked track to walk between the two *chatas*, and the actual ascent of the pass is not a walk at all but a scramble up what seems like a near-vertical cliff face, with walkers using chains and ladders to help them up: a scary and potentially very dangerous experience which forces many to turn back. Zbojnicka Chata is also situated at the head of a rocky valley, near many small lakes. From here it is a 3-hour walk along the blue-marked track back down to Hrebienok.

The above trip takes 8 hours. One can, of course, just do the first part of it (past the waterfalls to Nálepkova Chata), which is easy and takes an hour, one way.

There are two variations on the above walk: from Nálepkova Chata, one can walk up to Skalnaté Pleso (red markers), a tiny lake (altitude 5,743ft/1,751m). From here, there is a cable car down to Tatranská Lomnica, from where, if necessary, one can take the train back to Starý Smokovec. Alternatively, from the Téryho Chata, instead of the difficult journey over the Priečne sedlo pass, one can take the green markers and cross the mountains all the way over to Javorina, from where there are buses back to Tatranská Lomnica, for train or bus back to Starý Smokovec. The initial climb from the *chata* over the Sedielko pass is steep and rocky, but things get easier after this and much of the journey is along a long, quiet river valley. This, again, is a whole day's journey.

*Waterfalls in the High
Tatras, above Starý
Smokovec*

From Tatranská Lomnica

Not really a good place from which to walk; most people come here to take
the cable-car up to Lomnický Štít (see previous section). There is a steep
green-marked path up through the forest, following the cableways to the
lake, Skalnaté Pleso, but if you want to walk up to this lake it is better to start
from Hrebienok (see walk 2, from Starý Smokovec).

Eastern High Tatras

This is less busy, but still dramatic, part of the High Tatras. A good walking
destination is the lake, Zelené Pleso, which has a *chata* on its shores. There
are two paths up to it — the yellow-marked track from the Biela voda bus
stop on the Tatranská Lomnica — Tatranská Kotlina road; or the longer
track up from Tatranská Kotlina (blue/green, then green markers up to the
ruined *chata* on the shores of Biele pleso — about 3 hours; then ¹/₂ hour by
red markers over to the lake). From the *chata* at Zelené Pleso it is a steep,

2-hour climb, following the yellow markers, up Jahňaci Štít (7,311ft/2,229m); a good peak to aim for, with fine views and fewer people at the summit compared to western peaks such as Kriváň or Rysy.

From Ždiar

Ždiar is overlooked by the dramatic ridge of the Belianske Tatry, the northern ridge of the High Tatras. These mountains are closed to all walkers and skiers for conservation reasons; there are no paths through them. There is some more gentle, and generally deserted, countryside to the north of Ždiar.

There are a number of possibilities from the upper station of the chairlift to the immediate east of the village (reached via a turning off the road): for instance, east along the green-marked track to Jezerske lake and village, or into Ždiar itself along the blue, then red, markers.

From Tatranská Javorina

There is a path right across the northern part of the High Tatras, from Tatranská Javorina, along the Zadne Medodoly valley, over the Kopske sedlo pass and then down, past the Biele Pleso lake, to either Tatranská Kotlina (green markers) or, a longer walk, to Tatranske Matliare (blue markers), which is very close to Tatranská Lomnica. A lot of the walk is through forest, although it gets high and rocky around the pass; allow perhaps 5 to 6 hours for the walk. There is also a green-marked track from Javorina to Hrebienok, above Starý Smokovec, which goes over the Sedielko pass and past the Téryho chata; but this walk is better done going in the other direction, as there is much less walking uphill to do compared to walking downhill if you use Hrebienok as the starting point.

From Łysa Pol'ana

There is a path from here right across the mountains, to Tatranská Polianka, which will take a whole day to walk. Again, though, it is better to do this walk in the other direction, using Tatranská Polianka as a starting point.

The Slovak Paradise

The Slovak Paradise (Slovenský Raj) is an area of tiny streams, gushing waterfalls, narrow canyons and underground caves, to the south-east of Poprad. Covering a large area, much of which is fine walking countryside, the region makes for a good day-trip from Poprad or the High Tatras, and attractions fall into two main areas: that around the village of Hrabušice, 9 miles (15km) south-east of Poprad, where there are a number of interesting gorges and waterfalls, many of which lie deep in the hills; and secondly a smaller area, around Dedinky and the Dobšiná Ice Cave, on or just off the main road which runs south from Poprad to Rožňava.

The Gorges near Hrabušice

Limestone produces steep-sided gorges when rainwater — which is slightly acidic — is able to dissolve the rock when it flows into, and through, the naturally occurring joints and cracks. Near Hrabušice, half a dozen narrow gorges have been cut into the limestone of the area, by the fast-flowing mountain streams which still flow through them. The gorges can be walked through by means of ladders, steel and wooden walkways, and chains, which are built into the sides of the vertical cliffs above the waterfalls. Often, walkers in the caverns are dwarfed by the towering cliffs above them, which in some places are over 492ft (150m) high. There are dozens of possibilities for walking in this region, and those intending to walk here should buy a map, such as the one entitled *Slovenský Raj*, number 124 in the series published by VKU (Harmanec), available in many bookshops — and including a certain amount of information in English. Thorough advance planning is necessary before setting out on trips: many of the paths are one-way only, and are indicated as such on the map by arrows. This means that it is usually only possible to walk *up* the canyons: one cannot walk back down them, and usually the return journey must be made by other routes which lead over the hills. The main gorges to explore, easily identifiable on the map, are described below.

The **Hornád Gorge** (Prielom Hornádu) is the most popular part of this region to visit. It runs between Čingov, a short distance west of Spišská Nová Ves, and Podlesk, a short distance to the south-west of the village of Hrabušice. Both places are chalet camps, rather than villages, and can be reached by road. However, the gorge itself that runs between them can only be seen on foot. A 10 mile (16km) long blue-marked track runs the whole length of the gorge, over footbridges, steps, metal ladders and built walkways. This is not a one-way track, so it is possible to walk only one way along the gorge, and then turn back. Note that there is also a yellow-marked track linking Hrabušice with Čingov. This track runs parallel with the gorge, and above it, giving good views over it, especially from the viewpoint Tomášovsky Výhlad. To walk the complete length of the blue-marked track takes 3 hours, the yellow track 2 hours.

From the chalet camp at Podlesok, it is possible to walk right into another beautiful gorge, the **Suchá Belá Gorge**, parts of which are ascended by means of ladders. This gorge can get crowded at busy times, however. The path is wet and a bit of a scramble in places. It is a one-way track; it takes about 2 hours to get to the top from Podlesok, and one must return by a different route.

From Podlesok there is a green-marked track running all the way over to the Dobšina Ice Cave (see below; a 3 to 4 hour walk, mostly through forest). This path provides access to the **Piecky Gorge**, and, further on, the deepest gorge in the Slovak Paradise, **Velký Sokol**.

Deep in the hills, and only accessible after a very long walk, is the **Sokolia Dolina Gorge**, a walk along which will reveal a number of high, isolated waterfalls, including the Zavojy Vodopád falls, the highest in the Slovak Paradise. The best way to approach this gorge is from Podlesok, via Kláštorisko and through the valley Tomášaská Belá.

Many paths in this area lead to or through **Kláštorisko**, an isolated chalet community, campsite and restaurant situated on a mountain meadow. Archaeologists are slowly excavating an old thirteenth-century monastery here, to which the native Slavs of the region fled during the Tartar invasions.

Around Dedinky and the Dobšiná Ice Cave

The other part of the Slovak Paradise worth visiting is accessible by car or bus, heading south from Poprad on road 67. After leaving behind the rather dismal housing estates on the outskirts of Poprad, after 6 miles (10km) one comes to Hranovnica and the turn-off to Hrabušice. The road then enters the Slovak Ore Mountains, a range of dark and slightly forbidding hills which occupy an area to the south-east of the High Tatras. After passing through the village of Vernár, the road ascends a short, sharp pass over a limb of the Low Tatras and then comes down into the valley of the River Hnilec, which rises close to here. The pass itself is over 3,477ft (1,060m) high. A junction is reached after the road reaches the valley from the pass, where a left-turning should be made. After a short distance, the road crosses the boundary into the Slovak Paradise National Park and the car park and hotel-restaurant complex next to the path up to the **Dobšiná Ice Cave** (Dobšinská Ladová Jaskyňa) is reached (it is a short walk from the road up to the cave entrance).

The Dobšiná Ice Cave is the only cave open to the public in the Slovak Paradise National Park, but it is one of the world's most extensive ice cave systems. It lies at an altitude of 3,182ft (970m) on the slopes of a limestone hill called Duca. The cave was formed by the action of the River Hnilec on the limestone rocks of this region. However, the lower sections of the river became blocked off, and favourable conditions then resulted for the formation of ice in the cave. The bottom floor of the cave is covered with ice 82ft (25m) thick; there are also other ice columns and waterfalls. The cave has been open to the public since its discovery in 1870 and in 1887 it became the first cave in the world to be illuminated by electric lighting. The total known length of the cave system is about 4,592ft (1,400m), but the circuit the public walks is only about a third of this. The temperature inside the cave is a constant — 7 degrees centigrade (19 degrees fahrenheit) — so bring something warm; an early start is also advisable as the caves can become very crowded on summer afternoons and at weekends. Although the caves are situated at a fairly high altitude, there is a railway station very close to them called Dobšinská L'adová Jaskyňa, on the very scenic line that runs between Banská Bystrica and Košice via Margecany. Do not confuse the Dobšiná Ice Cave and the town of Dobšiná which lies a fair distance to the south-east.

A short distance beyond the Dobšiná Ice Cave, soon after the village of Stratena, a left-hand turning leads towards the village of Dedinky. After a short while this road skirts the side of a small artificial lake, called Palcmanská Maša, a very pleasant spot which in summer is popular with swimmers and windsurfers. Just before the road enters the village, a track on the right leads to the bottom station of a chairlift (*lanovká*) up to the Geravy Karst Plateau at an altitude of 3,411ft (1,040m). There is skiing here in winter, and a couple of skilifts have been built near the top station.

The Spiš Region

The Spiš region lies immediately to the east of Poprad and the High Tatras. In the thirteenth century, this region was devastated by the Tartar invasions, and most of the local population fled or were killed. Later, when the region was ruled by the Hungarians, Saxon settlers from Germany — who called the area Zips — were encouraged to come and colonize the area that had been formerly laid to waste by the Tartars. They founded, in all, twenty-four new towns, which gradually became a semi-autonomous kingdom within a kingdom, where all the inhabitants spoke German rather than the Slovak of the indigenous population. The towns were given special military and administrative rights, which lasted up until the nineteenth century, and which frequently brought the town councils into conflict with both the church, and with the local Hungarian magnates. The colonists originally came to work in the mines in the area. Later, the towns they founded grew very wealthy through trade, and metal and wood-working industries. Virtually all of the German-speakers have left, and the region is now as poor as the rest of Eastern Slovakia; nevertheless, evidence of the former wealth of the towns can be seen everywhere — particularly in the beautifully decorated Gothic churches, and also in the Renaissance merchants' houses which line most town squares, and which give an architectural unity to many of the towns.

Slovakia came under the influence, and later the rule, of the Hungarian Habsburgs, who treated the region and its people with a neglect bordering on cruelty when Slovakia became a dominion of Hungary in 1867. The cultural history of the Spiš region is thus curiously eclectic — with Slovak, Hungarian and German elements all thrown in. Any visit to a village or town cemetery will show this — the writing on various gravestones might be in German, Hungarian, or, on the simplest but best cared for stones, Slovak.

Relaxing by the lake next to Téryho Chata, surrounded by the spectacular mountain scenery of the High Tatras (Chapter 9)

The Tatran Electric Railway is a popular means of getting around in the High Tatras (Chapter 9)

These walkers are using chains, fixed into the rock, to negotiate a tricky stage on the path up to the summit of Rysy, one of the most challenging walks in the Tatras (Chapter 9)

The Spiš Region East of Poprad

The main town in the Spiš region now is **Spišská Nová Ves**. There is next to nothing to see here, although it is a useful centre for both the Spiš region, the Slovak Paradise and even the High Tatras — there is a main-line railway station here, and it is the start of a branch-line to Levoča. Once a rival of Levoča, and selected as the regional capital by the Habsburgs in 1772 (which brought about the demise of the former capital, Levoča), the town boasts a main square in the form of a wide, leafy avenue (a typically East Slovak arrangement), where you can find the town theatre (dating from 1905) and Gothic church (with its 282ft/86m high steeple), which contains a couple of minor works by Master Pavol of Levoča; there is also a small museum on the square. There are other, equally minor points of interest in Poprad itself — otherwise an ugly, drab sort of place, but its ancient suburb of **Spišská Sobota**, while still fairly ordinary, does at least provide an introduction to the Spiš region. It is 1 mile (2km) north-east of the railway station in the centre of the town. Here, the richly decorated Gothic church, whose fifteenth-century chapel is the burial place of the Zápol'skýs, a local Hungarian aristocratic family, and the sixteenth-century free-standing belfry, testify to the previous prosperity of the region. The eaves of the prosperous-looking medieval Burgher's houses, once owned by the rich merchants of the region, overhang the square, in whose centre is a Renaissance Town Hall and belfry. Inside the late Gothic church (of sv. Juraj — St George), a carved wooden altar dating from 1516, similar to that at Levoča, and carved by Master Pavol sits beneath some beautiful vaulting. There is also a small museum on the square. That said, there is little reason not to press on from both these places, to the real delights of the Spiš region — the town of Levoča, and, beyond it, the ruined castle at Spišske Podhradie, both of which lie on the main Poprad-Prešov road (along which frequent buses run).

Half way between Poprad and Levoča is a roadside village called **Spišský Štvrtok**, its small thirteenth-century church crowned with a wooden, pinnacled spire, rising above the houses and fields. It is noted for its perfect late Gothic (1473) side chapel, designed as a mausoleum for a local Hungarian magnate, Count István Zápolya, who was also canonized; its architect was Hans Puchsbaum, who also worked on St Stephen's Cathedral in Vienna. The painting on the altar shows the incumbent dying in the arms of the Virgin Mary. From the crypt there is an ancient underground passageway which runs next door to the former seventeenth-century monastery (now a hospital).

Levoča is 16 miles (26km) due east of Poprad. In the Middle Ages, Levoča was the capital of the Spiš Region, its wealth founded on trade and craft industries which in turn led to the flourishing of fine art and rich

*The ornate façade of
the Town Hall at
Levoča*

architecture, paid for by the rich German merchants who settled here. For
four centuries, this was the site of the Spiš government and administration
— the judiciary, the clergy, the merchants and the manufacturers all had
their base here. In 1321, King Charles Robert granted a Law of Storage to
the town; this meant that every merchant who passed this way had to stay
for 2 weeks, had to pay various taxes and dues and had to offer his goods to
the inhabitants and traders of the town; by the same law, Levoča merchants
were exempted from similar taxes when they passed through neighbouring
towns! Trade routes once ran from here in four directions — north to
Cracow, west to Nürnberg and Prague, east to Kiev and south to Budapest.
The trade, and the merchants, have now gone, but the rich architectural
legacy is left for today's travellers to appreciate. The town was founded by
its German speakers as Leutschau — reputedly derived from the German
leuth schaut (people look), the cry of the sentries when any Mongol
attackers were sighted from the lookout towers.

The main road that runs through Levoča skirts the medieval walls that surround the Old Town before opening out into Námestie Slobody, the largely featureless main square of the New Town. From here, it is possible to go through the Košice gate (Košická brána) which takes one through the walls and into the Old Town. From the gate, and the colourful New Minorite Church next to it (nicely decorated altars and ceiling decorations inside — if you can get in), Košická Street runs into the centre of things — the main square of the Old Town, a large rectangular medieval showpiece called Mierové Námestie. Levoča's medieval ground plan, a chess-board pattern of straight streets built around a central rectangular square, has survived, as have its medieval burgher's houses which line the square. However, it is the cluster of buildings in the centre of the square which more immediately command attention.

The first building one comes to is an undistinguished and now rather neglected old Weighing House, with the Coat of Arms of Levoča above the door; it was in this unlikely building that most of medieval Levoča's money was made, however, for it was the old trading centre of the medieval town. The money that was made here by the Levoča merchants funded the building of the church behind it, dedicated to St James, now the principal attraction of the town and the second most important church in Slovakia after St Elizabeth's Cathedral in Košice. Most of the church was built in the 1330s (although the tower is nineteenth century). Inside, the most outstanding work, amidst all the incredible late Gothic decoration, is the remarkable High Altar, created by a carver named Master Pavol (Paul) of Levoča and carved out of the wood of lime trees between 1507 and 1517. Over 59ft (18m) high, it is a unique work which is reputedly the largest Gothic High Altar in the world. The carving is entitled *The Last Supper*. Such was the egotism of Master Pavol's patrons, the Levoča merchants, that it was they who posed as models for the portraits of the disciples. Master Pavol, and his apprentices, can be seen lurking behind the figure of St James on the central panel. St John can be seen asleep on Christ's lap; Judas can be seen with thirty pieces of silver around his neck. Pavol was meant to have depicted a particularly mean and untrustworthy Levoča merchant as Judas! The altar was fully restored in the 1950s. There are a number of other carved altars in the church, some by the same builder. One can put a coin into the machine in the central aisle of the church, which gives a good tape-recorded description of the altar, and other decorations in the church, in English.

Just below the church is another distinctive building, the Renaissance Town Hall, with its distinctive arches, arcades and clock tower, built mostly in the sixteenth century. It now houses the museum of the Spiš region and a gallery of contemporary art. In front of the building is a preserved sixteenth-century pillory, designed for women. Other parts of the Spiš museum are housed in another building on the square, opposite, at number

The Kostel Marie Katédralá domed church sitting on the hillside above Levoča

20, the house in which Master Pavol is supposed to have lived. There is an exhibition here, devoted to his life and works, and to the efforts of two brothers named Kotrba, who restored Pavol's carvings in the 1950s. The other church in the square, an uninspiring Protestant church, dates from the early nineteenth century. The other parts of the old town, dusty, shabby and deserted, are worth a wander round; just pick any street that leads off the main square. The whole of Levoča is surrounded by ancient medieval walls, most of which can be walked along. Those who walk all the way around the walls will pass a grandiose German grammar school, the Gymnazium.

On a hill overlooking the town, called Marianska Hora, is a distinctive domed church called Kostel Marie Katédralá, from where there is a good view over the town. It is possible to walk up the hillside to the church. On the first Saturday in July, the church plays host to the biggest Marian festival in Slovakia, when over 250,000 Catholics from all over Slovakia descend on the church for a night of prayer, feasting, drinking and dancing. Many walk all the way to the church from wherever they live, taking several days to do so; some ascend the hill up to the church on their knees. High Mass is usually celebrated at the church at 6pm on the Saturday evening, and the religious celebrations go on at the church and in the fields surrounding it well into the next morning. An interesting festival to witness. The church is open — and considerably more peaceful — at all other times of the year, too. This pilgrimage demonstrates, visibly, the strength of Slovak Catholicism, as powerful and as unifying a force as it is in Spain or Italy, and palpably much more prevalent here than in Moravia or Bohemia.

Road 18 continues east from Levoča for 9 miles (15km) to **Spišské Podhradie**, another ancient Spiš town, which is overlooked by Spiš Castle (Spišský Hrad), one of the biggest ruined castles in Europe. The main road bypasses Spišské Podhradie, but entering the town itself, the first thing one comes to on the road that runs through its centre is the complex of buildings which make up **Spišská Kapitula**. This is a fortified ecclesiastical settlement, still surrounded by a high wall, which was the religious centre of the Spiš region. It was fortified against the repeated Tartar invasions. The main feature is the twin-towered thirteenth-century basilica of St Martin, a remarkable building whose origins are Romanesque. Forbidding and austere like many buildings of its age, it has been heavily restored over the centuries, although the church still retains its original Gothic appearance and the fourteenth-century frescoes, showing the coronation of King Charles Robert, remain. On the south side is the burial chapel of the local Zápolya family (1493). The Bishop's Palace, in the same complex, dates from the eighteenth century. In 1989 a new Bishop of Spiš was appointed, after the see had been vacant for many decades. Beyond the picturesque medieval frontage, the site is eerily deserted and overgrown, but despite the neglect of many of the buildings here, Spišská Kapitula is still a fully-functioning religious centre, thanks to the recent establishment here of a Catholic seminary. The best views of the castle can be obtained from beside the road which runs down, northwards, from Spišská Kapitula — an irresistible location for photographers, who can often be seen lining the road here. In fact, the view of the castle from here is probably better than inspection of the ruins close to, although the view from the hill on which the ruins sit is excellent.

From Spišská Kapitula, the road runs down into the centre of Spišské Podhradie itself. One can walk up to **Spiš Castle** from the centre of town (it takes about 15 minutes); the road up to the castle is a turning off the main Poprad-Prešov road, a short distance beyond Spišské Podhradie. The castle ruins are strung out along the top of a rocky plateau at a height of 2,080ft (634m), and they dominate the landscape for miles around. Because of its prime defensive position, the hill on which it stands has been occupied since the Stone Age by various tribes who built fortified settlements here. The present day stone castle was founded in about the thirteenth century. By 1450, over 2,000 people were living within its confines, including members of the nobility, their servants and soldiers. Throughout the next few centuries, it was owned by various aristocratic families, and it was partly rebuilt, in Gothic and then Renaissance style. The last military activity that the castle saw was in 1710, when it was captured by the Imperial Army. Soon

The ruins of Spiš Castle dominate the landscape east of Levoča

afterwards, it was damaged by an extensive fire, and became neglected; it was gradually allowed to become a ruin. Between 1969 and 1979 the castle was extensively restored, and was eventually opened to the public. The castle palace within the walls has been extensively rebuilt and restored; its rooms now contain a museum showing finds from nearby prehistoric sites, and a large collection of torture instruments.

Just south of the castle is an archaeological site called Dreveník. There are many rock formations here, and the plant life is unique. A path leads around it, starting from just below the castle. Paths lead on to the village of **Žehra**, where the tiny thirteenth-century church sitting on top of a hill comes complete with black onion dome, white perimeter walls and original, and now faded, frescoes.

The Spiš Region North-East of Poprad

Nine miles (14km) up the road from Poprad, **Kežmarok** (derived from its old German name, Käsmark, meaning 'cheese market'), is, like Levoča, easy to reach from Poprad and the High Tatras. Once one of the most important Spiš towns, its houses with overhanging eaves and wooden gables are distinctive of all Spiš towns. The town is dominated by its Protestant church, a huge building constructed in the 1880s by an architect named Theophil von Hansen, who also supervised the building of much of late nineteenth century Vienna; like the church at Levoča, its building was financed by the wealthy merchants of the town. Protestant churches are rare in Slovakia and the lack of decoration inside the church is startling: the tomb on the right-hand side is of Count Imre Thököly, a Hungarian (hence the tricolour) Protestant leader who led the Kuruc Revolt against the Habsburgs in the late seventeenth century. Next door to the church is a huge wooden Protestant church (plastered on the outside) built in 1716 and in theory able to seat 1,500 people. Its Teutonic grandness (it was also built by a German architect) could not be any further removed from the tiny traditional East Slovak wooden churches that exist in villages around here. It was built of wood because of the regulations of the Diet of Sopron (1681) which allowed Protestants in Hungary to build their own churches, but only if they were outside the town walls, and constructed of wood without stone foundations. The ceiling paintings were damaged in 1922, when the houses nearby caught fire, and the whole church was doused with water to prevent it from igniting too. There are plans to use the building as a local museum; in any case, the building has been closed for many years.

Both these churches are situated outside the town's old fortification walls. The main town is situated along a square and two streets which lead off it, with the main square forming the apex of a 'v' shape arangement. In the centre of the main square is the Renaissance Town Hall, dating from the sixteenth century, with the clock tower and façade added in 1799. Near the main square (take Dukelská street, then Kostolné street to the right) is another tiny square, Požiarnikov Námestie, which contains the Catholic Church (sv. Kríž) built in the fifteenth century but with a Renaissance belfry next to it, built 100 years later, whitewashed and adorned with decorative gables and *sgraffito* designs at the top. The church itself has magnificent Gothic vaulting and an altar-piece built by a student of Master Pavol of Levoča. Along the right-hand fork from the main square is the castle. Once owned by the local Hungarian aristocrats, the Thököly family, who turned it into a sumptuous residence, it was taken over by the Habsburgs after the family supported the Kuruc revolt against their Imperial overlords. Its white plastered walls and gable-like crenellations are typical of the Spiš region. Some of the original fourteenth-century parts of the castle remain, such as the Gothic chapel (which was later given Baroque embellishments). Now, like many castles of its type, it is a heavily-restored and fairly dull jumble of rooms and exhibitions.

Eight miles (5km) due south of Kežmarok is the drab town of **Vrbov**, where the curious sulphur smell which hangs in the air along the road to the south of the town points the way (almost) to its open-air swimming pool, fed by the hot, gassy sulphurous which naturally bubbles up from the ground. There is a collection here of cheap restaurants, hotels and campsites, but despite its proximity to the Tatras the clientele is Slovak rather than international, which keeps the prices low and the level of decrepitude of the place high.

Further up along the main road from Kežmarok, **Stará L'ubovňa** is similarly forlorn and neglected, with a back-of-beyond feel to it which it shares with many other Slovak towns. Overlooking the town is a partially ruined castle, built by the Hungarians to guard the northern border of their kingdom. It was later owned by a local Polish noble, to whom this part of the Spiš region was sold by the Hungarians, who wanted the money for military campaigns. The upper part of the castle was allowed to turn into a ruin, but the lower part was rebuilt as a Palatial residence, and this part is now a museum and memorial to those who were tortured in the castle by the Nazis. Behind the castle is an open-air *skansen* (folk museum) where villages from the surrounding, remote region of the Spišská Magura hills have been brought and reconstructed. Like many regions of Slovakia, this area experienced extreme poverty during the nineteenth century, and many people simply abandoned their cottages as they left the area, many going to the United States. The nineteenth-century wooden Orthodox church, richly decorated inside, is also typical of many remote regions of Northern Slovakia: ask around for the key.

The real reason for heading in this direction from Poprad, however, is to go rafting on the River Dunajec, which marks the border between Slovakia and Poland, to the north-west of Stará L'ubovňa. The place to head for is **Červený Kláštor**, the site of a former monastery, built in the early fourteenth century. One of its most famous abbots was one Brother Cyprian, who in 1768 was said to have invented a flying machine, which he glided from a hill near the monastery all the way to the High Tatras. Unfortunately the veracity of this considerable feat is not supported by any written evidence. Brother Cyprian was also a botanist and a scientist, and his former laboratory, as well as some Monks' cells can be seen today, but most of the building is now a catering school and district museum. At a landing site below the monastery, tickets can be bought for a raft trip along the river. Rafts are punted along by locals dressed in the traditional rafters' costumes, and the whole trip along the steep-sided limestone gorge and over its (usually) gentle rapids takes about an hour. The trip can also be organized from the Polish side of the river. A beautiful riverside path (red markers) also runs along the side of the gorge from Červený Kláštor (6 miles/10km in length). There are usually buses at the other end, taking people back to the start point. In September a canoe slalom is held on the river here. Note that the river forms an international border for most of the length of the raft trip, and in theory you are not allowed to cross over to the other side. The region around here is the Pieniny National Park, a remote limestone region which straddles the border. Maps are available for those who wish to plan walking trips in the area.

Further Information
— The Slovak Mountains —

Places to Visit

Žilina and Malá Fatra

Martin
Slovak National Museum
Muzeálna
Open: daily except Monday 8am-5pm.

Folk Skansen
On main road south of Martin
Open: daily except Monday, April to
September only.

Terchová
Budatín Château Museum
On the main street in village
Open: daily except Monday 8am-4pm.

Žilina
Považská Galéria
Námestie Dukla
Open: daily except Monday 10am
(11am weekends)-5pm.

The Western Tatras and Orava Region

Oravský Podzámok
Orava Castle
Open: May to October 8am-6pm
(4.30pm May, September, October),
daily except Monday.

Brestova
East of Zuberec
Orava Village Museum
Open: January to April, Monday to
Friday 8am-3pm; May to October
8am-4pm daily, except Monday.

Limestone Caves in the Low Tatras

Demänovská Jaskyňa Slobody
Open: mid-May to mid-September,
daily except Monday, tours on the
hour, every hour 9am-4pm.

Bystrianska Cave
Open: 1 April to 15 May, 16 September to 31 October, daily except
Monday, tours at 9am, 11am, 2pm; 16
May to 15 September, daily except
Monday, tours on the hour, every hour
9am-4pm.

Važec Caves
Open: as for Bystrianska Cave, above.

The Low Tatras

Liptovský Mikuláš
Hodža Museum
Tranovského 8
Open: Tuesday to Friday 9am-12noon,
1-4pm.

Král Museum
Open: Tuesday to Friday, 8.30am-
3.30pm. Saturday and Sunday, 9am-
12noon.

The High Tatras

Tatranská Lomnica
Tatra National Park Museum
Open: daily, 8.30am-12noon, 1-5pm
(mornings only at weekends).

Tatranská Kotlina
Belianska Jaskyňa Caves
Open: mid-May to mid-September,
daily except Monday, tours at 9.30am,
11am, 12.30pm, 2pm, 3.30pm. Rest of
year: daily except Monday, tours at
9.30am, 11am, 2.30pm.

Ždiar

Folk Museum
Open: daily 9am-4pm (to 12noon at weekends).

The Slovak Paradise and Spiš Region

Dobšiná Ice Cave
Open: mid-May to mid-September, daily except Monday, tours at 9am, 11am, 1pm, 3pm.

Levoča
St James's Church
Normally shuts daily at 4pm and is closed on Mondays. Tourists not admitted during services (which are frequent).

Museum and Town Hall
Opens: daily except Monday, 8am (Sunday 1pm)-4pm.

Spišská Kapitula
Spiš Castle
Open: daily except Monday, May to October only 9am-5pm.

Stará L'ubovňa
Museum
In castle
Open: weekdays except Monday 8am-4pm, weekends 9am-5pm.
Skansen, below castle: open daily except Monday 10am-11.30am, 12.30-4pm.

Tourist Information Offices

Čedok offices in:

Liptovský Mikuláš
Námestie Osloboditelov 6
☎ (0849) 22985

Poprad
Námestie Dukelskych Hrdinov 60
☎ (092) 23287

Ružomberok
Ulica Cervenej Armády 1
☎ (022) 22463

Starý Smokovec
On main street in town, just above railway station
☎ (0969) 2417

Tatranská Lomnica
Lomnica Hotel
☎ (0969) 967428

Žilina
Hodžova 9
☎ (089) 23347

There are many private tourist and accommodation offices in the main centres of this region.

10 • Central Slovakia

This chapter essentially revolves around four main urban centres, Banská Bystrica, Zvolen, Banská Štiavnica and Kremnica. The focus of the chapter is not so much upon walking, although possibilities are suggested, but more on the treasures to be found in the numerous surrounding small villages, from which many urbanised Slovaks are but a generation removed. The regional capital is Banská Bystrica, easily the largest town in the area (population 85,000) and with the best road and rail communications. In terms of the number of hotels and restaurants available here (and it being the only place with anything resembling a night-life), it is probably the best bet for a base from which to explore the region. Banská Bystrica was the centre, during World War II, of the Slovak National Uprising which took place over 2 months in late 1944, when partisans came down from the surrounding hillsides and occupied the town. Monuments to this brave but ultimately costly action cover especially the area between Banská Bystrica and Zvolen. As retribution the Nazis destroyed many of the small villages in the vicinity, killing many civilians, including women and children; some of the villages have had to be completely reconstructed since the end of the war. Many of the towns described in this section, including Banská Bystrica, were medieval mining towns; the prettiest of these to visit is undoubtedly Banská Štiavnica, which seems to be in the process of revamping itself as one large mining museum. This is probably the highlight of the region though art lovers might want to head for Zvolen, whose château now houses a very good art museum. Kremnica gained fame for its coin mint. When its castle finally reopens after refurbishment, it will be one of the most attractive destinations in the region. The area also has one of the most scenic railways in the country (from Banská Bystrica east along the Hron valley to Košice), which makes it a pity that the services are so infrequent.

The villages of the region have their fair share of ruined castles and châteaux. Many still hold the scars of the German response to the Slovak National Uprising and so many hold monuments dedicated to the 30,000 or so who lost their lives. There are a plethora of interesting churches (the most unusual is the large wooden church at Hronsek) and remarkable folk

CENTRAL SLOVAKIA

architecture (there is an especially good folk festival held at Detva) as well as caves, nature reserves and recreational lakes all of which linked, more or less, by hiking trails. The most attractive hiking trails are to the south of Banská Štiavnica, though the area between Banská Bystrica and Kremnica is also popular. Just for good measure, the region also boasts a couple of reasonable spa towns, the largest being Turčianské Teplice.

Banská Bystrica

Banská Bystrica is the administrative capital of Central Slovakia. Silver was mined here at least as far back as the eleventh century and between the fourteenth and sixteenth centuries the town was one of the most important copper-producing centres of Europe. An important centre of Communism between the two World Wars, Banská Bystrica played a significant part during the Slovak National Uprising when for 2 months from 29 August

1944 it was the seat of the illegally formed Slovak National Council; Nazi units recaptured the town on 28 October 1944, though it was 'liberated' by Soviet troops relatively soon after on 26 March 1945. The timber, engineering, textile and cement industries arrived during the Communist era.

The main bus and train stations are 10 minutes walk east of the town centre. The heart of the old town is the Square of the Slovak National Uprising (námestie SNP) originally formed in the thirteenth century. At the eastern end of the square there is a clock tower dating from 1552 (it leans noticeably from the vertical) which also used to serve as a watch tower and during the eighteenth and nineteenth centuries buglers' concerts held in the top gallery could be heard down below in the square. Adjacent to this, at the south-eastern corner of the square, is the baroque church of Francis Xavier which was built in 1715 (the two towers were added in 1844). A little way westwards along the southern side of the square, beyond the information office, is the so-called Thurzo's House created in 1495 from two older burghers' houses and intended as a representative building for the Fugger-Thurzo mining company. In the early sixteenth century it was given a Renaissance façade and today it houses the town's Historical Museum. In the archway of the house at number 7 is the fragment of a medieval wall painting. Across the other side of námestie SNP at number 16 is Beniczky's House, one of the most beautiful houses on the square, created in the last third of the sixteenth century from two Gothic burghers' houses. The Renaissance portal is decorated by Szentiványi's coat of arms, the arcaded loggia was added in the seventeenth century by the Italian architect Jacopo di Pauli. A little way back up the square (towards the clock tower) is the baroque Bishop's Palace which was built in 1787 under the reign of Berchtold. The house at number 22 is remarkable for its precious portal and vaults and its Renaissance bay dating from 1636. In the middle of the square there is a volcanic-looking fountain and a black obelisk — a monument to the Soviet army.

The oldest part of Banská Bystrica is the area of the town castle which is situated just off the north-eastern corner of námestie SNP. The large Church of the Assumption of the Virgin Mary was originally built in the thirteenth century in Romanesque style; in the late fifteenth century it underwent substantial Gothic reconstruction and it was given a new baroque interior and furnishings after a fire of 1761. Its most famous chapel, completed in 1509, is dedicated to St Barbara, the patron saint of miners. The altar comes from the workshop of Master Pavol of Levoča (see previous chapter). Behind this stands the younger Church of the Holy Cross, next door to which is the Matthias House, a five-storey late Gothic building with a Gothic portal and stone console balcony named after the Hungarian king Matthias Corvinus who used to reside here. On the façade are the coat of arms of the

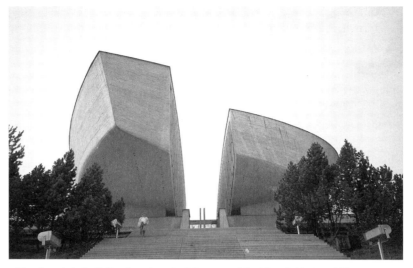

The futuristic building housing the Museum of the Slovak National Uprising in Banská Bystrica

town and of King Matthias and the year 1479. The Old Town Hall originally dates from the year 1510 and contains Gothic, Renaissance and baroque elements. In time of war it was used as a bastion and it presently houses the town's Art Gallery. The gallery mainly puts on temporary exhibitions culled from its collection of twentieth-century Slovak artists. The Barbican (1521) next door, once the entrance to the castle, also shoulders some of the burden of the gallery. The Barbican Tower's present day appearance dates from after the fire of 1761. It has three bells, the largest of which weighs 99 quintals. The column of the Virgin Mary was moved here from the main square in the 1960s.

Beyond the castle area the road splits into Horná and Skuteckého. The former is the more attractive with houses covering late Gothic, Renaissance, baroque and *fin de siecle* styles. During August 1944 the house at number 21 housed the Independent Slovak Transmitter. Skuteckého leads you in the direction of the Jewish cemetery where the town's most famous painter Dominik Skutecký (1849-1921) is buried. His detailed work, often of local scenes, is represented in the Old Town Hall Art Gallery.

Leave námestie SNP at its south-eastern corner along Kapitulská then turn left along Cikkera which will lead you to the great symbol of the modern town, the Memorial to the Slovak National Uprising (designed by Dusan Kuzma in 1969), looking something like a giant intergalactic hard-boiled egg that someone has sat on and sliced in half — the architect's own explanation is that the dividing line between the two segments symbolizes the great breakthrough which the Slovak National Uprising represented in the history of the Slovak people. It is actually a museum containing weapons, clothing, documents and photographs commemorating the uprising. In the surrounding park there are two medieval bastions and the scant remains of the town's fortifications as well as a World War II Outdoor Museum of sorts with an aeroplane armoured train, Soviet and German tanks, cannons and a partisan bunker.

The Slovak National Uprising

The first ever Slovak state was actually established between 1938 and 1939 while Hitler was helping himself to large portions of Bohemia and Moravia. Initial Slovak enthusiasm for their new country was quickly dampened however when it became clear that they had little real independence from Germany and realising this many Slovak soldiers left the army to join the partisan groups hiding in the mountains. By 1944 partisan activity in the hills around Banská Bystrica had become widespread and the London-based government-in-exile began preparing plans for a national coup to coincide with the expected imminent arrival of the liberating Soviet troops. On 29 August 1944 with the Red Army seemingly poised to enter Slovak territory the uprising was officially declared on Independent Slovak radio and the partisans came down from the surrounding hillsides, quickly establishing control over the region and setting up a governing Slovak National Council in Banská Bystrica. Unfortunately however the expected Soviet advance took longer than expected; supply lines had been stretched to the limit and it eventually took several months and 84,000 lives to wrestle the Dukla Pass from the Germans. Even without their assistance the Slovaks kept going for nearly 2 months but on 28 October 1944 the Germans finally regained control of the region and the reprisals continued on for months after; whole villages were destroyed (women and children being among the victims) and in all some 30,000 Slovaks are thought to have died as a result of the uprising.

Leaving námestie SNP along Národná at its south-western corner we find at number 10 a neo-Renaissance style former bank and at the bottom of the street the Národný dom (National House) built between 1924 and 1929 according to the design of Emil Belluš which contains a hotel, a restaurant, a night-club and a theatre all in one building. The western end of námestie SNP narrows into Dolná which has been magnificently preserved. The dwellings here, built in Renaissance and baroque styles, originally belonged to rich burghers. The house at number 8 dates from the fourteenth century and over the entrance portal is the Latin inscription *Benedictio domini divites fac 1610*, meaning 'The Blessing of the Lord makes people rich'. It is called the Bethlen House because in 1620 an Hungarian Assembly elected the prince of Sedmohrad, Gabriel Bethlen, as king of Hungary here. The house at number 19 holds a massive chain used to close off the street at the time of the aforementioned assembly. At the end of the street is the small white Church of St Elizabeth, one of the oldest buildings of the town. Originally dating from 1303 it was rebuilt in baroque style in 1750. Inside is a precious Gothic vault and an altarpiece of St Elizabeth by Jozef Murgaš.

Running from námestie SNP at its most north-westerly exit (through a narrow arch) is Horná Strieborná. The house at number 16 bears the Latin inscription *Benedict domini divites facit AD1610*. Also down here is a very good restaurant called the Kurian which is open until 2am. At the end of Lazovná, the next exit on the northern side of námestie SNP (walking eastwards) is the building of the former evangelical school which today houses a literary and musical museum. At number 32 Lazovná is Slovakia's first kindergarten dating from 1829.

Near Banská Bystrica town railway station (not the main one but the one at the end of Národná) is the baroque chapel of St Jon of Nepomuk dating from 1770. Hiking trails lead from here up the hill Urpín (from where there is a good view of the Low Tatras ridge) to Vartovka, where a former watchtower against Turkish invasion was rebuilt as an observatory between 1958 and 1961.

In the Sásová district about 1¹/₂ miles (2¹/₂km) north of the old town centre is the small Gothic Church of the Hermit Saints Anthony and Paul dating from the first half of the fourteenth century. Further alterations took place in the first half of the sixteenth century under the direction of Master Anton Pilgram, architect of St Stephen's Cathedral in Vienna. The late Gothic high altar dates from around 1500.

In the southern part of town known as Radvaň there is a fourteenth-century Catholic church which was fortified against a Turkish threat and a monument to the poet Andrej Sládkovič who is buried in the cemetery at Kráľova (a little further south) as well as a sixteenth-century Renaissance manor house which belonged to the Radvanský family that now houses the regional archives, a late seventeenth-century manor house belonging to the Bárczy family and, in the middle of a modern housing estate, the Tihányi manor house which contains the science department of the Central Slovak Museum. A little further south of this is the village of Kremnička (still within the town limits) where between 5 November 1944 and 11 February 1945 as a response to the Slovak National Uprising the Germans killed 747 people

A picturesque setting for the lake at Štrbské Pleso (Chapter 9)

The summit of Lomnický Štít in winter (Chapter 9)

Orava Castle in the Western Tatras (Chapter 9)

The fortified religious centre at Spišská Kapitula (Chapter 9)

(including 211 women and 58 children). The victims were buried in mass graves; a pink stone monument marks the execution place.

Popular Slovak writer Jozef Gregor Tajovský was born in **Tajov** 5 miles (8km) west of Banská Bystrica. There is a memorial room dedicated to him in the house where he spent a good portion of his life. Both Tajovský and his wife, Hana Gregorová are buried in the local cemetery. Another memorial room, in the old school on Tajov square, is devoted to the inventor of radiotelegraphy Jozef Murgaš who was also born here though he spent most of his life in America. The oldest building of the town is the church, originally built in Gothic style. It was rebuilt and enlarged in Renaissance style and then again in baroque style during the eighteenth century. A myriad of hiking trails lead from Tajov, Kordíky and Králiky across the Kremnica range of hills and back via Suchý Vrch (2,624ft/800m) to Banská Bystrica.

North of Banská Bystrica

Eight miles (13km) north of Banská Bystrica is the village of **Špania Dolina**, with one of the most beautiful locations in Central Slovakia. Declared a reserve of folk architecture in 1960, this town, formerly devoted to copper mining, is now renowned for its lace-making and during the summer it is not unusual to see women making lace in the streets outside their houses. Small former miners' houses stand around the dominant white church and pepper the hillsides. The nearby village of **Baláže** (only accessible from Špania Dolina on foot) was destroyed by the Nazis on 20 March 1945 and rebuilt at the end of the war by youths from Bulgaria, Greece, Yugoslavia, Canada and the USA. Memorials today commemorate the events of the Slovak National Uprising.

Accessible by bus or an infrequent train from Banská Bystrica 10 miles (16km) along the Harmanec valley is the **Izbica karst Cave**, discovered in 1932 and opened to the public in 1950. There is a railway station at the cave's entrance and from the terrace at the entrance there is a good view of the Veľká Fatra mountain range. The length of the sightseeing circuit that the public is taken on is 2,361ft (720m). Bones of primeval animals have been found in the Dolná and Horná Túfna caves in the Harmanec valley but these are not open to the public. The rail line that leads up the Harmanec valley is one of the most beautiful in the country. It has twenty-two tunnels, the longest of which is 1,475ft (4,498m) long.

The town of **Staré Hory**, 10 miles (16km) north of Banská Bystrica, is one of the very oldest mining settlements — there is evidence of copper being mined here in 1006. In the town stands an originally Gothic Church of the Virgin Mary featuring a very precious sixteenth-century sculpture of the Virgin, a spring with a statue of the Virgin (an important pilgrimage site) and a baroque building of the former mining office.

Turn left off the main road at Staré Hory to reach the small village of **Turecká**, located in a narrow valley in the Velká Fatra. Some houses which formerly belonged to miners here have been converted into weekend cottages and indeed this is quite a popular place to begin walks as there is a chairlift leading from the village to the top of Križna (5,163ft/1,574m) from where it is an hour's walk to the summit of Ostredok (5,223ft/1,592m), the highest peak in the Veľká Fatra. The views on this walk are quite spectacular and on a clear day you can even see as far as the peaks of the High Tatras. The slopes of Mount Križna are very steep, having been created by avalanches. In 1924 the biggest recorded avalanche on these slopes killed eighteen people in the nearby villages of Prašnica and Rybie. Every year a race is held from the top of Križna to Turecká using two-person home-made peasant sleds known at 'krnačky'.

Further up the road from Staré Hory, a total of 17 miles (28km) from Banská Bystrica, is the settlement of **Donovaly** which claims to be the second largest ski resort in Slovakia (the place, renowned for its wealth of flowers in the spring, is consequently much given over to recreational facilities). The focal point for skiers is the hill Zvolen (4,599ft/1,402m) while down in the town probably most noteworthy of attention is the classical church featuring an altar painting of St Anthony by the local painter A. Stollman and an organ dating from 1850. Many houses in the town are in fact precious relics of folk architecture while in front of the Sport Hotel there is yet another memorial to the Slovak National Uprising.

East of Banská Bystrica

Seven miles (11km) east of Banská Bystrica stands the town of **Slovenska Lupča**, over which stands a mid-thirteenth-century Gothic castle. Owned in the fifteenth century by the great Hungarian king, Matthias Corvinus, it is presently used as a seminary. Down in the town there is a Gothic church built between 1611-20, a mid-eighteenth-century Marian column and a Town Hall dating from 1659. A short detour from here would take you to the village of **Podkonice** which boasts a baroque-classicist church dating from between 1813 to 1819. Inside is a Gothic statue of the Virgin dating to the second half of the fifteenth century.

Further on along the Hron valley from Slovenska Lupča is the spa of **Brusno**. Five springs of mineral water (used for the treatment of the digestive system and gall bladder) were discovered here in 1829. In the spa area of the town there is a chapel dating from 1910. The original spa buildings were built in classical style. In the main part of town there is a fifteenth-century church built in Gothic style.

A little further up the valley is **Nemecká**. Just before the town itself is the stone figure of a kneeling woman with hands outstretched, a memorial to the 900 people killed by the Germans in January 1945 in a lime-quarry located at the entrance to the Ráztocky valley. As well as Slovak partisans some Soviet and French partisans, members of an Anglo-American military expedition and a number of local women and children were murdered.

The section on the Low Tatras in the previous chapter has information on the area to the east of Nemecká, including the Hron valley east of Brezno, and the southern limb of the Low Tatras around Hotel Srdiečko.

South of Banksá Bystrica

There is a Gothic church dating from the thirteenth century and an eight-eenth-century classical church in the town of **Horná Mičiná**, 5 miles (8km) south-east of Banská Bystrica. An other mile (2km) further south in **Dolní Mičiná** there is a Renaissance castle dating from the second half of the sixteenth century which used to belong to the Beniczky family. In the nearby village of **Čerín** is the early fourteenth-century Gothic Church of St Matthew, close to which is a wooden belfry.

From here continue south-west along the road to Sliač until you reach the village of Vel'ká Lúka where you should detour right to **Hronsek**, home to one of Slovakia's more unusual wooden churches. The church was built at the height of the Counter Reformation in 1726 when Protestants were only allowed to build their churches under special conditions; the building had to be made entirely of wood (there is not a single metal nail), the belfry had to be separate and the entire construction had to be completed within a year. The 110 pews inside are capable of holding about 1,000 people. In order to look inside one must recover the key from the local priest who lives nearby; the address should be posted. Also in the town is an eighteenth-century baroque manor house that used to belong to the Geczy family.

From Hronsek it is a short drive or two stops on the railway to the spa town of **Sliač**. The curative springs here were known about since the mid-thirteenth century though they were not fully exploited until the nineteenth century. For a long time the springs were considered to be harmful because of the number of dead birds and animals found near the mouth of the source. It was not until the eighteenth century that it was discovered that the carbonated waters, though safe for humans, could asphyxiate small animals. Heart and blood circulation problems are treated here. The nearby airport, Tri duby, until recently used by the Soviets, was an important partisan airforce base during the National Slovak Uprising and so in the spa park there is a monument to the dead war pilots. The actual town of Sliač was formed by the merger of two thirteenth-century fishing villages on either side of the River Hron; Hájniky on the west bank and Rybáre on the east. In

Hájniky there is an early Renaissance manor dating from the mid-sixteenth century and an early thirteenth-century Gothic church renovated in 1668 after damage sustained from the Turks in 1627. From Silač it is a mere 3 miles (5km) south to Zvolen.

Zvolen

The site of Zvolen has been inhabited by man as far back as the fifth century BC. Archaeological finds from Pustý hrad (site of the original town castle) and the large Lužice burial ground date back to the Bronze Age and there is also evidence of a Celtic settlement here and of a Roman foray into the

Zvolen Castle, now an art gallery

region. During the sixth century Slavic tribes settled here and silver is known to have been mined here as far back as the twelfth century. In 1244 Zvolen was granted a town charter by Hungarian King Béla IV and between 1370 and 1382 King Louis the Great built a huge hunting lodge in the style of an Italian castello on the hill above the town. This subsequently became one of the favourite residences of King Matthias Corvinus after whose death in 1490 Johann Thurzo, a Hungarian magnate and mine-owner, took over the building and converted it into a fortress. As the century progressed and the Turkish threat became ever greater the castle became linked to the town's fortifications. In 1628 the Eszterházy family acquired the property and began converting it into a grand residence. A large hall was created in the west wing in 1712, its ceiling decorated with portraits of the Holy Roman Emperors up to the reigning Charles VI, and in 1784 the chapel was given a baroque renovation. Today the rather stern looking castle, thoroughly restored between 1956 and 1971, houses an art gallery displaying a range of mainly fifteenth- to eighteenth-century European masters including Hogarth, Breughal and Caravaggio. Another section concentrates on the work of sixteenth-century sculptor Master Pavol of Levoča while the top floor houses temporary exhibitions of modern Slovak art.

In the late nineteenth century, after the construction of a railway linking Budapest to Banská Bystrica, Zvolen became an important railway junction with maintenance workshops and in the park below the castle there is an armoured train, one of three made in Zvolen during the National Slovak Uprising. The train was made in 2 weeks and could hold up to seventy men and on 21 September 1944 it took part in a battle at Stará Kremnička. Zvolen was liberated on 14 March 1945, and the military cemeteries east of the town house nearly 17,000 Soviet and 10,000 Romanian soldiers who gave their lives for the liberty of Southern Slovakia.

At the heart of the town is the long square námestie SNP which is dominated at its northern end by the Gothic Church of St Elizabeth. Originally built between 1281 and 1290, it was reconstructed in 1500 when it was given a charming Renaissance decoration. In the middle of the southern end of the square are monuments to the SNP and the Soviet army. The former Town Hall at number 21 on the square houses the local history museum with exhibits covering archaeology, furniture, clocks, china and folk costumes. Short term exhibitions are also held here. A plaque commemorates the election here on 30 October 1847 of L'udovít Štúr to deputy of the Hungarian Assembly. Also of note on the square is the house at number 70 dating from the sixteenth century which has a beautiful oriel window on corbels, next door to which at number 71 is an originally late Gothic house reconstructed in baroque style that has some remarkable arcades in the yard.

The town's main railway station (1951) was built on top of some mineral springs and one of the springs is actually in the concourse of the station. Opposite the railway station and behind the bus station is the huge Technical University, near to which is the Old Jewish Cemetery where in the winter of 1944 to 1945, 127 people were murdered by the Nazis. On the hill above the railway station are the extensive ruins of the old Zvolen castle (Pustý hrad), eclipsed and deserted after the construction of the present day castle in 1370 to 1382. The climb is quite steep but it offers a good panorama of the town. In the very northern part of town, known as Borová hora, there is an Arboretum belonging to the Technical University which is particularly renowned for its rose growing. To the south-east of the town, the Môtová reservoir is a popular recreational area. In the winter it serves as an ice-rink.

South and East of Zvolen

Ten miles (16km) east of Zvolen, via the village of Zvolenská Slatina, stands the small agricultural settlement of **Očová** renowned for its strong folk traditions. First written mention of the village comes from 1406 when it was inhabited by royal hunters. Destroyed by the Turks several times the village was only given market rights in the eighteenth century. The Catholic church is a fourteenth-century Gothic construction later rebuilt in baroque style. A sixteenth-century relief by Master Pavol of Levoča has been preserved in the altar and the church also features the gravestone of the Turkish soldier Arnaut who joined the community. The village also boasts a Reformed church dating from 1785 with an altar painting by J.B. Klemens (1868). Beyond the village of Očová is a blue walking trail leading down the Hrochot valley. Until the 1970s a narrow-gauged railway used to run down here. The trail passes beyond the impressive rocks known as Jánošikova skala and Bátovský balvan to the lumber settlement of Kyslinka (3 hours 15 minutes) and finally to the Poľana chalet (6 hours).

Nine miles (14km) east of Zvolen, along the main road to Lučenec, is the village of **Vigľaš**, above which stand the ruins of a fourteenth-century castle that was fortified against the Turks, rebuilt in the nineteenth century and then demolished in February 1945. The nearby village of Pstruša has the dubious distinction of holding the record for the lowest temperature ever recorded in Slovakia (-41°C/-42°F on 11 February 1929).

The town of **Detva** is 15 miles (24km) east of Zvolen. During the nineteenth century the town was most famous for its specially salted sheep cheese (*bryndza*) but nowadays most people come here for the town's excellent folk festival, held every year in the second week of July, when locals present themselves in their richly embellished traditional costumes and demonstrate their traditional songs and dances. Through the town traditional stone houses have been preserved, as have their richly engraved gates and the carved wooden peasant headstones found in the local grave-yard. Detva is also another starting point for walks to the Poľana chalet (4,284ft/1,306m) via either the interesting rock formations at Kalamárka (on the red trail, 3 hours 15 minutes) or the high waterfall Bystré (on blue and then green after Skliarovo, 3 hours 30 minutes). The walk from Poľana chalet to the peak of Poľana mountain (4,782ft/1,458m) takes an hour. Poľana chalet could also be reached from Hriňová (about a 2¹/₂ hour walk), though the town has little to recommend it.

The small village of Podzámčok, (6 miles/10km) south of Zvolen on the road to Krupina, basically rose up around the thirteenth-century castle of **Dobrá Niva**, built to defend an important trade route. In 1583 it successfully fought off a Turkish attack but in the eighteenth century the building fell into disrepair and today only one wall remains from the original two-storeyed palace. A mile (2km) south in the town of Dobrá Niva itself there is a Catholic church originally built in Romanesque style in 1241, though rebuilt in baroque style during the seventeenth century, and some interesting stone semi-detached houses with common gates and yards dating from the nineteenth century. From Dobrá Niva it is a 3-hour walk westwards along the yellow path to Tri Kamene (2,736ft/834m) in the Štiavnica mountains. The path continues on to Banská Štiavnica. If travelling by car, one could return from Dobrá Niva to Zvolen via the villages of **Bacúrov**, where there is a late eighteenth-century baroque church, and **Ostrá Lúka**, where there is a Renaissance manor dating from 1636 to 1641 that was partially rebuilt in the mid-eighteenth century and which today houses the state archives.

West from Zvolen to Banská Štiavnica

The village of **Budča** 3 miles (5km) west of Zvolen in the Hron valley, was the seat of the second Czechoslovak parachute brigade during the National Slovak Uprising. Its Catholic church dates from the fourteenth century and was rebuilt in the seventeenth and eighteenth centuries. By the Budča railway station there is the beginning of a 3 mile (5km) long path through the **Boky Nature Reserve** which ends near the town of Hronská Dúbrava. The portected hillsides of the reserve feature many precious species of flora and fauna and oak trees up to 200 years old as well as a huge volcanic rock called the Čertova skala (Devil's Rock).

On the road south from Budča to Banská Štiavnica one will pass through the towns of **Kozelnik** (which has an eighteenth-century coach house and traveller's inn) and **Banská Béla** where there is a late thirteenth-century Romanesque church enriched by Gothic and Renaissance decorations (around which is a defensive wall) and a smaller church of the Virgin Mary dating from 1708 which has a rococo chapel (1756). From Banská Béla it is about 2 miles (4km) south-west to Banská Štiavnica.

The historical importance of **Banská Štiavnica** is due to its gold and silver mines. The first documentary mention of a mining settlement here is in 1075 when there was already a castle in the town. In the twelfth century German miners arrived here and replaced the open-cast mining then used with underground mining. Local mining activity reached a peak in the late fifteenth century but then went into a slight decline. The town was fortified and the 'New Castle' was built in the mid-sixteenth century in response to the Turkish threat (they had taken Buda in 1541) and improved mining techniques in the seventeenth and eighteenth century — such as the use of gunpowder and steam-powered engines. In 1760 the world's first Mining Academy was opened here, though the seams became exhausted in the early nineteenth century and since then the town has stagnated; the Mining Academy was closed in 1918 and today the population of the town is a mere 10,000.

The old centre of Banská Štiavnica

Walking to the old town centre up the hill from the bus station (along Andreja Kmeta) to the right one will eventually come across a sculpture of Andrej Kmet, the founder of the Slovak National Museum. His robe shows him as a priest, the book as a scientist, the rose as a botanist and the urn as an archaeologist. A little behind the sculpture is the Church of the Assumption of the Virgin Mary dating from the thirteenth century, though rebuilt in classical style, beyond which may be found a Botanical Garden founded in 1938 which features some two hundred timber species from around the world. The large complex of buildings across the street from the sculpture of Anrej Kmet is the so-called Kammerhof which was formed from several Romanesque houses that were joined together around the mid-fifteenth century to house the royal mining chamber. The two Renaissance bastions formed part of the sixteenth-century fortifications. The building presently houses that part of the town's Mining Museum concerned with mining technology.

Continue up Andreja Kmeta to námestie SNP where you will find backing onto you the Gothic Church of St Catherine, originally built in 1500. Its late Gothic vault, figurative consoles and spiral staircase are sixteenth century. The beautifully decorated yellow building on the corner of the square is the so-called Fritz's House, presently the seat of the State Central Mining Archive. Before going into the church take a look at the Town Hall next door (there is a very good information office inside). The present day look of the building dates from 1788 as does the clock, unusual in that the

St Catherine's Church, in the centre of Banská Štiavnica, on the sloping square námestie Trojičné

small hand shows the minutes and the big hand the hours. Opposite the Town Hall is a late eighteenth-century Lutheran church, built shortly after the 1781 Edict allowing greater religious tolerance in Slovakia. The entrance to the church of St Catherine is on Trojičné námestie. In the middle of the square stands a very impressive Holy Trinity Statue built in 1710 by Dionýz Stanetti. Half way up the square to the right is the Berggericht, built in the fifteenth century as the seat of the Court of the Hungarian Mining Towns and given its present baroque appearance in the eighteenth century. Today the building houses that part of the town's Mining Museum dealing with mineralogy. A little further up from this is an art gallery named after the local painter Jozef Kollař which houses temporary exhibitions.

At the back of the Town Hall you will find a sculpture of the Virgin Mary (1748) and steps leading up to the Old Castle. This was originally a thirteenth-century Romanesque church that was converted into a castle in the mid-sixteenth century during the Turkish invasion of Hungary (the fortification is also where the precious metals were stored). Presently undergoing restoration, there are plans to establish a museum devoted to the history of mining in Slovakia within.

Return down the steps and begin walking up along Sládkovičova. To the right is the newly-restored, gleamingly-white Renaissance Belházy house (1616), one of the former residences of the Mining Academy and now a hospital. Further up the street, again to the right, is the Klopačka tower (1681) in which is situated the 'clapper'. Every morning at 5am the miners of the town used to be woken by the sound of an oak hammer being hit against a wooden board and today there is a 'clapping' every day at 10am during the summer months. There is another mining museum annexed to the tower with a display of various miners' lamps and tools. Further up the road, on the left, is the Church of the Virgin Mary (1512) just opposite which is the Piarist Gate, built in 1554 as part of the fortifications to defend the town from the Turks. Only one of the bastions presently survives. The other was destroyed during World War II. From here one could walk to the white-washed Renaissance New Castle built in 1571 upon Frauenberg hill as a watchtower against Turkish attack. A bugle is sounded from here every 15 minutes and a bell every hour. The building houses a museum dedicated to the anti-Turkish struggles of the sixteenth and seventeenth centuries. Alternatively, a further mile (2km) along the road from the Piarist Gate — one could either walk or wait (and wait!) for a bus — is an outdoor Mining Skansen. Above ground there are various mining towers, miners' houses, workshops and the like while underground there is a half mile (1km) long mining shaft that one may only visit as part of a group of fifteen or more — one might have to wait for an organized tour party to turn up. Hard hats and overcoats are provided.

One final place that may be visited in the town is the Štiavnica kalvária standing on the volcanic mountain Scharffenberg which you will probably have seen approaching the town. A zig-zag path, along which are seventeen stations of the cross dating from 1751, leads up to a two-storey baroque chapel at the top of the hill.

Around Banská Štiavnica

The two most popular recreational areas near to Banská Štiavnica are around the nearby lakes at **Richnavské**, and **Banský Studenec**. Both lakes were constructed in the early eighteenth century and provide starting points for walks in the surrounding hillsides. Probably much more worthwhile though is a visit to the late baroque château at **Antol** (1744-50), 2 miles (4km) south-east of Banská Štiavnica, which was constructed to symbolize the divisions in the year with 4 entrances, 52 rooms, 12 chimneys and 365 windows. The château was built by the Hungarian general Andreas Kohar on the site of a former castle and is furnished with valuable paintings, prints, daguerreotypes and hunting trophies. The most interesting rooms are the Louis XVI-style Audience Room, the early eighteenth-century rococo Chinese Salon, the Golden Salon and the small Gaming Room. Around the château is a 74 acre (30 hectare) park, with small lakes, waterfalls, a cave and an aqueduct which merges with the surrounding forest.

A green-marked walking trail leads from Antol through the village of **Elija**, where there is a small thirteenth-century Romanesque church, to Sitno (3,301ft/1,009m) the highest hill in the area and once the site of an old hill-fort. Today there is a watchtower on the top, built by the Kohary family in 1727, housing a museum of history and nature. There are a plethora of hiking trails leading down from the top, probably the most attractive leads down to the lake Počúvadlo from where one could return to Banská Štiavnica via Štiavnické Bane, where there is an eighteenth-century monastery and two surviving bastions, or Štefúltov where there is a late baroque church (1799) with a still-intact late baroque interior. Another place one could potentially walk from is Prenčov, a little further down the road from Antol, where there is a memorial room to the Slovak patriot Andrej Kmet in the rectory. Kmet, who founded the Slovak National Museum, was a priest here for 30 years. There are two churches here; the Catholic one dates back to the eighteenth century and the Protestant one to 1900.

Podhorie is a small village lying to the north of Banská Štiavnica. A shortish walk north of the village is the ruined castle of **Žákylsky.** The village itself boasts a baroque church (1717) and a wooden belfry in the cemetery. To the north-west of this is the old spa of **Skelné Teplice** which has twelve thermal calcium sulphur springs (temperatures vary from 39 to 52°C/102 to 126°F). A little way south-east of here is the former spa of **Vyhne** which has a baroque church (1776), above which is the 'kamenné more' ('sea of stone') nature reserve.

Žiar to Turčianske Teplice and Martin, via Kremnica

Žiar is most famous for its aluminium works, said to be the largest in the world, and is a town split pretty evenly either side of the main road with no discernible centre but a few good restaurants. The only point of interest is in the southernmost part of town where there is a former Bishop's Palace which has been converted into a school with a memorial room to Stefan Moyses, the first chairman of the Matica Slovenská — an institution founded in 1863 dedicated to the promotion of the Slovakian language, culture and education (as opposed to the then dominant Hungarian). A mile (2km) east of Žiar, at the turning to Kremnica, are the impressive hill-top ruins of **Šášov Castle**, first mentioned in 1235 and abandoned at the beginning of the eighteenth century. The only thing of any interest on the main road north to Kremnica is in the village of **Horná Ves** where there is an eighteenth-century baroque Holy Trinity column which originally stood in the town square in Kremnica.

Silver was mined in **Kremnica** as far back as the eleventh century; in the thirteenth century gold mining was started. One year after being granted royal privileges in 1328 the town began minting silver coins, and 6 years later, gold ones. Kremnica eventually became the most important mining town of Upper Hungary. Commemorative coins and medals are still minted here though the town's heyday was between the fourteenth and sixteenth centuries after which mining became steadily less profitable. Other industries rose to take its place and today Kremnica is an important centre of lace and ceramic production.

Standing above the town is the Town Castle complex, built up between the second half of the thirteenth century and the end of the fifteenth century. This functioned as the seat of the royal court and the storage place of the precious metals extracted here. On the left as one enters the complex is the round thirteenth-century Romanesque Charnel House above which is a fourteenth-century Gothic chapel dedicated to St Andrew. A covered stairway leads to the so-called Parish Bastion. At the centre of the complex is the two-nave Gothic Church of St Catherine. The bell tower is the former castle keep. Next to the church is a fourteenth-century Clock Tower, while opposite the portal of the church is the fifteenth-century Old Town Hall used by the town council until 1560.

The unwieldy town square below has existed in its present shape since the early fourteenth century and is surrounded by the originally Gothic houses of the most important burghers that have taken on Renaissance and baroque characteristics over the centuries. The grey and white Town Hall at the top of the square has served that function since 1783 when the original Gothic house here was rebuilt and enlarged. The Catholic Parish House next door dates its present day appearance from the second half of the eighteenth century. The house at number 7 houses the Museum of Coins and Medals (and indeed paper money) while at the bottom of the square there is a Franciscan Church and Monastery (1660) next to which is a Ski Museum of all things (it is not so odd really, the nearby Kremnica mountain range has several ski resorts). The Mint at number 24 is a nineteenth-century building of fourteenth-century origin — there is no admission. The 66ft (20m) high Plague Column in the middle of the square was built between 1765 and 1772 according to the design of Dionýz Stanetti (who designed the one in Banská Štiavnica).

Around the main square runs the town's fifteenth-century fortifications. Only one gate has been preserved (leading to the bus station). In 1530 a barbican was built in front of the gate, the semi-circle bay window over the portal was built to provide the guards with a better view. The fortification wall runs from the Black Tower, near the bus station, to the Red Tower, which once functioned as a prison. A short walk east of the centre along Malinovského there are a couple of original-style miners' houses and in front of the Miner's House at number 362 (present number 494/40) there is a small late baroque chapel. There are some more similarly preserved wooden miners' houses in the mining village of Kremnické Bane, 2 miles (3km) north of Kremnica. It goes without saying that Kremnica is obviously an ideal place to begin a walk in the Kremnica mountains.

The road continues north from Kremnica to **Turčianske Teplice** — included in this chapter more for the sake of completeness than anything else as one may well need to change bus or train here. It is a very modern and very dull spa town that is not recommended as a destination in its own right. Boring and charmless by turns, it is not even a viable base for exploring the Veľká Fatra as there is nowhere for non-patients to stay. By far the brightest thing in the town is the sky-blue bathhouse known as the Modrý kúpel. The road continues on to the town of Martin, a good base from which to explore Malá Fatra and Veľká Fatra (see previous chapter).

Further Information
— Central Slovakia —

Places to Visit

Antol
Château
☎ 239 32
Open: Tuesday to Sunday 8am-3pm.

Banská Bystrica
Historical Museum
Thurzo Palace
SNP námestie
☎ 251 93
Open: Monday to Friday 8am-4pm, Sunday 9am-4pm.

Art Gallery
Old Town Hall
Moysesovo náměstí
☎ 24167
Open: 9am-5pm Tuesday to Friday. Saturdays and Sundays 10am-4pm.

Museum of the Slovak National Uprising
☎ 25781
Open: 8am-6pm (8am-4pm October to April) closed Mondays.

Museum of Literature and Music
Lazovná 44
☎ 23690
Open: Monday to Friday 8am-4pm and on Sundays in summer.

Natural History Museum
Tihányi Manor House
Radvaň
☎ 31994
Open: Monday to Friday 8am-4pm, Sunday 9am-4pm.

Banská Štiavnica
Mining Museum
Trojičné náměstí
☎ 22544
Open: May to September 8am-4pm, April and October 8am-2pm, closed Mondays.

Jozef Kollař Art Gallery
Trojične náměstí
☎ 23431
Open: 8am-3pm, closed Mondays.

Klopačka (The Clapper)
Sládkovičova
☎ 23765
Open: May to September 8am-3pm,
closed Mondays. October to April
Monday to Friday 8am-3pm.

New Castle
☎ 21543
Open: May to September 8am-3pm,
closed Mondays.

Open-Air Mining Museum
☎ 22971
Open: 8am-4pm, closed Mondays.
April to October only.

Harmanec
Caves
☎ 981 22
Open: May to October 10am-4pm,
closed Mondays.

Kremnica
Museum of Coins and Medals
Štefánikovo náměstí
Open: 8.30am-1pm and 1.30-5pm
Tuesday to Saturday. Sunday 9am-
3pm.

Ski Museum
Štefánikovo náměstí
Open: 8.30am-1.30pm and 2-5pm,
closed Mondays.

Tajov
Tajovský's House
Open: by appointment ☎ 972 01

Zvolen
Art Gallery
Inside the Château
☎ 243 11
Open: 10am-5pm, closed Mondays.

Town Museum
Námestie SNP 21
☎ 235 26
Open: 9am-5pm Tuesday to Friday
and Sundays.

Tourist Information Offices

Banská Bystrica
Čedok
Náměstí Slobody 4
☎ 32575

Slovakotourist
Dolná 6
☎ 23025

Intertour
Partizánska cesta 9
☎ 44783

Banby Tour
Ul. ČSA 14
☎ 52565

Banská Štiavnica
Čedok is on Akademická though a
better source of information is the
Town Hall on Antona Pecha.

Cultural Events

Banská Bystrica boasts an opera house
(Divadlo J.G. Tajakovského) and also
a puppet theatre on J. Kollara. Anyone
looking for something slightly more
upbeat could head either for the
Melod Club or the Omega Club (both
on Skuteckého), both of which have
discos or live bands most nights. In
June and July plays and operas are
performed in the courtyard of Zvolen
Castle, check also for performances at
the Tajovský Theatre in Zvolen (221
91 or ask at the information office on
the main square). Cultural events of a
varying kind are held during the
summer months in the spa of Sliač and
the folk festival held at Detva in the
second week of July is recommended.

11 • Košice and Carpatho-Ruthenia

Eastern Slovakia is arguably where visitors after the 'real' Slovakia will find it: away from the commercialism and bustle of Bratislava or the High Tatras, this is a region where traditionalism is still important and where visitors are still uncommon enough for locals to view them, by turns, with suspicion, interest or profound disdain — but never with the indifferent cynicism that comes from the impact of tourism in areas such as the High Tatras. Košice is the principal town in the area and one through which most people are likely to pass. Interesting in its own right, it is located centrally enough for many day trips to be made into the surrounding countryside. To the south-west, around Rožňava, Hungarian-speaking villages pepper the bleak countryside — but the principal attractions lie underground, in the fabulous limestone caves of the Slovak Karst. To the north is the land of the Rusyns, the peoples of Carpatho-Ruthenia who follow their own Uniate religion and whose tiny rural communities often focus around distinctive wooden churches. In the very easternmost corner of Slovakia, Zemplínska šírava — a large man-made lake — is an obvious draw, as are the low mountains, the Vihorlat vrchy, which come down to its northern shores. Unlike other parts of Slovakia, there is a patchwork of cultures and landscapes here — from bleak limestone moorland and deserted beech-covered mountains to the flat Zemplín plains which stretch on into the Ukraine and Hungary; and the peoples include significant gypsy, Ukrainian and Hungarian minorities, whose presence many Slovaks feel unhappy about, even though their communities have existed here for centuries. All, though, are united by a common history — one of poverty, hardship and emigration to better opportunities elsewhere. All of which makes travelling in this neglected, isolated part of Europe an exciting experience.

Košice

The city of Košice is the capital of Eastern Slovakia, and the region's principal transport centre. This means that most people visiting the region are likely to find themselves at least passing through Košice or, more probably, staying there. Košice is so accessible, and on so many transport

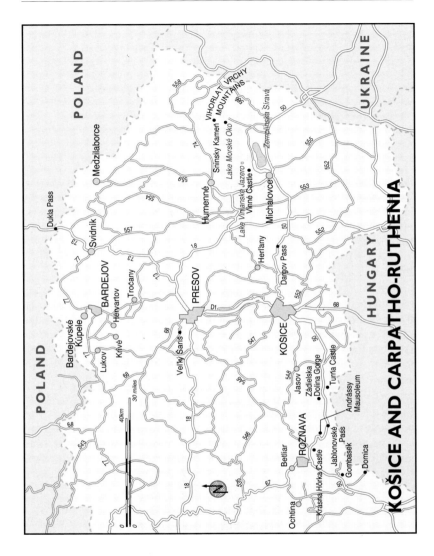

routes, that it is in fact difficult for travellers in Eastern Slovakia to actually *avoid* passing through it. It is a stop on the north-south rail routes linking Cracow (Poland) with Miskolc and Budapest in Hungary. There are through-trains running into Ukraine (and even to Moscow and Kiev), and trains west to Poprad (frequent; 1 hour 30 minutes), Prague (10 to 11 hours, some overnight trains with sleeper and couchette cars), Bratislava (via Poprad and Žilina; frequent — about 8 hours), Brno and many other places in the Czech and Slovak Republics including Cheb, the westerly-most town in Bohemia.

By road, Košice is 422km (262 miles) from Bratislava, 293 miles (473km) from Brno, and 414 miles (667km) from Prague. The E50 road from Prague via Brno, Trenčín, Poprad and Prešov runs through Košice and on through Michalovce to Kiev and Moscow. The E71 is a fast route that runs south from Košice to Budapest. Some people may want to fly to Košice, which is well served by internal flights from Prague and Bratislava.

The *Spiš Chronicle*, one of the oldest documents recording the history of Eastern Slovakia, tells that a monastery was founded at Košice in 1216. Other, less easily authenticated records tell of the present day site of the city being inhabited by Slavic peoples as long ago as 400BC. Whatever its origins, the town's importance began to grow during the fourteenth century, when the first ramparts surrounding the town were constructed. By 1400, Košice was one of the most important cities in the Hungarian empire after Buda (now part of Budapest), and was (and sometimes still is) known by its Hungarian name, Kassa. The town played an important part in repelling the Turks from Hungarian territory, and in fact it became the capital of Hungary for a short while in its own right, after the fall of Buda to the Turks.

The character of the town changed in the nineteenth century when industry arrived, including a steelworks, and during this time there were increasing demands from the citizens of the town to be released from the control of an increasingly brutal Hungarian government. During World War II the town was occupied by Hungarian forces and in 1945 it became one of the first Slovak towns to be liberated from Nazi control by the Russian Army as it swept westwards through Czechoslovakia. Later in the same year, it was briefly the capital of a newly-liberated Czechoslovakia before Prague was liberated and was made the capital. Tremendous growth since 1945 has meant that the population has swelled, making it the largest city in Slovakia after Bratislava. Now it is the natural focal point for two of Slovakia's minority peoples, the Hungarians and the gypsies, both of which have become the subject of recent unwanted attention from the new ultra-right wing groups which have grown up in Slovakia since 1989.

Košice is one of the most important industrial cities in Slovakia, but this fact does not seem to lessen the character of the city and there is much here to interest visitors. At the centre of the town is a long, elongated square, called Námestie Slobody, lined with buildings that used to house the offices of the Hungarian administration. In the middle of the square is **St Elizabeth's Cathedral**, the biggest church in Slovakia, built between 1382 and 1508. The western façade is framed by two towers, one tall and octagonal, the other squat with Gothic detailing. Both the exterior (the striped roof tiles are similar to those on St Stephen's Cathedral, Vienna) and the interior (full of exuberant Gothic detailing) are worth seeing. St Elizabeth was the daughter of King Charles of Anjou, with whom the city had a long argument (concerning its perceived monopoly of the salt trade, through which its merchants became wealthy and funded the building of the cathedral). The huge winged altar showing scenes from her life contains forty-eight panels and was built in the 1470s. Elizabeth was noted for devoting her life to the poor, sick and elderly, and was canonized in 1235 (only 4 years after her death). The relief work above the north and west doorways depicts the Last Judgement and Christ and the Disciples on the Mount of Olives. In May and June the organ in the church is used for the Košice International Organ Festival. In a crypt on the left hand side of the church is the tomb of Ferenc Rákáczi II, a Transylvanian prince who led Košice's struggle against the ruling Hungarian Habsburgs in the eighteenth century, and whose remains were brought here from Turkey in 1906. Next to the cathedral is its belfry, called the Urban Tower, built in the sixteenth century but reconstructed in 1628, with the arcade around the bottom dating from the 1940s. In the arcade are gravestones, with German inscriptions, from the cemetery that used to surround the cathedral. The building was damaged in a fire in 1966 and extensively rebuilt. It houses a museum of metal working. The attractive building of the State Theatre, dating from the nineteenth century is also an obvious feature of the square. A pleasant area of greenery and fountains separates the cathedral and the theatre.

Beyond the theatre, on the right, on the corner of Adyho Street and the main square, is a Jesuit church, dating from the seventeenth century. Walking down Adyho Street brings one to the buildings of the Košice Museum, and the Katova Bastion, part of the defences from the medieval era which also houses a museum. A little way beyond these buildings, walking along Hrnčiarska Street and then turning left along gen Petrova Street, brings one to **Jacob's Palace** (Jacabo Palác), an interesting looking pseudo-Gothic mini-palace built by a rich Hungarian aristocrat at the beginning of the twentieth century. The fact that Edvard Beneš, the first president of Czechoslovakia after World War I, lived in this house is recorded by a plaque on the wall. The interior of this building is not open to the public.

There are a number of museums in Košice. On the main square, at number 72, is the art gallery Východoslovenská Galéria, which exhibits twentieth-century paintings and sculpture by Slovak and Hungarian artists. Just up from this, walking away from the theatre and cathedral, one comes to the Technical Museum, on the same side of the square. This museum, like that in the Urban Tower, in the centre of the square next to the cathedral, concentrates on the wrought ironwork that has traditionally been manufactured in this region. Here the square simply narrows into a road, but walking up this road brings one to the square Maratónu Mieru and the East Slovak Museum (Východoslovenské Múzeum), with displays relating to the archaeology and history of Eastern Slovakia and — more interestingly — the Košice gold treasure in the basement, a hoard of 3,000 gold coins dating

The north doorway of Košice Cathedral

from between 1400 and 1700. The coins were all minted at Kremnica (see previous chapter) and were hidden by city burghers in the 1670s when Košice was under threat of being taken by Hungarian rebels. They were discovered by builders in 1935, renovating a house on the main square in which the money was walled up. Behind the museum is a tiny wooden Uniate church, originally from Carpatho-Ruthenia and reconstructed here. Another part of the same museum is at 10, Pri Miklušova Väznici Street, approached from the main square along Adyho Street. From the sixteenth century these two houses were the location of the **Mikuloš Prison** (Miklušova Väznica), and along with displays relating to the history of Košice there are medieval torture chambers, secret passages and cells dating from this time. Next to this building in the Katova Bastion on Hrnčiarska Street is a zoological museum.

Košice has quite a strong cultural life. Aside from the Hungarian and Slovak theatre performances, there are regular concerts in the cathedral or at the Dom umenia on Ždanovova, and operas are performed in the grand theatre across the small park from the cathedral.

Eleven miles (18km) north-east of Košice is the geyser at **Herľany**. The village is reached by taking the E50 towards Michalovce and turning left (north) after 10^1/$_2$ miles (17km) on the minor road leading towards Vranov nad Toplou. The geyser gushes every 32 to 35 hours for a period of about 20 minutes and the water jet is anything up to 131ft (40m) high. After this the water and carbon dioxide must accumulate again beneath the surface of the ground for the next eruption to take place. The geyser was discovered in the 1870s by accident, when speculators were digging into the ground, trying to find out whether there was enough natural warm water in the area to merit the construction of a spa (there was not). One should enquire at the Čedok office in Košice (in the Hotel Slovan, at the southern end of the main square), to find out when the geyser will be active. The same information is also available by telephoning 116 and listening to the recorded information (in Slovak only) about the weather conditions in the area, which is followed by an indication of the next time the geyser will play. Try asking a hotel receptionist to ring this number and listen for you. Neither source of information is particularly reliable.

Košice is excellently placed for a number of day excursions. Most places mentioned in this chapter are within a comfortable day trip by car from Košice, although those using public transport will find that travel times are so much longer by bus or train to make journeys of any length impracticable.

South-West from Košice

The area to the south-west of Košice, like many parts of Eastern Slovakia, receives few visitors. It is a barren region of rocky moorland and limestone outcrops, with remote agricultural settlements and hill-top castles dotting the countryside. Close to the Hungarian border, the region has very strong cultural connections with that country, with large Hungarian-speaking communities in many places, particularly around Rožňava. There are also a number of large gypsy communities. In the village of Medzev, in 1990, the gypsies complained that they were being discriminated against by the Slovak authorities in terms of housing provision — to which the authorities responded by bulldozing the gypsy residences and re-housing them all in cheap prefabricated houses on the outskirts of town. This incident, which has parallels in many parts of Eastern Slovakia, is indicative of the problem, which the gypsy community is seen as being.

Once the area became wealthy through the mining of ores (iron, copper and gold). Now little mining takes place, and a dusty air of neglect has fallen across many of the towns, where any evidence of previous prosperity is limited, if visible at all. The principal attraction in this area are the stunning limestone caves of the Slovak karst, and Rožňava is the best base from which to see some of the area, though many places are also accessible on day trips from Košice, particularly for those with a car.

The limestone in this region is up to 1,640ft (500m) thick in places, and water flowing through this rock has created a number of underground caves with their fascinating stalactite and stalagmite formations that are the result of millions of years of geological evolution. In contrast to the Slovak Paradise (see previous chapter), the attractions of the Slovak Karst lie mainly underground. Four of the caves have been opened to the public. In addition to the caves, there are two castles in the region which might be worth visiting, and there are numerous possibilities for walks in the deserted countryside with its high bluffs and narrow valleys. The map *Slovenský krás: Domica* is a good investment and shows most of the places covered in this section. Over the border in Hungary there are more caves (the Domica cave system actually runs under the border; in Hungary it is known as the Aggtelek system), although (at the time of writing) the border crossings at Domica and Turna nad Bodvou could only be used by Slovaks and Hungarians. Western nationals must use the crossing places much further away from this region to get into Hungary, making visiting the Aggtelek region from this part of Slovakia difficult.

It is 43 miles (69km) from Košice to Rožňava, along road 50 (E571). There are a number of interesting things to see along this road. Twelve miles (19km) from Košice at Moldava nad Bodvou there is a road leading to the right to **Jasov** and its cave, called Jasovská Jaskyňa. The cave was hollowed out by the underground River Bodva. Archaeological evidence attests to the fact that this cave was inhabited in the Stone Age (footprints of Palaeolithic man have been discovered here), and the cave itself used to be inhabited by the monks of Jasov Monastery; graffiti scrawled on the cave walls by Czech Hussites in 1452 can be seen. The cave is seen on a tour 2,034ft (620m) in length. The monastery in the village is considered to be one of the most impressive baroque structures in Slovakia. Although founded in the early Middle Ages, its present buildings all date from the eighteenth century. The monastery is currently being restored and may be opened to the public one day. There are impressive ceiling and wall frescoes inside, and the buildings are set in a huge park. The cave at Jasov is not the most spectacular in the region — there are better examples of underground limestone formations beyond Rožňava. However it is still worth seeing, if only because it is far less busy than the other caves in the region. Another 6 miles (10km) beyond Moldava nad Bodvou, **Turňa Castle** looms into view on the right, above the road on a vineyard-covered hillside (access to the castle is difficult; the best view of it is from the road).

A few miles further on along the road is the **Zádielska Dolina Gorge**, one of the most interesting sights of the Slovak Karst area. Access to the gorge is from a car park in the village of Zádiel, which the main road bypasses; the gorge can only be seen on foot, by walking through it along the red-marked path which begins in the car park at Zádiel. The road along the bottom of the gorge, although metalled, cannot be used by private motorists. The entrance to the gorge, which is visible from the main road, leads into a steep, narrow valley, which leads off the main wide valley of the River Turňa. The gorge itself is 2 miles (3km) long, and in some places is only 33ft (10m) wide with soaring, vertical limestone walls up to 1,312ft (400m) high. The River Blatnica, whose erosive action formed the gorge, still flows down the middle of it. It takes an hour to walk up to the gorge — a pleasant but spectacular stroll. There are other possibilities for hiking in this region: for instance there is a blue-marked track which runs along the top of the gorge and then takes one down to Turnianske Podhradie, to the east of Zádiel; there are also paths across the hills to Jasov.

Beyond Jablonov nad Turňo the road ascends the **Jablonovské Pass**, which crosses over a low arm of the Slovak Ore mountains. There are excellent views to the west as one descends the pass on the other side, over to Rožňava and Krásna Hôrka castle, on its distinctive hillock. At the bottom of the pass, on the right, is the **Andrássy Mausoleum**, built in 1904 and reputedly the most beautiful art-nouveau building in Slovakia. The mausoleum is a small, simple domed structure, set back from the road in its own carefully tended gardens, close to a big motel and in sight of the castle where the family of its deceased incumbents lived. It was built by Count Dionysus

Andrássy in memory of his wife, Francesca Hablatz, who was a Viennese opera singer. The interior is a riot of gold and marble; the sarcophagi, of the Count and his wife, are made from Carrara marble. The count was disowned by the Andrássy family because he did not marry a member of the aristocracy. Even those who do not decide to look at the castle, a little further on, should stop off here for a while. **Krásna Hôrka Castle** itself can be seen from miles around. It sits on top of a conical hill which rises above the village of Krásnohorské Podhradie. Motorists must turn off the main road and drive through the village to reach the castle. The first castle was built on this site in 1320; later reconstructions turned it into a Renaissance fortress against the Turks who always threatened to extend their vast empire into Slovakia. From the sixteenth century the castle was the seat of the Andrássy family. In 1910, they turned the place into a museum all about themselves (having other castles in which to actually live), which still occupies the building, and which is not particularly inspiring, with displays of period furniture and weapons which must be seen on a guided tour (likely to be on offer only in Slovak). There is a folk museum in the village itself, which is much more interesting.

Just beyond the castle is Rožňava. Košice and Rožňava are also linked by a railwayline: Jasov is accessible on a minor branch line (change trains at Moldava nad Bodvou); use Dvorníky station for the gorge at Zádlel (short walk — the red-marked track up the gorge actually starts from the station here); use Lipovník station for Krásna Hôrka Castle (which is a fair distance away from the station). Unfortunately, the railway goes through a tunnel under the Jablonovské Pass, so rail travellers do not get the same views as road users.

The town of **Rožňava** itself is uninspiring, but it is an excellent base from which to see the Slovak karst, with its caves and gorges. It is the focus of public transport routes in the region (the main railway station is 1 mile/2km south of the town centre). There are a few hotels here. Rožňava grew up as a gold mining town in the Middle Ages, when it was populated by German mining prospectors; it became a bishopric and gained a mint. Those who have some time to spend in the town may care to visit the mining museum on Šafárikova Street. Round the back is a reconstructed mine shaft — the inscription *Zdar boh* means 'good luck'. The statue is of Lajos Kossuth, the hero of the Hungarian independence movement. There is a Renaissance observation tower on the town's main square. There is also a small Gothic cathedral (now parish church) in the town. Its sixteenth-century altarpiece shows scenes from the working life of the old gold miners who created this town's medieval prosperity.

From Rožňava, road 50 (E571) leads south towards Plešivec, Šafárikovo and Rimavská Sobota. The second village one passes through, travelling

Krásna Hôrka Castle west of Košice

along this road, is Slavec. After the village there is a turning off to the left, to the village of Silica. Along this road on the right is **Gombasek Cave** (Gombasecká Jaskyňa). This cave was discovered in 1951, and is famous for its slender white 'quills' that are anything up to 10ft (3m) in length, but only a few millimetres wide. Returning to the main road, one must continue south to the small town of Plešivec. From the junction in the centre of this town. A road leads left towards Dlha Ves and the **Domica Cave** (Jaskyňa Domica), which is reached after a short drive up a bleak valley. The Domica-Baradla cave system is 13 miles (21km) in length and is one of the fifteen longest cave systems in the world. In fact, the majority of the cave system actually lies under Hungarian territory, but nevertheless, the length of the tour taken on the Slovak side is about 1 mile (2km) in length, which normally includes a boat ride on the underground River Styx, which was responsible for hollowing out the cave on its three levels. On occasions, low water levels in the river may mean that this trip cannot be made. A number of archaeological finds have been made in the cave, including painted ceramics, from 5,000 years ago when it was inhabited by prehistoric man. A yellow-marked track runs from Gombasek towards Domica (3 hours in total); on the way the path passes an ice cave, called Silická l'adnica, which is closed to the public but you can see the ice encrustations around the barred entrance. Shortly after the ice cave you must change on to red markers and follow them over the bleak limestone hills to get to Domica.

To reach the **Ochtina Aragonite Cave** (Ochtynská Aragonitová Jaskyňa) one must head in a different direction to the caves mentioned above. From Rožňava, take the minor road leading west towards Štítnik and Jelšava. After the village of Štítnik, 8 miles (13km) from Rožňava, the road heads along a steep, narrow valley. At the highest point in the road, about 5 miles (8km) from Štítnik, is the car park for the caves, which cannot be reached by road. It is a walk of less than 1 mile (2km) to the entrance, up a fairly steep path. There are many pretty rock features in the cave, including the small aragonite 'flowers' which cling to the rocks like limpets, but the formations, while beautiful, are by no means as spectacular as those in the other cave systems.

Finally, at **Betliar**, on the right hand side of the road running north from Rožňava towards Poprad and the Dobšiná Ice Cave (see Chapter 9), there is a small hunting château, set back from the main road surrounded by its own estate. It was once a hunting lodge owned by the Andrássy family. Founded as a medieval fort, the Andrássy's gradually rebuilt it as a sumptuous hunting lodge in the heart of thick forests which, presumably, contained enough game for parties to stay here for long periods. Inside is a predictable array of hunting trophies, stuffed animals, hunting rifles and period furniture; the gardens, formally laid out in English style, have an array of small follies, rotundas, pavilions, sculptures and fountains.

North from Košice

Košice is the capital of Eastern Slovakia and is about as far east as most people get — if they get here at all. To the north is empty countryside consisting of rolling, forested hills dotted with tiny villages which might well be some of the most remote, tradition-bound and poverty-stricken rural communities anywhere in Europe. This is Carpatho-Ruthenia, an area with indefinable boundaries which roughly covers the part of Slovakia north and north-east of Košice, leading up to the Polish and Ukrainian borders. The people of the area are known as the Rusyns. They follow their own branch of the Greek Orthodox (or Uniate) religion and their attractive wooden churches can be found in many villages in this part of Slovakia. Mass emigration has affected this area more than any other part of Slovakia, as people tried to escape the poverty and lack of opportunity here; one émigré was Robert Maxwell, the former media mogul who set off from here on foot to sell trinkets on street corners in Bratislava. Others were the parents of the American artist Andy Warhol, and a museum has recently been established in the area from which they came. Travelling in this area by public transport is difficult, and many destinations are remote and only practical to visit by those who own a private car. Nevertheless, rewards for those who venture here are considerable — if only to glimpse an aspect of Europe that ought to be part of the past by now.

Geographically in the centre of Eastern Slovakia, **Prešov** is a bustling and pleasant market town (although there is little to see beyond its attractive main square) and is also a good base from which to see many places of interest in Eastern Slovakia. It is 22 miles (36km) due north of Košice along the E50 road. The town is an important industrial centre, particularly in the branches of food and engineering. Prešov is the cultural centre of the Rusyns in Eastern Slovakia, and bears witness to this in its architecture and history. It is also the centre of an important wheat producing area, and many agricultural markets are held here. The bus and train stations are ¹/₂ mile (1km) to the south of the main square, linked to it by most bus and trolley-bus routes.

The town's main square is called Námestie Slovenský Republiky. There are beautifully preserved eighteenth-century buildings along its sides, coloured in pastel shades with ornate gables and pediments. There are a

Prešov's town centre

number of interesting churches in Prešov, built in different styles and home to three different faiths. On the square, next door to Čedok, is the principal church of the Rusyns, known as the Grecko-Katolická Katedrále, where Eastern Orthodox decorations (including a huge iconostasis) fill the interior of a typically baroque Catholic church building. In the middle of the square is the Gothic Church of St Nicholas, dating from the fourteenth century, with a baroque altarpiece; the stained glass is modern and comes from Moravia. Behind it is a plainer Protestant church, built in the mid-seventeenth century. This region has always been sufficiently remote for religious reformism to be a powerful focus, and this Protestant church was established when many other parts of Slovakia were experiencing the full force of the counter-reformation. However, in 1684 the Habsburgs finally caught up with the Protestant reformers in Prešov, and twenty-four Lutherans were publicly hanged in the main square. There is a memorial to them which stands near by; the main figure is one Count Caraffa, who organized the trial. Also on the main square is the town's art gallery (number 326), featuring works of Slovak art, and the Town Hall, from whose balcony the Hungarian Red Army leader, Béla Kun, declared the existence of a Socialist Republic of Slovakia in 1919 (inspired by the recent Russian Revolution), a fact that Slovak Communists have commemorated ever since — although Kun had very little support for his actions. There are other fine old buildings in the town, in the vicinity of the square (including the so-called Rákociho dom, near the Town Hall, once the site of the town's museum which used to concentrate almost exclusively on its Communist past). There are also many areas of the town (particularly to the north) which consist of hideous, angular grey estates and government buildings, a reminder in concrete and stone of the architectural brutality of 1950s Stalinist Czechoslovakia.

The large ruined castle of **Veľký Šariš** sits on top of a high hill, 4 miles (6km) to the north-west of Prešov. There is a good view from the top. The castle dates from the thirteenth century and was burned out in a fire in 1687. The castle ruins can be approached from the village of Veľký Šariš, which is a turning off road 68 which runs north from Prešov. Note that 9 miles (30km) along road 18, which runs west from Prešov, is Spiš Castle, and beyond that, the historic town of Levoča; both are described towards the end of Chapter 9.

Just over 40km (25 miles) north of Prešov and close to the Polish border, **Bardejov** is one of Slovakia's best preserved medieval towns. Founded in the twelfth century and made a royal free town in 1376, Bardejov prospered during the fifteenth and sixteenth centuries due to its position on an important trade route between Hungary and Poland and the town became an important centre of cloth manufacture. The old centre of the town, about 5 minutes walk south-west from the bus and train stations, is still surrounded

The attractively preserved medieval centre of Bardejov

by much of its medieval fortifications and the old town square is surrounded almost entirely by attractive gabled pastel-coloured houses originally dating from the fifteenth and sixteenth centuries though rebuilt after numerous town fires. At the northern end of the square is the Gothic Church of St Giles originally built in the mid-fifteenth century on the site of a Cistercian abbey church though substantially restored after a fire in 1878. Inside are eleven side altars dating from the fifteenth and sixteenth centuries, the neo-Gothic high altar by Moritz Hölzel dating from between 1886 to 1889. In the centre of the square is the Renaissance Old Town Hall (1505-11) inside of which is an historical exhibition. At the southern end of the square on the corner of Rhodyho there is a museum housing the largest collection of icons in Slovakia (dating from the sixteenth to the nineteenth century) and a number of models of the region's Uniate churches, while a third museum, on Rhodyho, is devoted to nature. At the end of Rhodyho is the Gunpowder Gate. Visible to the right from here is the so-called Monastery Bastion. Eight of the town's bastions are actually still standing — the sloping Veterná street leads down from the main square to the most impressive, Hruba a Mala (Thick and Small) Bastion, which was at one time used as a granary.

A 2 mile (4km) bus ride north from Bardejov (or an hour's walk through the woods on the red trail) takes one to the quiet and pleasant spa town of **Bardejovské Kúpele**. The curative properties of the waters here have been known about since the thirteenth century though they were not commercially exploited until the mid-seventeenth century. In the late eighteenth century the place developed into a very exclusive aristocratic resort and among the visitors to the spa were Napoleon I's wife Marie Louise (1809), Tzar Alexander (1821) and the Empress Elizabeth, wife of the Habsburg Emperor Franz Josef (1895) in whose honour a row of lime trees was planted (there is also a bronze statue of her dating from 1903 in front of the Hotel Dukla). Unfortunately the resort was built largely out of wood and was for the most part destroyed by fires in 1910 and 1912. The spa has only really been revived to anything like its former glory since the 1960s when a number of modern hotels and bath houses were constructed. The waters are used for the treatment of diseases of the alimentary canal. There is a small museum in the town with a rare collection of icons, near to which is the entrance to Slovakia's oldest *skansen* (founded in 1955) featuring various constructions transported from the surrounding Šariš region, the centrepiece of which is a wooden Uniate church dating to 1706.

About 12 miles (20km) east of Bardejov is the town of **Svidník** which was almost completely destroyed during heavy fighting in October and November 1944. Unsurprisingly the town today is rather lacking in charisma though there a few points of interest. A couple of doors away from Čedok on the main shopping street is the Museum of Ukrainian Culture devoted to the folk traditions of the Rusyn people (there is a large minority in the town) while a couple of minutes from the bus station, on Partizánska, is the Dezidera Millyho Art Gallery which is largely devoted to the works of contemporary Rusyn artists but which also features some works by the Expressionist Milly and some icon paintings. Beside the main road leading to Bardejov there is a large white War Museum devoted to the bloody so-called Duklian Operations that took place to the north-east of the town during World War II. Clearly visible above the trees from here, past the display of tanks and planes, is the 121ft (37m) high Soviet War Memorial commemorating the estimated 84,000 Soviet soldiers who lost their lives during the operations. About 6,500 Czechoslovaks also died in the fighting. On the opposite side of the road from this, up the hill beyond the football stadium, there is a *skansen*. Amongst the farmsteads is a wooden Uniate church brought here from the nearby village of Nová Polianka in which services are still held.

The **Dukla Pass** is situated 9 miles (15km) north of Svidník. For many centuries it was the main mountain crossing point on the trade route from Hungary to the Baltic and from 8 September to the 27 November 1944 it was the scene of one of the toughest military operations of World War II when the Soviet army, with Czechoslovak support, fought to wrestle the pass from the hands of the Germans; some 300,000 soldiers were involved. Near to the border-crossing with Poland stands a large Monument to the 'Dukla Heroes', behind which is a cemetery with a statue of a woman giving thanks to a

The Dukla Pass, scene of some of the fiercest fighting during World War II

liberating soldier. Along the road from the memorial leading to Krajná Polana there is an open-air war museum featuring various tanks, aircraft, bunkers and the like, all of which were used in the fighting. The first Czechoslovak town to be liberated was Vyšný Komárnik (on 6 October), some 2 miles (3km) from the pass.

There are a large number of wooden Uniate churches in the villages of this region, built by Greek Catholic Rusyns (their religion is a combination of Greek Orthodox and Roman Catholic). Most date from around the eighteenth century and many are still very much in use today. The easiest way to see one of these churches is to visit one of the *skansens* at Bardejovské Kúpele, Svidník or Humenné but for anyone with the determination to visit one of the churches in situ there are a cluster of them to the south and east of Bardejov and to the north-west of Svidník on the way to the Dukla Pass. The latter group are very much more easy to visit for those without private transport as distances between the villages are small and there is a bus service running up and down the road to the pass. The key (*klúč*) can usually be gained from the local priest *(kňaz)* whose address will normally, but not always, be posted to the door. Sometimes there is a fixed charge, other times not — a contribution would be in order. Uniate churches are divided into three sections (from west to east: the entrance porch, the nave and the sanctuary). The screen separating the sanctuary from the nave is usually very richly decorated, only the priest is allowed to pass through its central door. A gruesome depiction of the Last Judgement usually covers the wall of the entrance porch (or narthex). High trees are often planted near to the churches to serve as lightning conductors.

The church of St Lucas in the village of **Tročany**, 7 miles (12km) south of Bardejov, was declared a national cultural monument in 1971. It was built in 1739 in the place of an older church, the seventeenth-century iconostasis and altar of which have been preserved within the newer structure. The church was restored in 1933 and 1968 and is particularly renowned for its lurid icon depicting the Last Judgement. About 7 miles (12km) north-west of Tročany in **Hervartov** is one of the most remarkable of all the churches, constructed out of red spruce between 1593 and 1596 though it has been renovated on several occasions since. The paintings within of *Adam and Eve*, *St George and the Dragon* and the *Wise and Foolish Virgins* date to 1594; they were restored during the 1660s and again in 1969. There is another church in **Krivé** about 6 miles (10km) north-west of here, dating back to 1826 and dedicated to St Lucas. A little more out of the way (9 miles/14km due west of Bardejov) is the church at **Lukov**, renowned for its fantastic depiction of the Last Judgement dating back to the sixteenth century. On the way from Svidník to the Dukla Pass there are churches at Ladomirová, Dobroslava, Hunkovce, Nižný Komárnik and Vyšný Komárnik — though two of the finest churches are a little to the south-east in Bodružal and Mirol'a.

The Greek-Catholic church was established within the Roman Catholic church by the Union of Brest-Litovsk (1596). Today the religion, tied to Rome but with most of the external forms of the Greek Orthodox Church, is the great embodiment of the identity of the Rusyn (or Ruthenian) people who are generally reckoned to have originated in the Ukraine and who settled in the hills that provided a natural border between Hungary and Poland. According to the last census some 40,000 people in Slovakia regard themselves as Rusyn. The first Rusyn nationalists, led by Uniate priests, emerged in the late nineteenth century as a reaction to the increasing attempted Magyarization of the Rusyn population. Poverty and the strangulation of Hungarian rule induced many Ruthenians to emigrate around this time, especially to the United States where they concentrated in Pennsylvania. After the Great War the province of Ruthenia was established within the new Czechoslovak Republic, situated to the east of the River Už and containing some 370,000 Ruthenians as well as large minorities of Hungarians, Jews, Germans and Romanians. A Rusyn minority of some 100,000 was meanwhile left to the west of the Už in the province of Slovakia. In March 1939 when the Germans marched into Czechoslovakia Ruthenia declared itself to be the independent state of Carpatho-Ukraine, though one day later it was annexed by Hungary with German approval. At the end of the war the Už river became the permanent border between Czechoslovakia and the Soviet Union and Ruthenia ceased to be. Following the Communist takeover, in an effort to destroy cultural individuality, the name Rusyn was declared to be an 'anti-progressive label' (they were henceforth to be known as Ukrainian) and the Uniate church was amalgamated with the Orthodox church with Pavol Gojdic, the church's only bishop, being thrown into Leopoldov prison where he died in 1960. In addition to this many tradition-ally hill-dwelling peasants were rounded up, urbanised and put to work in factories (thus encouraging assimilation with the Slovak community) and the language of instruction in Rusyn schools was changed to Ukrainian — of which the Rusyn language is a western dialect. It was only in 1968 that the ban on the Uniate church was finally lifted and since then the Uniates have spent most of their time arguing with the Orthodox church over the return of property handed over during the 1950s. Bishop Pavol Gojdic has meanwhile been canonised.

Buses wind their way from Svidník to **Medzilaborce** only very infre-quently so it is probably best to approach by train from Humenné instead (26 miles/42km to the south). The basic reason for coming here is to visit the Andy Warhol Family Museum of Modern Art which is difficult to miss as it has two giant Campbell's soup tins outside the main entrance. At first glance Medzilaborce might seem an odd place to house an Andy Warhol museum, indeed it does not seem any less odd after one has learnt the circumstances in which it came to be. Warhol (real name Andrej Varchola) was born in Pittsburgh but both his parents hailed from the village of Miková 5 miles (8km) north-west of Medzilaborce, from where they emigrated to the USA in 1918. In 1987, following Warhol's death, his elder brothers John and Paul journeyed to Slovakia to trace their family roots. The brothers generously offered to donate an original screenprint, the bright pink *Head of Cow*, to the art gallery in nearby Medzilaborce but were told in fairly plain terms that they could keep it. One revolution later the brothers, backed by some hard currency from the Andy Warhol Foundation for Visual Arts, had another go and in September 1991 the world's first Andy Warhol family museum was opened in the town's former Communist cultural centre — it was originally to be housed in the dilapidated former post office but the 6 million *koruna* renovation grant 'went missing'. The Warhol Foundation and the Warhol family donated twelve silk screens and fourteen paintings to the museum. They may well have wished they had not when in January 1992 (only 4 months after opening) the museum's dodgy heating system very nearly accounted for the all silk screen works. The damage (and the heating system) had to be rectified by the Warhol Foundation.

In addition to the Warhol exhibits, the museum puts on temporary art exhibitions and organises a varied programme of cultural events. The

One of the many wooden churches that can be seen in many parts of Eastern Slovakia; this one is at Ladomirová

gallery shop sells Warhol souvenirs (if one can refer to a tin of soup as such) as well as information on the Rusyn culture — Warhol and his two brothers were brought up speaking both English and Rusyn.

East from Košice

The E50 road runs east from Košice towards the only border crossing between Slovakia and the Ukraine, at Vyšné Nemecké-Užgorod (where, in theory, visas for Ukraine can be purchased on the spot by most western nationals — though do not bank on this). The main features east of Košice are the Vihorlatské Vrchy, a desolate area of low mountains covered with beech forests, which rise from the northern shores of Zemplínska Šírava (the 'Slovak Sea'), a large man-made lake which is popular in summer with sunbathers, anglers, boaters and watersports enthusiasts.

Road 50 (E50) links Košice with Michalovce, 37 miles (60km) to the east. After passing through the small town of Svinica, the road goes over a low range of hills called the Slanské Vrchy, via the **Dargov Pass**. In 1944 this pass was the scene of heavy fighting between the Soviet Red Army and the occupying Nazi forces, during which 22,000 Red Army soldiers were killed. There is a high Victory Memorial by the road side and a rose garden next to it. The road descends from the Dargov Pass onto the Zemplín Plain, which stretches east into the Ukraine and south-east into Hungary.

In **Michalovce** there are three hotels. Although it is not a place to linger, the Zemplín Museum, concerned with the area, is next to the bus station, and the Čedok office for this region is in the town's main street. Along the northern shores of Zemplínska Šírava there are other hotels and many camp sites.

Zemplínska Šírava, just beyond Michalovce, is a large reservoir, covering an area of 13sq miles (35sq km). Those who are not staying in Michalovce can simply travel through the town and onto the road that runs along its northern shore, linking all the resorts. The shores of the southern side of the lake are inaccessible; all the resorts are on the northern and western sides. The chief resort is Hôrka. Other resorts include Biela Hora (on the western shore), and Medvedia Hora and Kamenec which are beyond Hôrka on the northern shore. There is little difference between the resorts as all are pretty soulless and grey. Tourist cruise ships ply between the resorts, and it is possible to rent small boats, swim and sunbathe on the beaches. Beaches are, of course, a rarity in Slovakia, and the area is crowded in high summer (and dead for most of the rest of the year). The area is hotter, and has more hours of sunshine every year, than any other place in the Czech and Slovak Republics.

The small village of Vinné is immediately to the north of the lakeside town and resort of Hôrka. It is reached by a turning off the road which runs along the northern shore of the lake. From the church in the middle of the village, there is a marked track which runs up to the ruins of **Vinné Castle** (Viniansky Hrad), which are situated on a hill high above the village, inaccessible by road. It takes half an hour or so to reach the castle, up a very steep slope and along a path which is not properly marked (in theory, one should follow the blue markers almost all the way up to the castle, and then the yellow markers up the last slope). The ruins are more extensive than they appear from the bottom of the hill, and are eerily neglected and overgrown with trees that seem in some places actually to sprout from the castle walls. There are good views from some parts of the castle, however.

A road continues on from Vinné towards Humenné. The next village beyond Vinné, continuing in a northerly direction and travelling away from Zemplínska Šírava, is Chemko Strážske, with its associated **Lake Vinianské Jazero**. This is a much nicer lake than Zemplínska Šírava, though it is far smaller in comparison — more, in fact, of a large pond rather than a serious lake. It is much more pleasant to swim here than at Zemplínska Šírava, and there is the usual collection of boats to hire and narrow beaches from which to swim. The lake is pleasantly situated in the low hills of the Vihorlatské Vrchy. By the bus stop on the southern shores of the lake is the start of another, longer path up to Vinné Castle (1 hour 30 minutes, yellow markers).

The Vihorlatské Vrchy are a pleasant range of low volcanic hills that lie immediately to the north of Zemplínska Šírava. Their southern slopes, rising from the northern shores of the lake, are covered with vineyards. They are really another part of the Carpathians — as are all the mountain ranges in Slovakia. By far the nicest part of the hills is around the **Lake Morské Oko**, set in a beautiful isolated position surrounded by low hills and overlooked by a rocky peak called Sninsky Kameň. It is reached by travelling along the road that runs along the northern shore of the lake from Michalovce, through the resorts of Hôrka, Klokočov and Kusín to Jovsa, at the far north-eastern end of the lake; then through the village of Poruba and at the next junction taking a left turn towards Remetské Hámre. The road continues through this village and terminates in a car park for the lake 6 miles (9km) from the village, from where the lake itself is a short walk (this road does not appear on some atlases and maps, though it is perfectly easy to drive along — in fact, buses and logging lorries regularly use it). It is a pleasant journey along the scenic valley of the River Okna to the parking area, where there are refreshments on sale in season. There is no swimming or boating in the lake itself, as it is in a nature reserve. The fact that it is in a nature reserve has unfortunately not prevented large-scale tree felling taking place in the area. In July and August there is an infrequent bus service from Michalovce right to the lake itself. At other times of the year buses only get as far as the village of Remetské Hámre.

Overlooking the lake is the rock outcrop **Sninsky Kameň**. It is 3,296ft (1,005m) high and provides a spectacular view over the whole of the Vihorlat region. It is interesting to walk up to it from Morsek Oko, following the blue-marked track which starts from the southern end of the lake (1 hour 30 minutes walking time). The path goes via sedlo tri table, a low pass. From the top of Sninsky Kameň, it is a walk of about $1^1/2$ hours back down the other side, via the village of Zemplínske Hámre to Belá nad Cirochou, from where there are trains back to Michalovce.

Sninsky Kameň and Morské Oko are both about 8 miles (13km) or so from the heavily guarded border with the Ukraine. One can often hear or see military activity in the area, although all the places mentioned above should stay open at all times. There is a detailed walking and touring map of the region, called *Vihorlatské Vrchy-Zemplínska Šírava*, but it is not very easy to find. Keep looking out for the map in bookshops in Košice or Michalovce, although it may be much easier to find it in bookshops in Bratislava, for those visiting the city and intending to journey on to this region.

Further Information
— Košice and Carpatho-Ruthenia —

Places to Visit

Košice
Východoslovenská Galéria
Corner of main square and Šmeralova
Open: daily except Monday, 10am-6pm (2pm Sunday).

Košice Museum
Urban Tower, on the main square and at Ulica Pri Miklušovej Väznici 10
Open: daily except Monday, 9am-5pm (1pm on Sundays).

East Slovak Museum
Námestie Maratónu Mieru
Open: as for Košice Museum, above.

Technical Museum
Námestie Slobody
Open: daily except Monday 8am-5pm (1pm Sundays).

North from Košice
Bardejov
Museum
Open: Tuesday to Sunday, 10am-4pm.

Bardejovské Kúpele
Skansen
Open: daily except Monday 8.15am-4.15pm; closed winter.

Medzilaborce
Andy Warhol Family Museum of Modern Art
Open: daily except Monday.

Prešov
Art Gallery
On main square
Open: daily except Monday 10am-6pm (1pm weekends).

Svidník
Galéria Dezidera Millyho & Skansen
Open: daily except Monday 8.30am-4pm (weekdays), 9am-2pm (weekends).

War Museum
Open: Tuesday to Sunday, 10am-5pm.

East from Košice
Michalovce
Zemplin Museum
Open: Tuesday to Sunday, 10am-4pm.

South-West from Košice
Andrássy Mausoleum
Open: daily, shutting at 6pm (April to September) and 4pm rest of the year. Closed for lunch 12noon-1pm.

Domica Cave
Open: mid-May to mid-September, daily except Monday, tours at 9am, 10.30am, 12noon, 2pm, 3.30pm. Rest of the year, tours at 9am, 11am, 2pm, daily except Monday.

Gombasec Cave
Open: 1 April to 15 May, 16 September to 31 October, daily except Monday, tours at 9am, 11am, 2pm. 16 May to 15 September, daily except Monday, tours on the hour, every hour, 9am-4pm.

Jasov Cave & Ochtina Aragonite Cave
Open: as for Gombasec Cave.

Krásna Hôrka Castle
Open: daily except Monday 8am-4.30pm (April to October) 9am-2.30pm (rest of the year).

Rožňava
Mining Museum
Šafárikova 43
Open: daily except Monday 9am-4pm
(1pm Sunday).

Ruined Castles
There is open access at all times to
Turna, Vinné and Veľký Šariš Castles.

Tourist Information Offices

There is a Čedok office in most large
towns in the region, which also deals
with accommodation:

Košice
Rooseveltova 1 (in Hotel Slovan)
☎ (095) 23121&20764

Michalovce
Námestie Osloboditelov 12
☎ (0946) 21455

Prešov
Slovenskej Republicky Rad 1
☎ (091) 24040

Rožňava
Námestie Baníkov 22
☎ (0942) 2343

Accommodation and Eating Out

ACCOMMODATION

Finding accommodation can sometimes present a problem in the Czech and Slovak republics as they continue to adjust to the market economy. Before 1989 visitors were traditionally just shepherded into pre-booked state-owned accommodation — often at grossly inflated prices. Anyone feeling a little nervous still has the option of booking accommodation from home at one of the Čedok offices, the only snag is that they generally only deal with the more expensive hotels in the largest cities. Good news though is that cheaper accommodation (ie mostly bed and breakfast or self catering flats) specialists are beginning to emerge. Here are a few addresses in England:

Czechbook Agency
52 St John's Park
London SE3
☎ 0181 853 1168

Czech-in Ltd
63 Market Street
Heywood
Rochdale OL10 1HZ
☎ 01706 620 999

Czechscene
63 Falkland Road
Evesham
Worcs WR11 6XS
☎ 01386 442 782

Czech Travel Ltd
21 Leighlands Road
South Woodham Ferrers
Essex CM3 5XN
☎ 01245 328 647

One can of course ring or fax a hotel but there is no guarantee that they will understand — try a bit of German and you should be okay. As a general rule though if one makes a habit of arriving in towns on a weekday within normal working hours few problems will be presented.

Hotels

The real problem following the fall of Communism is the lack of hotels catering for the cheaper price range. After having been sold off in state auctions or given back to their former owners under the restitution law many hotels are either undergoing modernisation or have been converted for another use. The new hotels that are being built are almost exclusively luxury ones, often with Western capital (expensive hotels will accept payment by credit card). Hotels used to be classified from A* de luxe to C according to price and facilities but most have now switched to the star system though be warned that prices and conditions can vary dramatically within each category and do not be incensed if you are being charged a higher price than domestic tourists as this merely reflects the gross disparity of incomes. The town's main Čedok office will have a list of hotels and their relative prices and should be prepared to phone ahead to check if there is space available (they also own some hotels). The addresses of Čedok offices are given at the end of each chapter. Alternatively, most hotels are predictably gathered on or just off the main town square or around the main railway station (or between the two). All but the most expensive hotels tend to be drab with grossly underlit corridors and quite sparsely furnished (often just a bed, table, chair and wardrobe). If you are lucky you may have a radio but it may well be permanently tuned to the state radio station, a Communist hangover. Televisions are more common in double than in single rooms, do not count on there being one and be prepared to pay extra if there is. Each room normally has a sink though hot water and heating can be erratic. Most hotels have a restaurant and some will have a bar. If breakfast is included you will be given a token to hand to the waiter in the morning. It usually consists of a large table spread of rolls, cheese, tomatoes, meat, eggs and the like and coffee or tea or hot chocolate. Single rooms can be hard to find and when you do they tend to be only just cheaper than a double so it may be a better idea if travelling alone (or even if not) to seek out a private room where prices are invariably charged per person.

Private Rooms

Since 1989 (before which they were illegal, though tolerated) there has been a rapid increase in the availability of private rooms which do a sterling job in plugging the gap in the market while the cheaper hotels sort themselves out. The best place to seek them out will be the town's main Čedok office; alternatively there may be agencies in town centres advertising their availability or else just knock where you see the 'Zimmer Frei' (or even occasionally 'Bed and Breakfast') signs. When not dealing through an agency one will obviously pay less and often if you just book in for a couple of days with an agency and then decide to extend your stay by a private arrangement with the owner you will be charged a cheaper rate (though do not bank on it). Most private rooms are kept to a very high standard of cleanliness and are regularly checked if being dealt with through an agency. One can never be entirely sure what one is going to get; in terms of living space it can often be much larger than a hotel room, your host or hostess may feel the urge to ply you with beer and food or you may not even see them. Cooking facilities (if there are any) and bathrooms may be shared but hosts are generally quite conscious of minding out the way. Breakfast is almost always available; it may be included in the price or it may not, so ask in advance. Hosts may be prepared to cook extra meals for extra money.

Youth Hostels and Student Accommodation

For an even cheaper bed one may prefer to seek out one of the limited number of youth hostels in the republics. It is worth bringing your own sleeping bag although some do rent out blankets and sheets. The CKM hostels (Cestovní kancelář mládeže) are affiliated to the IYHF (International Youth Hostel Federation). It is not necessary to have a card to stay here but there is a reduction if you do. Pressure on places is very high so book in advance if at all possible. In university towns during July and August student accommodation is let out very cheaply. Usually there are two or possibly three beds in a room which will be rented out as a unit to single travellers so it is not necessary to share a room and one also has the reassurance of possessing the only key. The rooms themselves are inhabitable if a bit tatty (it is student accommodation after all); there might be a sink or there might not. As well as these rooms there are usually also some dormitories so it is worth asking in advance. The local CKM office deals with all this. Their whereabouts are listed where appropriate in the Further Information section at the end of the chapters. Alternatively, if in Prague one may pay a visit to the main CKM office at Žitná 12, Nové Město, Praha 2 (☎ 02 20 54 46) for further information.

Camping

Campsites (*autokempink*) are quite plentiful, most are quite simple basic affairs (ie just a stretch of grass with basic toilet and washing facilities) though some are more extravagant with shops, swimming pools and restaurants. There are two categories, A and B. Many sites also feature bungalows — the cheapest are very basic wooden shelters with a hard bed and no heating while the more expensive are really just small chalets. Very few sites open all year round, most just from early May to mid-September. If in Prague one may pick up information on camping from Sportourist at Národní 33, Praha 1 or just ask at any Čedok office for a camping map (either inside or outside the country). In the Krkonoše and High Tatras Mountains there are a number of mountain huts called *bouda* or *chata*. These range in quality from very cheap wooden shelters to small hotels. None are accessible by road and one should not really take the chance of just turning up. To book in advance see Čedok in Vrchlabí for the Krkonoše and Slovaktourist in Nový Smokovec for the High Tatras.

Prague
The hotel situation in Prague is notoriously bad with just 10,000 beds in the city and most of them overpriced. If one is determined to stay in a hotel in Prague then one should seriously try to book a room before leaving home at Čedok (though their choice of hotels is limited and very expensive) or by contacting the hotel yourself by letter, telephone or fax. Čedok in Prague have a better selection though do not bank on any availability if turning up on spec. Do not waste your time walking around the city with a list of hotels, these places should be contacted in advance or not at all. Most people visiting the city choose instead to opt for a private room. There is a very large supply of these though in July and August the choice becomes smaller (do not worry, something will be available). AVE, Hello and Agentura are the names of three accommodation agencies which deal with private rooms, they have offices at the airport and main railway stations. These agencies should also have details of any beds available in student accommodation during July and August, their location is usually central and they are cheap but they can often be very noisy at night — they are places to drink and meet people rather than to get a good night's sleep. Official IYHF hostels are few and far between and often full though CKM at Žitná 12, Nové Město will have the details (☎ 02 20 54 46).

CURRENCY AND CREDIT CARDS

The Czech and Slovak republics now have completely different currencies though they both still use the *crown (koruna)* which is divided into 100 *heller (haléř)*. The old Czechoslovak notes and coinage are presently valid only in the Slovak republic but they are being gradually phased out — for the latest information ask at Čedok. The two currencies began at parity but the value of the Slovak crown has since fallen to about 80 per cent of the Czech one (making Slovakia a cheaper place to stay) so expect a different exchange rate for each country.

Traveller's cheques are the safest and easiest way to carry funds. Most banks will accept them (though try and opt for a well-known brand). Banking hours are Monday to Friday 7.30am-12noon and 1.30-3.30pm. Čedok only changes cash and one is strongly advised to consider taking an amount in Sterling, US dollars or Deutschmarks to see one through any potential inconvenience. Eurocheques are accepted in some hotels and shops, one can also use them to withdraw cash from most banks. Well-known credit cards are accepted in most of the more expensive hotels, restaurants and shops though it will be harder to find banks that will advance cash on them. If credit cards are lost phone the credit card hotline — ☎ 236 66 88.

EATING OUT

The most obvious place to go for a full meal is either to a restaurant (*restaurace*) or to one of the larger hotels. A *vináma* will always serve food but only wine, not beer. They are usually very smart establishments, often situated in historic cellars. To eat more cheaply one might prefer to visit a *pivince* or *hostinec* — basically lively, beer-stained and smoke-filled pubs. Very much lower down the scale are the stand up buffets offering anything from snacks to full meals which will probably be of most value when filling up at one of the railway stations before a hike as they generally open as early as 6am. The food served here can be of a quite decent quantity though it is worth remembering that probably the easiest foods to get food poisoning from are chicken and rice. As a final option there are often various street takeaway vans serving hot dog (*párek*), and open sandwiches. At present there are two Western fast food restaurant chains in the areas covered (there is a McDonald's in Brno and Ostrava) though there has been a great increase in the number of pizza parlours opening all over both republics producing fare of varying quality.

Because they tend to get up very early (about 5 or 6am) Czechs and Slovaks actually make little fuss of breakfast and tend to eat the main meal of the day at lunchtime — which accounts for the fact that some places may stop serving by about 9am or 10am though with the increase in tourists this trend is on the decline. A menu (*jídelní lístek*) is often available in German and sometimes in English. Often menus will list the price of the meal as regards to the weight listed, thus it is possible for the price to vary according to the size of the portion. Tipping only exists by rounding up the bill to the nearest few crowns. Occasionally there are cloakrooms. Anyone resisting the advances of the little old ladies that man them will be frowned upon but tolerated.

Most menus start with soup (*polévky*, often the tastiest dish on offer), the most popular of which is potato soup (*bramborová polévka*), the only other choice of starter is usually a selection of cold meats. The main courses are overwhelmingly meat based, usually pork and often beef. The variety of preparative techniques are many though the most popular way to serve it is

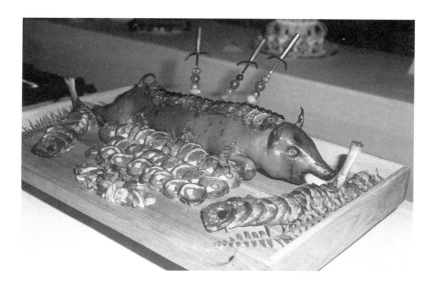

to dip it in a mixture of flour, breadcrumbs and egg (known as *řízek*). Often menus provide little help to foreign guests by their bizarre naming of dishes (eg *klaštemy tajemství* translates as 'mystery of the monastery'), the chances are that if you have little idea of what you are ordering pork will come back, even if you are pretty sure that you have not ordered it. In Slovakia the cuisine tends to be a bit more spicy, a hangover from the Hungarian addiction to paprika. The Hungarian influence accounts for the great availability of goulash (*segedinsky guláš*), stuffed peppers (*plnene papriky*) and paprika chicken (*kuře na paprice*) in the republic. Fish is not that common and are generally listed under a separate heading along with chicken and other fowl. Trout and carp are the cheapest and most widely available — they are usually served either grilled or roasted. Chips, boiled potatoes, rice or, in the Czech republic, dumplings (often in a form resembling heavy white bread) usually accompany the main meal. Salad must be ordered separately, usually it will just be a small plate of vinegar-sodden tomato or cucumber. Vegetarians are not well catered for, indeed until recently the concept was unknown — meat consumption here is one of the highest in the world. One could possibly try a pea omelette (*omeleta s hrášem*) if one does not approve of fish or maybe *knedliky s vejce* (dumplings and egg).

Ice cream is fairly common and very popular outdoors all year round but the only speciality to look for on the menu are the pancakes filled with chocolate or fruit or cream. They are not to everyone's taste. Coffee is generally of the small black variety (*turecka*, Turkish), tea is a bit of a DIY job; one will normally be given a glass of boiling water, a tea bag, a slice of lemon, optional sugar and (maybe) some milk. Milk in either republic, generally speaking, is not to be trusted.

With Czechoslovakia's recent split into two the Czech republic has at a stroke leapt over the Germans to become the world's number one beer consumers per head. Without doubt Czech beer is amongst the best in the world and no visit to the republic would be complete without a jar of the stuff, the usual accompaniment to meals. Virtually every town with any sense of civic pride has its own brewery though the more expensive restaurants will serve probably either Pilsner Urquell (from Plzeň) the most famous export and the original Pilsner lager, or Budvar (from České Budějovice). Restaurants are usually quite happy if people only want to drink there, though obviously more so down the price range. Consumption is such that it will usually be assumed by the waiter that another beer is required when one is finished so if this is not the case state so explicitly by whatever hand or facial gestures one has within one's repertoire. Often in the cheapest restaurants most tables will be taken by people drinking and smoking rather than eating and along with the beer being much cheaper it will also be served out of a tap creating a thick creamy head, which is nicer. Beer is drunk at all times of the day, by all ages and by both sexes.

The Slovaks by contrast have no great tradition in beer drinking (though they have been fast learners with consumption increasing tenfold since 1945), their traditions are more orientated towards their moderate quality wines grown in the very south of the country which use the same grapes as those in northern Hungary. There are some vineyards in Moravia to the south of Brno. In terms of spirits there is an enormous variety on the shelves. Most domestic brands originate from Slovakia or eastern Moravia. The best and most famous is the delicious plum brandy *slivovice* from Vizovice in Moravia. Others to look out for include the juniper-flavoured gin *borovička* and the herb flavoured liquor known as *becherovka*, a speciality of Karlovy Vary which has a taste all to itself.

Polévky — **soups:**		*Maso* — **meat:**	
Bramborová — potato		*Hovězí* — beef	
Fazolová — bean		*Kuře* — chicken	
Hovězí — beef		*Salám* — salami	
Hrachová — pea		*Sekaná* — meat loaf	
Kuřecí — chicken		*Slanina* — bacon	
Zeleninová — vegetable		*Šunk*a — ham	
		Telecí — veal	
		Vepřové — pork	

Ryby — **fish:**
Kapr — carp
Pstruh — trout
Zavináč — herring

Zelenina — **vegetables:**
Cibule — potatoes
Brambory — mushrooms
Hranolky — chips
Hrášek — peas
Knedlicky — dumplings
Rajče — tomato
Rýže — rice
Špenát — spinach

Zelí — cabbage
Zákusky — dessert
Palačinky — stuffed pancakes

Napoje — **drinks:**
Čaj — tea
Káva — coffee
Koňak — brandy
Minerální voda — mineral water
Mléko — milk
Pivo — beer
Víno — wine

Chléb — bread
Omeleta — omelette

TELEPHONE SERVICES

Dialling codes to the Czech and Slovak republics are: from Britain 010 42, from the USA and Canada 011 42 and from Australia and New Zealand 0011 42. From the Czech or Slovak republic dial 0044 for the UK, 00353 for Eire, 001 for the USA or Canada, 0061 for Australia and 0064 for New Zealand. When dialing the UK miss out the first zero of the town area code.

The best place to make an international telephone call is either from a telephone exchange (situated in major post offices) or, more expensively, from a hotel. Hand over the number required to the clerk or receptionist and then wait to be told which booth to enter — pay at the end of the call. International calls can also be made at one of the card phones which are springing up around the country, phonecards (telecarty) are available from post offices. Public phones are generally in a pretty sorry state — yellow boxes are for local calls only, to call outside the local area code one must find a grey box (from where one can theoretically make international calls). A dialling tone is a short and then long pulse, a ringing tone is long and regular and an engaged signal is short and rapid. Put your money in the slot when you hear a reply (the usual response is prosím), when the money has run out a recorded voice will tell you —do not count on getting any unused coins back but it is possible. An English-speaking operator should be available on 0135. Telegrams can be sent from any post office or by phone (though not from a phone box) by dialling 127, for telex and fax services ask at one of the larger hotels.

TOURIST INFORMATION OFFICES

Čedok
49 Southwark Street
London
SE1 1RU
☎ 0171 378 6009

Čedok
10E 40th Street
New York
NY 10016
☎ 212 689 9720

Do visit these offices beforehand if you can. Čedok is the old state controlled travel agency and has offices in most towns in both republics (open Monday to Friday 9am-12noon and 1-5pm and sometimes Saturday mornings). Čedok's original purpose was to organise tours for Czechs and Slovaks around the other Eastern bloc countries and not to dispense local tourist information and so they are not always the most useful of sources. However, they should at the very least be able to provide maps and information concerning accommodation as well as money changing facilities.

Accommodation and Eating Out

***	Expensive
**	Moderate
*	Inexpensive

Hotel restaurants are not included in the listings.

Chapter 1
Prague

Accommodation

Evropa ***
Václavské náměstí 25
Praha 1
☎ 236 52 74

Paříž ***
U Obecního domu 1
Praha 1
☎ 232 20 51

Ungelt ***
Štupartská 1
Praha 1
☎ 232 04 71

International ***
Podbaba
Praha 6 - Dejvice
☎ 331 91 11

Pyramida ***
Bělohorská 24
Praha - Břevnov
☎ 311 32 96

Merkur *
Těšnov 9
Praha 1
☎ 231 68 40

Axa **
Na Poříčí 40
Praha 1
☎ 232 72 00

Barbora **
Uranová 1259
Praha 5 - Zbraslav
☎ 591 223

Hybernia *
Hybernská 24
Praha 1
☎ 220 431

Balkán *
Svomosti 81228
Praha - Smíchov
☎ 540 777

Juventus *
Blanická 10
Praha - Vinohrady
☎ 255 151

Libeň *
Rudé armády 37
Praha - Libeň
☎ 828 227

Moravan *
U Uranie 22
Praha - Holešovice
☎ 802 905

Eating Out

The Centre

Bellevue **
Smetanovo nábřeží 18
Staré Město
☎ 235 95 99

Nebozízek **
Petřínské sady 411
Malá Strana
☎ 537 905

U čerta ***
Nerudova 4
Malá Strana
☎ 530 975

Na rybárně **
Gorazdova 17
Nové Město

U Pinkasů ***
Jungmannovo náměstí 15
Nové Město

The Suburbs

CG-čínský restaurace **
Janáčkovo nábřeží 1
Smíchov
☎ 549 164

Mateo **
Arbesovo náměstí 15
Smíchov

China restaurace **
Francouzská 2
Vinohrady
☎ 252 643

Principe **
Anglická 23
Vinohrady
☎ 259 614

*Toscana pizza
    restaurace* *
Vinohradská
Vinohrady

Rebecca *
Olšanské náměstí 8
Žižkov

Chapter 2
North from
Prague:
the Elbe Valley

Accommodation

Děčín
Grand Hotel **
Benešovo náměstí
☎ 04 12 270 41

Hotel Sever *
Benešovo náměstí
☎ 04 12 221 66

Hřensko
Hotel Labe **
☎ 0412 981 88

Litoměřice
Hotel Sechezy **
Vrchlického 10
☎ 0416 24 51

Teplice
Hotel de Saxe *
Masarykova
☎ 0417 266 11

Hotel Thermia **
Masarykova
☎ 0417 282 21

*Hotel Prince de
    Ligne* ***
Zámecké náměstí
☎ 0417 247 55

Ústí nad Labem
Interhotel Bohemia ***
Mírové náměstí
☎ 047 286 11

Interhotel Máj ***
Hoření 15
☎ 047 452 51

Hotel Vladimír **
Masarykova 36
☎ 047 223 11

Hotel Racek **
Litoměřická 1023
☎ 047 412 49

Hotel Lipa **
Tisá 356
☎ 047 902 83

Eating Out

Děčín
Asia **
Teplická
(closed Saturday and
Sunday).

Litoměřice
Hotel Rak *
Mírové náměstí

*Restaurace na
Mostné hoře* **
    Mostné hoře (park 1
mile/2km from centre)
☎ 412 01

Terezín
Teresian *
Náměstí Čs. armády

Ústí nad Labem
Merkur **
Masarkova 34
☎ 275 97

Hai Phong *
Velká hradební 619
☎ 237 33

Savoy **
Pařížská 20
☎ 238 60

Cleopatra *
Masarykovo 90
☎ 229 37

Horizont *
Mírová 2861
☎ 400 62

Chapter 3
North-Eastern Bohemia and the Krkonoše Mountains

Hotel Accommodation

Broumov
U svatého Václava *
Máchova 187
☎ 0447 964 37

Praha *
Mírové náměstí 49
☎ 0447 213 94

Dvůr Králové nad Labem
Central *
Main Square
☎ 0437 24 75

Harrachov
Juniorhotel Fit Fun *
☎ 0432 92 93 76

Hořice
Beránek *
Husova 32
☎ 0435 2598

Hradec Králové
Interhotel Alessandria ***
SNP 733
☎ 049 450 50

Zimní stadion **
Komenského 1214
☎ 049 326 31

Pařiž *
Baťkovo náměstí
☎ 049 242 01

Hrubá Skála
Stekl **
Hrubá Skála 5
☎ 0436 916 284

Jaroměř
Černý kůň *
Náměstí 15
☎ 0442 2208

Jičín
Start **
Revoluční 1061
☎ 0433 233 63

Malá Skála
Jizera *
☎ 0428 772 02

Náchod
Beránek **
Náměstí T.G. Masaryka
☎ 0441 217 52

Pecka
Roubal *
Pecka 7
☎ 0434 9352

Podkost
Hotel Podkost *
☎ 0433 931 27

Police nad Metují
Ostat *
Main square
☎ 0447 943 44

Sobotka
Pošta **
Míru náměstí 251
☎ 0433 7119

Špinderlův Mlýn
Hotel Montana ***
☎ 0438 935 51

Labská Bouda ***
☎ 0438 932 21

Hradec *
☎ 0438 932 56

Teplice nad Metují
Orlik *
☎ 0447 933 66

Trosky Castle
Trosky *
☎ 0436 91290

Trutnov
IH Hornik *
Polská Ulice
☎ 0439 6967

Motel Horal *
Rout 14
☎ 0439 48 51

Turnov
Slavie **
Off main square

Železný Brod
IH Cristal **
Vaneckova 200
☎ 0428 72 445

Eating Out

Dvůr Králové nad Labem
Radnice **
Main square

Hradec Kralove
Pod věží *
Velké náměstí

Na hradě *
Špitálská

Pizzeria Pinocchio **
Masarykovo náměstí

Bašta *
Ulrichovo náměstí

Jičín
U Valdštejna **
Valdštejnovo náměstí

U Rynečku **
Chelčického

Hotel Praha *
Husova

U anděla *
Valdštejnovo náměstí

Chapter 4
The Šumava
Mountains

**Hotel
Accommodation**

Cesky Krumlov
Krumlov ***
Náměstí Svorností 14
☎ 0337 2255

Růže ***
Horní
☎ 0337 2245

Horní Planá
Smrčina *
☎ 0337 97228

Lipno nad Vltavou
Lipno *
☎ 0337 958 117

Prachatice
Park Hotel ***
U stadionu 383
☎ 0338 213 81

Národní dům **
Velké náměstí
☎ 0338 21561

Zlatá stezka *
Velké náměstí 46
☎ 0338 218 41

**Rožmberk nad
Vltavou**
Hotel Pegas **
☎ 02 463 451

Srní
Šumava ***
☎ 0187 922 22

Strakonice
Švanda dudák *
☎ 0342 222 11

Bílý Vlk *
Bezděkovská
☎ 0342 225 10

Bavor ***
☎ 0342 227 40

Sušice
Fialka *
Náměstí Svobody
☎ 0187 243

Vimperk
Zlatá hvězda *
1 máje
☎ 0339 210

Volary
Bobík **
☎ 0338 923 51

Vyšší Brod
Vzlet **
Namesti Miru
☎ 0337 926 69

Eating Out

Cesky Krumlov
U dvou marií **
Parkán

U hroznu *
Náměstí Svomosti

U města vidně *
Budějovická brána

Prachatice
U medvědků *
Velké naměstí

Chapter 5
Brno and its
Surroundings

**Hotel
Accommodation**

Blansko
Panorama ***
Obůrka 168
☎ 0506 5951

Dukla **
Náměstí Republiky
☎ 0506 5000-2

Macocha-Juříček **
Svitavská 35
☎ 0506 3203

Boskovice
Velen **
Dukelská
☎ 0501 2071

Slávia *
Komenskeho 55
☎ 0501 3239

Brno
Astoria **
Novobranská 3
☎ 225 41

Avion **
Česká 20
☎ 276 06

Continental ***
Kounicova 20
☎ 75 05 01

Grand ***
Benešova 18/20
☎ 264 21

Kozák *
Horova 30
Brno - Zabovresky
☎ 74 41 89

Slovan ***
Lidická 23
☎ 74 55 05

U Jakuba ***
Jakubské náměstí 6
☎ 229 91

Jedovnice
Riviera *
☎ 0506 932 09

Moravský Krumlov
Jednota *
Náměstí T.G. Masaryka
27
☎ 0621 2373

Nedvědice
U sokolovny *
☎ 0505 22 67

Eating Out

Bílovice
U lišky bystroušky *
☎ 05 654 39

Brno
Academická *
Gorkého

Bellevue **
Joštova 2
☎ 254 07

Bohémia **
Rooseveltova 1
☎ 284 29

Čemý medvěd **
Jakubské náměstí 1
☎ 272 76

Gourmand **
Josefská 14
☎ 232 84

U Jakuba **
Jakubské náměstí 6
☎ 229 91

Italia **
Zamečnická

U Lucerny *
Veveří 20
☎ 752 042

Petrov *
Masarykova 34
☎ 244 21

Shanghai *
Pekárská

Slavia **
Solniční 15/17
☎ 237 11

Stopka **
Česká 5

Chapter 6
South-Eastern
Moravia

Hotel
Accommodation

Holešov
Sokolský dům **
Palackého 546
☎ 0634 2535

Kroměříž
Hotel Oskol **
Oskol 3203
☎ 0634 242 40

Luhačovice
IH Alexandria ***
☎ 067 3311

Litoval *
☎ 067 93 30 40

Uherské Hradiště
Fojta *
Masarykovo náměstí
155
☎ 0632 3440

Morava **
Šafaříkova 855
☎ 8632 2673

Grand **
Palackého náměstí 362
☎ 8632 3055

Vsetín
Vsacan **
Žerotínova
☎ 0657 4401

Valasske Klobouky
Ploština *
Náměstí Míru
☎ 2064

Zlín
Interhotel Moskva ***
Náměstí Práce 2512
☎ 067 514

IH Družba ***
Revoluční 15
☎ 067 241 12

Ondráš **
Kvítková 4323
☎ 067 232 02

Garni **
Náměstí T.G. Masaryka
1335
☎ 067 258 71

Eating Out

Luhačovice
Havlíček **
Masarykova ul.
☎ 93 30 43

Miramare **
Bezručova ul.
☎ 93 20 59

Slovácká búda **
Spa park
☎ 93 30 46

U fojta **
Masarykova ul.
☎ 93 33 11

Valašské Klobouky
Beseda *
Náměstí Míru
☎ 2300

Vizovice
Lidový dům *
Masarykovo náměstí
☎ 95 26 90

Valašský šenk **
Lázeňská ul
☎ 95 26 52

Sokolovna **
Nádražní ul.
☎ 95 21 48

Zlín
Avion *
Rašínova ul.
☎ 257 95

Bistro *
Náměstí Míru 18
☎ 224 24

Chateau restaurant **
☎ 222 67

Januštice **
Zálešná
☎ 277 02

Koliba Kocanda **
Paseky 4369
☎ 422 73

Morava **
Bartošova 40
☎ 223 85

Rybena *
T. Bati 201
☎ 251 22

Chapter 7
Olomouc and
Central Moravia

Hotel
Accommodation

Litovel
Záložna *
Namesti Pr. Otakara 762
☎ 068 2290

Olomouc
Morava *
Riegrova 16
☎ 068 296 71

Národní dům **
8 května 21
☎ 068 251 79

Palác **
1 Máje 31
☎ 068 240 96

Flora ***
Krapkova 34
☎ 068 232 41

Gol ***
Legionářská 12
☎ 068 286 17

Eating Out

Olomouc
Drápal **
Havlíčkova 1
☎ 280 91

Fontána **
Smetanovy sady
☎ 412 402

Hanacká *
Dolní náměstí 38
☎ 252 96

Litovelská **
Opletalova ul. 2
☎ 235 70

Maxim Grill Club **
Divadelní 2
☎ 243 27

Orient **
Divadelní

Pizzeria Verona **
Ostružnická 23
☎ 280 19

Chapter 8
Silesia and the
Beskydy
Mountains

Hotel
Accommodation

Frýdek-Místek
Dolu Paskov **
Pionýrů 1757
☎ 0658 324 91

Centrum ***
Na poříčí 494
☎ 0658 215 51

Frenštát pod Radhoštěm
Vlčina ***
1 mile ($^{1}/_{2}$km) from town on green path
☎ 0656 5351

Sport **
Školská 1393
☎ 0656 5120

Fulnek
Jelen **
Náměstí Komenského 48
☎ 0656 923 134

Hradec nad Moravicí
Belaria **
Žimrovická
☎ 0653 917 82

Kopřivnice
Tatra **
Tr. Odboje Záhumenní
1161
☎ 0656 421 55

Stadión **
Masarykovo náměstí
541
☎ 0656 424 01

Nový Jičín
Praha **
Lidická 6
☎ 0656 209 11

Kalač **
Dvořákova 1947
☎ 0656 222 52

Štramberk
Šipka *
Náměstí 37
☎ 483 14

Opava
Park Hotel **
Městské sady
☎ 0653 213 745

Koruna **
Náměstí Republicky 17
☎ 0653 216 915

Ostrava
Imperial ***
Tyršova 6
Ostrava 1
☎ 069 236 621

Palace **
Tř. 28 října 59
Ostrava 1
☎ 069 236 660

Atom ***
Zkrácená
Ostrava 3
☎ 069 353 821

Chemik ***
28 října 170
Ostrava 1
☎ 069 261 320

Brioni *
Stodolní 8
Ostrava 1
☎ 069 231 966

Vítek **
Adamusova 2
Ostrava - Hrabůvka
☎ 069 596 16

Eating Out

Kopřivnice
Severka *
☎ 419 65

Nový Jičín
Národní dům *
☎ 20843

Tatrovanka **
☎ 23757

Nové slunce **
☎ 23540

Jelen *
☎ 22122

Máj **
☎ 23655

Ostrava
Domino *
Masarykovo náměstí
Ostrava 1

Fénix **
Čs. legií 11
Ostrava 1

U jelena *
Masarykovo náměstí
Ostrava 1

Jindřiška **
Osvoboditelů 57
Ostrava 1

Lesanka **
Černá Louka
Ostrava 1

Pavilón **
Černá louka
Ostrava 1

Volha **
Nádražní ul.
Ostrava 1

Příbor
Slávie *
☎ 9117 10

Letka *
☎ 9110 62

Štramberk
Dělnický dům *
☎ 405 15

Chapter 9
The Slovak Mountains

Hotel Accommodation

Čičmany
Kaštiel *
☎ 089 9297

Dolny Kubín
Marina **
Hviezdoslavovo
namesti

Liptovský Mikuláš
El. Greco **
Štúrova
☎ 0849 227 13

Jánošík ***
Jánošíkovo nábrežie
☎ 0849 227 21

Kriváň *
Štúrova
☎ 0849 224 15

Tatran **
☎ 0849 240 63

Poprad
Európa *
Next to train station
☎ 092 327 44

Gerlach *
Hviezdoslavovc námĕstí
☎ 092 337 59

Ružomberok
Liptov *
☎ 0848 225 09

Hrabovo **
☎ 0848 267 27

Malina *
☎ 0848 250 70

Starý Smokovec
Grand ***
☎ 0969 25 01

Štrbské Pleso
Patria ***
☎ 092 925 91

Panoráma **
☎ 092 921 11

Tatranská Lomnica
Grandhotel Praha ***
☎ 0969 967 941

Slovakia **
☎ 0969 967 961

Slovan ***
☎ 0969 967 851

Žilina
Slovakia ***
☎ 089 456 72

Slovan **
☎ 089 205 56

Polom **
☎ 089 211 51

Metropol *
Opposite station
☎ 089 329 00

Eating Out

Dolny Kubín
Marina **
Hviezdoslavovo
namesti

Žilina
Fontana *
Main square

Atelier *
Republiky

Chapter 10
Central
Slovakia

Hotel
Accommodation

Banská Bystrica
Eurohotel ***
Komenského 22
☎ 088 539 66

Lux ***
Námĕstí Svobody 2
☎ 088 241 41

Urpín *
Cikkerova 5
☎ 088 245 56

Turist **
Tajovského cesta
☎ 088 355 90

Junior *
Národná 12
☎ 088 233 67

Národný dom **
Národná 11
☎ 088 237 37

Banská Štiavnica
Grand *
Antona Pecha - Andreja
kmeta

Kremnica
Vĕtmík **
☎ 0857 925 709

Žiar nad Hronom
Luna **
Námĕstí Mat. slov. 3
☎ 0857 4841

Zvolen
Polana ***
Námĕstí SNP
☎ 0855 243 60

Rates **
Mraziarenská cesta
☎ 0855 215 96

Eating Out

Banská Bystrica
Kurian **
Horná Strieborná

Atom **
Horná ul.

Bystrica *
Horná ul.

Národný dom **
Národná

Cechova **
Námestie SNP

Konzum *
Horná ul.

Banská Štiavnica
Presso Marína **
Trojičné

Strieborna **
Strieborna

Chapter 11
Košice and
Carpatho-
Ruthenia

Hotel
Accommodation

Bardejov
Republicka *
Dlhý rad 50
☎ 0935 2345

Bardejovské Kúpele
Minerál **
☎ 0935 4135

Mier **
☎ 0935 4524

Košice
Európa *
Mlynská
☎ 095 238 97

Hutník *
Tyršovo nábrežie 6
☎ 095 377 80

Slovan ***
Rooseveltova
☎ 095 273 78

Prešov
Dukla **
Slov. rep. rád
☎ 091 227 41

Savoy **
Hlavná 50
☎ 091 31062

Šariš *
Sabinovská 1
☎ 091 463 51

Svidník
Dukla **
☎ 0937 228 39

Eating Out

Košice
Maďarská **
Náměstí Svobody 65

U Maka *
Bočná

Slavia *
Náměstí Svobody

Prešov
Pizzeria *
Svätoplukova

Slovenská *
Hlavná ul. 13

Vrchovina **
Svätoplukova 1

Index

<u>TRAVEL GUIDE LIST</u>

Airline/Ferry details ....
....
....
....
....

Telephone No. ....

Tickets arrived ☐

Travel insurance ordered ☐

Car hire details ....
....
....

Visas arrived ☐

Passport ☐

Currency ☐

Travellers cheques ☐

Eurocheques ☐

Accommodation address ....
....
....
....

Telephone No. ....

Booking confirmed ☐

Maps required ....
....
....

DAILY ITINERARY

Date ....

Places visited

....
....
....
....
....
....

Accommodation ....
....
....
Telephone No. ....

Booking confirmed ☐

Notes:

Austria

Explore the quiet valleys of Bregenzerwald in the west to Carinthia and Burgenland in the east. From picturesque villages in the Tannheimertal to the castles north of Klagenfurt, including Burg Hochosterwitz. This dramatic castle with its many gates stands on a 450ft high limestone cliff and was built to withstand the Turkish army by the man who brought the original Spanish horses to Austria.

Britain

Yes, there are places off the beaten track in even the more populated areas of Britain. Even in the heavily visited national parks there are beautiful places you could easily miss — areas well known to locals but not visitors. This book guides you to such regions to make your visit memorable.

Greece

Brimming with suggested excursions that range from climbing Mitikas, the highest peak of Mount Olympus, the abode of Zeus, to Monemvassia, a fortified medieval town with extensive ruins of a former castle. This book enables you to mix a restful holiday in the sun with the fascinating culture and countryside or rural Greece.

Ireland

Ireland not only has a dramatic coastline, quiet fishing harbours and unspoilt rural villages, but also the natural friendliness of its easy-going people. *Off The Beaten Track Ireland* will lead you to a memorable holiday in a country where the pace of life is more relaxing and definitely not hectic.

Italy

Beyond the artistic wealth of Rome or Florence and the hill towns of Tuscany lie many fascinating areas of this ancient country just waiting to be discovered. From medieval towns such as Ceriana in the Armea valley to quiet and spectacular areas of the Italian Lakes and the Dolomites further to the east. At the southern end of the country, the book explores Calabria, the 'toe' of Italy as well as Sicily, opening up a whole 'new' area.

Germany

Visit the little market town of Windorf on the north bank of the Danube (with its nature reserve) or the picturesque upper Danube Valley, which even most German's never visit! Or go further north to the Taubertal. Downstream of famous Rothenburg with its medieval castle walls are red sandstone-built villages to explore with such gems as the carved altar in Creglingen church, the finest work by Tilman Riemenschneider — the Master Carver of the Middle Ages. This book includes five areas in the former East Germany.

Poland

Off The Beaten Track Poland is an invaluable guide full of itinerary based ideas for discovering the lesser known places in Poland. The country also has a truly astonishing variety of landscapes including 19 National Parks which range from the huge Sahara-like sand dunes on the Baltic coast. From the spectacular Alpine-type mountains of the Tatras to Europe's last remaining primeval forest and only remaining wetland, the haunt of hundreds of different bird species.

Portugal

Most visitors to Portugal head to the Algarve and its famous beaches, but even the eastern Algarve is relatively quiet compared to the more popular western area. However, the book also covers the attractive areas of northern Portugal where only the more discerning independent travellers may be found enjoying the delights of this lovely country.

Scandinavia

Covers Norway, Denmark, Sweden and Finland. There is so much to see in these countries that it is all too easy to concentrate on the main tourist areas. That would mean missing so many memorable places that are well worth visiting. For instance, there are still about sixty Viking churches that survive in Norway. Alternatively many private castles and even palaces in Denmark open their gardens to visitors. Here is your guide to ensure that you enjoy the Scandinavian experience to the full.

Spain

From the unique landscape of the Ebrodelta in Catalonia to the majestic Picos d'Europa in the north, the reader is presented with numerous things to see and exciting things to do. With the mix of cultures and climates, there are many possibilities for an endearing holiday for the independent traveller.

Switzerland

Switzerland offers much more than the high mountains and deep valleys with which it is traditionally associated. This book covers lesser known areas of the high mountains — with suggested walks in some cases. It also covers Ticino, the Swiss Lakeland area near to the Italian Lakes and tours over the border into the latter. In the north, the book covers the lesser known areas between Zurich and the Rhine Falls, plus the Lake Constance area, with its lovely little towns like Rorschach, on the edge of the lake.

Northern France

From the sandy inlets of Brittany and the well-watered pastures of Normandy, the hugh flower festival of La Tranche, the eagle reserve at Kintzheim in Alsace et Lorraine, to France's loveliest wine route in Alsace. See the France that most visitor's miss, this book is your key to going Off The Beaten Track in Northern France

Southern France

From the windy beaches and huge sand dunes of Aquitaine, the grandeur of the Pyrénées, the medieval villages of early English Kings, the spectacular chasm of the Verdon Gorges to the quiet areas of the Camargue. This book will take you to fourteen different areas of Southern France and show you the lesser known sights that reflect this country's true identity.

Scotland

Heather-clad mountains, baronian castles and magnificent coastal scenery, all combined with a rich historical heritage, combine to make this an ideal 'Off The Beaten Track' destination.